Intensive Participation in Children's Sports

American Orthopaedic Society for Sports Medicine

Bernard R. Cahill, MD
University of Illinois College of Medicine, Peoria

Arthur J. Pearl, MD
University of Miami School of Medicine

Editors

Human Kinetics Publishers

Library of Congress Cataloging-in-Publication Data

Intensive participation in children's sports / Bernard R. Cahill,
  editor, Arthur J. Pearl, editor ; American Orthopaedic Society for
  Sports Medicine.
      p.   cm.
  Includes papers presented at a workshop sponsored by the society
  and held Dec. 5-9, 1990 in Peoria.
  Includes bibliographical references and index.
  ISBN 0-87322-409-4
      1. Sports for children--Psychological aspects. 2. Sports for
  children--Physiological aspects. 3. Sports for children--Social
  aspects. 4. Sports for children--Accidents and injuries.
  I. Cahill, Bernard R., 1929-   . II. Pearl, Arthur J., 1930-
  III. American Orthopaedic Society for Sports Medicine.
  GV709.2.I58   1993
  796'.01922--dc20   92-26253

ISBN: 0-87322-409-4

Managing Editor: Julia Anderson; Assistant Editors: Moyra Knight, Laura Bofinger,
and John Wentworth; Copyeditor: Julie Anderson; Proofreader: Kathy Bennett; Indexer:
Theresa Schaefer; Production Director: Ernie Noa; Typesetting and Text Layout: Angela
K. Snyder; Text Design: Keith Blomberg; Cover Design: Discover Graphics; Interior Art:
Jim Hampton; Printer: Braun-Brumfield

Printed in the United States of America   10   9   8   7   6   5   4   3   2   1

Human Kinetics Publishers
Box 5076, Champaign, IL 61825-5076
1-800-747-4457

Canada Office: Human Kinetics Publishers, P.O. Box 2503, Windsor, ON N8Y 4S2
1-800-465-7301 (in Canada only)

Europe Office: Human Kinetics Publishers (Europe) Ltd., P.O. Box IW14,
Leeds LS16 6TR, England
0532-781708

Australia Office: Human Kinetics Publishers, P.O. Box 80, Kingswood 5062,
South Australia
374-0433

New Zealand Office: Human Kinetics Publishers New Zealand, P.O. Box 105-231,
Auckland 1, New Zealand
(09) 309-2259

Contents

Panel of Experts

Oded Bar-Or, MD
Team Leader, Physiological Representative, North American Society of Pediatric
Exercise Medicine

Cameron J.R. Blimkie, PhD
Speaker, Physiological
Assistant Professor, School of Physical Education at McMaster University,
Hamilton, Ontario

Bernard R. Cahill, MD
Workshop Chairman
Clinical Professor of Orthopaedic Surgery
Director, Great Plains Sports Science and Training Center
Chairman, Board of Trustees, The Foundation for Sports Medicine Education
and Research

T. Jeff Chandler, EdD
Director of Research,
Lexington Clinic Sports Medicine Center,
Lexington, Kentucky

Jay Coakley, PhD
Speaker, Sociological
Professor of Sociology and Director of the Center for the Study of Sport and
Leisure, University of Colorado at Colorado Springs

Peter Donnelly, PhD
Speaker, Sociological
Undergraduate Chair, School of Physical Education
Associate Professor and Associate Member of the Department of Sociology,
McMaster University, Hamilton, Ontario

James A. Farmer, EdD
Workshop Director
Associate Professor of Continuing Education and Coordinator of Graduate Pro-
grams in Continuing Education, College of Education, University of Illinois at
Urbana-Champaign

Steve Fleck, PhD
Representative, United States Olympic Committee

David Gallahue
Representative, National Association for Sport and Physical Education

William E. Garrett, Jr., MD, PhD
Team Leader, Clinical/Pathological
Assistant Professor, Orthopaedic Surgery and Cell Biology, Duke University
Medical Center, Durham, North Carolina

Steven Gordon, PhD
Representative, National Institute of Health
Musculoskeletal Disease Program Director, National Institute of Arthritis and Musculoskeletal and Skin Diseases

Daniel Gould, PhD
Speaker, Psychological
Professor, Department of Exercise and Sport Science, University of North Carolina at Greensboro

Sally S. Harris, MD, MPH
Representative, American Academy of Pediatrics

W. Ben Kibler, MD
Speaker, Clinical/Pathological
Medical Director, Sports Medicine Center, Lexington Clinic, Lexington, Kentucky

Greg Landry, MD
Team Leader, Sociological
Assistant Professor, Department of Pediatrics, Head, Section of Sports Medicine, University of Wisconsin, Madison, Wisconsin

Robert M. Malina, PhD
Representative, American College of Sports Medicine
Professor of Kinesiology and Health Education and of Anthropology, University of Texas at Austin

Bert R. Mandelbaum, MD
Speaker, Clinical/Pathological
Adjunct Clinical Assistant Professor, Orthopaedic Surgery and
Adjunct in Department of Kinesiology at University of California at Los Angeles

Rainer Martens, PhD
Team Leader, Psychological
President of Human Kinetics Publishers
Founder of the American Coaching Effectiveness Program

Arthur J. Pearl, MD
Publications Committee Chairman, American Orthopaedic Society for Sports Medicine
Associate Professor, Department of Orthopaedics and Rehabilitation, University of Miami School of Medicine

Peter D. Pizzutillo, MD
Representative, Pediatric Orthopaedic Society of North America
Clinical Professor, Department of Orthopaedic Surgery and Director, Pediatric Orthopedics, Thomas Jefferson University, Philadelphia

Thomas W. Rowland, MD
Speaker, Physiological
Director, Pediatric Cardiology, Baystate Medical Center
Associate Professor of Pediatrics, University of Massachusetts School of Medicine
Clinical Assistant Professor of Pediatrics, Tufts University School of Medicine

George Wade, MD
Publications Committee, American Orthopaedic Society for Sports Medicine

Maureen R. Weiss, PhD
Speaker, Psychological
Associate Professor, Department of Physical Education and Human Movement Studies
Director, Children's Summer Sports Program, College of Human Development and Performance, University of Oregon, Eugene

Preface

Olympic victors were those who did not squander
their powers by early training.
—Aristotle

This book contains the concerns and recommendations of a group of sports medicine experts on the effects of intensive training and participation in youth sports. The purpose of this book is to clarify what is known about this subject from the broad perspective of four separate domains: the psychological, the sociological, the physiological, and the clinical/pathological.

The youth sports specialists, sports medicine specialists, and researchers studying sport who read this volume will become familiar with the latest data, areas of disagreement, recommendations, and future research requirements on the subject of intensive youth sports. It is for these professionals that this book is written.

During the past 20 years the youth of North America, if not of the world, have been introduced to sports at earlier and earlier ages. Youth sports have been accompanied by the same practices seen in adult sports, namely year-round training, specialization in a single sport, increased hours of training per year, and compulsory strength training. In youth sports, adult supervision has intensified, and media coverage and the institution of local, regional, national, and international competition have ensued. Berryman (1988) extensively reviewed this development.

The magnitude of youth participation in sports was studied by Martens (1988). He stated that 44% of our youth ages 6 to 18 participate in nonschool sports and 5.13 million boys and girls participate in high school sports. Further, these percentages and figures are increasing.

Questions arising from these practices in youth sports are increasingly directed toward national sports medicine organizations such as the American Orthopaedic Society for Sports Medicine (AOSSM), the American College of Sports Medicine, the President's Council on Physical Fitness and Sports, and the United States Olympic Committee. Practitioners of sports medicine are called upon to address these questions.

The concerns of those involved with youth sports range from what age to begin participation in intensive activity to the applications of anabolic steroids, and many questions need immediate and detailed replies. The public, the consumer of youth sports medicine, wants to know the risks and benefits and how to minimize risks and maximize benefits. These questions about perceived risks and benefits of youth sports were the seeds that generated the concept of a workshop addressing intensive training and participation in youth sports, which the American Orthopaedic Society for Sports Medicine (AOSSM) held in 1990. This book is a result of that workshop.

The workshop was by no means the first group to critically examine youth sports. In 1937 the American Association for Health, Physical Education and Recreation (AAHPER) denounced highly organized sports for children and followed with proscriptions in 1947 and 1951. In 1984 the Olympic Scientific Congress considered youth sport risks and benefits (Weiss & Gould, 1986). In 1985 the Big Ten Committee on Institutional Cooperation studied the effects of competitive sports on children (Brown & Branta, 1985). Other educational, medical, scientific, and professional groups have conducted forums on youth sports, usually from a narrow focus. But the workshop studying intensive training and participation in youth sports was the first forum to consider youth sports from the psychological, sociological, physiological, and clinical/pathological viewpoints.

The roster of team leaders, speakers, and delegates representing national organizations leaves little doubt that the premier experts on youth sports, at least in North America, were present December 5-9, 1990, in Peoria, Illinois. The following national organizations were represented at the conference:

- American Academy of Family Physicians
- American Academy of Pediatrics
- American College of Sports Medicine
- American Orthopaedic Society for Sports Medicine
- National Association for Sport and Physical Education
- National Institutes of Health
- North American Society of Pediatric Exercise Medicine
- Pediatric Orthopaedic Society of North America
- United States Olympic Committee

The processing of information followed this format: Each participant developed a list of risks and benefits of intensive training and participation in youth sports. This tabulation formed the beginning discussions for each of the four domains or perspectives. Then in general sessions in which participants from all four domains met, decisions were made as to what risks and benefits stood the test of consensual validation. From this process the true risks and benefits were derived. Recommendations were then made to maximize the benefits and minimize the risks of intensive youth sports. The four team leaders, Bar-Or, Garrett, Landry, and Martens, were responsible for coordinating their two speakers and developing the discussion at the breakout sessions. They all performed admirably.

This was the second workshop on youth sports supported by the AOSSM. The first, entitled ''Strength Training for the Prepubescent Athlete'' (Cahill, 1988), provided a proving ground for the consensual validation process. This second workshop was funded by The Foundation for Sports Medicine Education and Research (FSMER), an affiliate of AOSSM.

The workshop itself was intensive with long days of stimulating debate and disputation. The results, however, are at least a beginning to the understanding of the good and bad in youth sports, and they provide information that will maximize the good and minimize the bad.

Special thanks are due to the Foundation for Sports Medicine Education and Research for funding this workshop and to the national organizations for providing delegates. The workshop would never have occurred without the work of our secretary, Peggy King, who became an adopted member of the workshop and who never failed to supply typing, make phone calls, and husband progress, always with a smile.

References

Berryman, J.W. (1988). The rise of highly organized sports for preadolescent boys. In F.L. Smoll, R.A. Magill, & M.J. Ash (Eds.), *Children in sports* (3rd ed., pp. 3-16). Champaign, IL: Human Kinetics.

Brown, E.W., & Branta, C.F. (1985). *Competitive sports for children and youth: An overview of research and issues*. Champaign, IL: Human Kinetics.

Cahill, B.R. (Ed.) (1988). *Proceedings of the conference on strength training and the prepubescent*. Chicago: American Orthopaedic Society for Sports Medicine.

Martens, R. (1988). Youth sport in the USA. In F.L. Smoll, R.A. Magill, & M.J. Ash (Eds.), *Children in sports* (3rd ed., pp. 17-23). Champaign, IL: Human Kinetics.

Weiss, M.R., & Gould, D. (Eds.) (1986). *Sport for children and youths*. Champaign, IL: Human Kinetics.

Bernard R. Cahill

Introduction

Bernard Cahill

The workshop on intensive training and participation in youth sports focused only on the prepubescent athlete, that is, boys and girls of the Tanner II classification or younger (boys age 12 or less and girls age 11 or less). However, some of the contributors to this book include children and adolescents up to age 18 in their respective chapters.

The major issues discussed in this book are those that our panel of experts agreed were the principal risks and benefits in intensive youth sports. The multidirectional approach to the workshop was founded on the diverse nature of motivational and environmental influences in youth sports. To examine intensive training in the young athlete from the physiological aspect alone would not cover the range of factors affecting these children. Both the reasons for the increasing magnitude of youth sports and the environmental influences on the young athlete dictated that even an overview would be incomplete if this topic was not also viewed from both the psychological and sociological domains.

Both of these domains were concerned with the following reasons for youth sport expansion:

- The belief that intensive training and participation in youth sports benefits the child
- Adult self-interest
- Media and their effects (e.g., role models)
- The child's desire to excel
- Social influences

Further, these two domains were concerned with the following environmental factors:

- Child athlete and peer relations
- Parental involvement or lack of such involvement
- Potential family discord
- Other adult supporters of intensive training and participation in youth sports
- Social issues

Three critically important individuals met in Chicago in March 1988 to plan the workshop: Oded Bar-Or, who provided a pediatric physiological perspective; Rainer Martens, bringing a psychological perspective; and James Farmer, who contributed his educational/information-processing methodology.

The original title for the workshop was ''The Effects of Intensive Training on the Young Athlete.'' The adjective *intensive* was chosen to characterize a physiological exercise dose that was high (e.g., higher than Little League baseball and similar to gymnastics or youth football). Dr. Martens argued that from a psychological perspective the physiological exercise dose may not be relevant, and the intensity factor may be psychologically relevant only to the competition or participation phase. As the reader of this volume will come to understand, this is a very cogent argument. Therefore, the noun *participation* was added to the title. For the physiological and clinical pathological domains, the higher physiological exercise dose retained its original distinction.

Thus the information presented and processed at the workshop was reviewed from two general perspectives: (a) The physical intensity of training and participation in youth sports and (b) The nonphysical, behavioral aspect of participation and competition in youth sports. The following sections explain technical terms that appear throughout this text.

Pharmacological Dose-Response Curves

It was Milo of Croton who, as a youngster carrying a growing calf on his back, discovered that exercise provoked desirable biological adaptations. He also practiced the principle of progression, which is an essential ingredient of any training program. From Milo's era to the 1970s, little scientific data were produced to create training programs that would consistently produce desired metabolic adaptations. Only in the last 20 years have sport scientists realized that exercise doses bring about responses, as do pharmaceuticals, in dose-response relationships.

On the vertical axis of Figure 1 the biological adaptation or response is plotted against the dose. In the case of exercise, which is one of our considerations, the dose is the stress of the physical activity. Our other consideration is psychological stress dose and the attendant psychological adaptations.

Psychological stress/dosing response is less predictable from the dose-response curve than physiological dosing. This is especially true when an entire team of athletes is studied. The reason for this is the inaccuracy of predicting what psychological stress dose will provoke a response: One athlete's stress may be another's challenge.

Figure 1 may represent the biological adaptation of the entire organism, specific systems, or anatomic areas. In the case of the entire organism, the desired biological adaptation could be fitness or conditioning; a specific system adaptation could be improvement in anaerobic power output; and an anatomic adaptation could be improvement of the vertical jump. A psychological adaptation could be enhancement of self-esteem.

There are, of course, doses that are too small to provoke desirable biological adaptations. As the dose increases (which is termed *progression*) the biological response increases to a level of an optimal dose beyond which no further dose increase provokes desired adaptations. At some point in this increasing dose range, undesirable biological adaptations will occur. Such adaptations within the

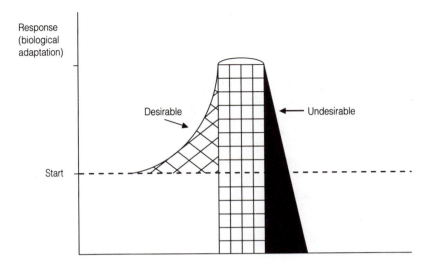

Figure 1. Dose-response curve.

musculoskeletal system are termed *stress failure syndromes* and are most often pathological symptoms of cellular destruction. In the psychological area undesirable adaptations may be ''burnout'' or ''bingeing'' (see chapter 2).

Selye's General Adaptation Syndrome

In 1950 Hans Selye published *The Physiology and Pathology of Exposure to Stress* (Selye, 1950). Although this treatise on general adaptation syndrome (GAS) principally considered the neurohormonal axis, the work's application extends to other physiological and psychological areas.

Selye postulated that stress to biological symptoms promotes adaptations that may be desirable or undesirable, and that there is a critical relationship between relief from stress (rest) and the stress itself (Figure 2).

For the sport scientist and this youth sports workshop, this balance point is like the Holy Grail of the medieval knights. The similarity of the GAS to dose-response curves is quite obvious, and it is not surprising that this dose-response, stress-rest relationship was cited by the workshop as the principal future research requirement.

Stress Failure Syndromes

Since the early 1970s the term *overuse syndrome* (OS) has been used to describe symptoms of undesirable adaptations following exercise dosing and is a diagnosis

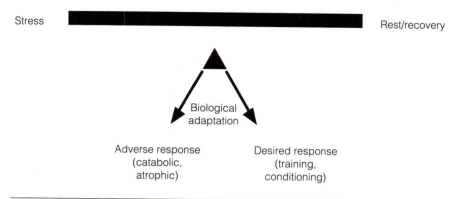

Figure 2.   Selye's general adaptation syndrome. *Note.* Based on data by Selye (1950).

frequently applied to the injured athlete/exerciser. Sports people have been dissatisfied with this term for the same period of time, because it is not descriptive and is pejorative. *Overuse syndrome* is accusatory, especially when applied to the young athlete. Parents and adult supervisors feel they must be guilty of some error of commission or omission when confronted with this diagnosis. Parents are unable to understand why their children have OS and others do not.

Overuse syndrome has mutated through *multiple reinjury syndrome* and *recurrent stress syndrome* to the currently accepted diagnosis *stress failure syndrome* (SFS). SFS is more descriptive, is remote, and is not accusatory. Using this term makes it much easier to explain to a parent, coach, or athlete why the undesirable adaptation occurred to the organism, system, or body part and to educate those concerned about the unique individuality of each organism, system, or body part. SFS simplifies the explanation of the lack of a uniform biological response (e.g., of an entire team) because of these unique individual biological characteristics, especially in children.

Few epidemiological studies in this hemisphere (see chapter 8) have investigated dose response and its relation to SFS. Japanese authors have published dose-response papers of SFS of the lumbar spine, wrist, elbow, and knee in children involved in numerous sports. Research in this area is urgently needed.

Categories of Exercise Doses

There are four categories of exercise doses:

- Conditioning
- Training
- Atrophic
- Catabolic

The effects of each dose category are plotted against their effects on biological adaptation over time (Figure 3). The degree of biological adaptation on the vertical axis may be for the organism, a system, or a body part.

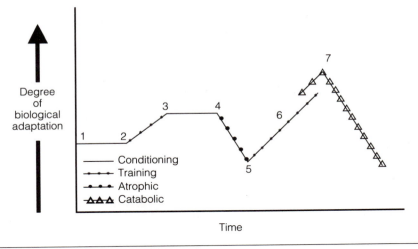

Degree
of
biological
adaptation

——— Conditioning
•—•—• Training
•—•—• Atrophic
▲▲▲ Catabolic

Time

Figure 3.   Categories of exercise doses.

The four exercise categories may be best explained and defined by example. In this text we will use fitness as the desired biological adaptation.

- *Conditioning:* Each person is at some level of biological adaptation or fitness (Point 1, Figure 3). If the physiological stress (size of exercise dose) remains constant, that level of fitness will be maintained. Thus the conditioning exercise dose is the dose that will maintain a level of fitness. This dose would have to increase for the person to maintain fitness when moved to an area of decreased gravity (a space-life problem).
- *Training:* Training must always be conducted at a dose higher than the conditioning dose. At Point 2 the exercise dose increases, and over time a new higher level of fitness is obtained (Point 3). All training doses require progression. If at Point 3 the dose does not continue to progress, the individual will enter a new conditioning period but will need a higher exercise dose to maintain fitness level at Point 3 than at Point 1.
- *Atrophic:* If for any reason (e.g., illness, personal conflict) the person decreases the exercise dose (Point 4) to a level below Point 1, a new lower level of fitness will be reached (Point 5). The atrophic exercise dose is that dose that will lower a given level of fitness.
- *Catabolic:* At Point 5 the exerciser embarks on a new training program and progresses to Point 6, a new higher level of fitness (above Point 3). At some point in this training dose the exerciser will reach the catabolic dose (beyond Point 6). The catabolic exercise may destroy tissue for months, faster than rest can rebuild it, before symptoms occur (Point 7). Thus the onset of symptoms in catabolic exercise doses occurs months after the onset of net tissue destruction and is a time when gross tissue damage is present. The level of fitness rapidly deteriorates and SFS is diagnosed. This failure usually affects a body part (e.g.,

the tendon) and not the organism or an energy system. Nonetheless, the fitness level will decrease. SFS may psychologically involve the entire organism as in depression or burnout syndrome.

Components of the Exercise Stress Prescription

Quantification of exercise involves three important parameters:

- Frequency
- Duration
- Intensity

In addition, the performance factor to be trained (the desired biological adaptation) must be preferentially stressed in order for the exercise to be most efficient. For at least a decade the principles of sport-specific training have been practiced. Now, however, it is recognized that we must be even more specific. Current training programs are aimed at one of the two energy systems, aerobic or anaerobic. Selection of the energy system to be trained is based on the energy requirements of the sport or exercise, that is, power (anaerobic) or work (aerobic) sports.

- *Frequency:* Frequency defines the number of training sessions per week; the most common frequency is three. Intensive anaerobic training requires at least 24 hr rest between sessions; however, six to seven anaerobic sessions can be held per week if different body segments are trained on alternate days.
- *Duration:* Duration, the amount of time in hours or minutes of training per session, is highly variable depending on the intensity and the energy system being trained (Fleck & Kraemer, 1987); 30 min per session is considered to be the threshold of a training effect.
- *Intensity:* Intensity is the percentage depletion or exhaustion of the energy system being trained (Figure 4). It is also the rate of work or power output.

Most training intensities are at approximately the 70% depletion area (Figure 4, Point 1). To arrive at these training intensities the athlete should select an intensity below well-known individual best maximal efforts. In aerobic distance training this may mean exercising 10 to 30% slower than an athlete's best times. In the anaerobic system it can mean lifting weights 10 to 50% below maximal best efforts.

The total exercise dose obviously is a blend of frequency, duration, and intensity, and effective training programs logically manipulate these factors. As intensity increases, duration must obviously decrease (see Fleck & Kraemer, 1987).

Overview of Intensive Participation in Children's Sports

During this workshop the factors discussed in this introductory chapter took on a monolithic relevance in both the psychological and physiological domains. The

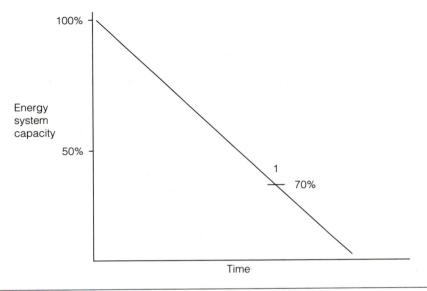

Figure 4. Training intensity (percent exhaustion).

relativity of dose-response curves, the general adaptation syndrome, categories of exercise doses, stress failure syndromes, progression, and exercise/stress dosing become inseparable.

All workshop participants supported the conclusion that there were more benefits than risks from youth sports. However, areas of concerns and questions remain unanswered.

- What is the earliest age a child should begin sport participation and does this differ for gender and for individual sports?
- What is the tolerable effective exercise dose for a child?
- What is the safest and most beneficial sport for children to pursue?

This book is structured to effectively organize the information presented and discussed at the workshop and the conclusions and recommendations the workshop participants reached concerning intensive participation in youth sports.

Each domain—psychological, sociological, physiological, and clinical/pathological—will follow this pattern in its respective sections:

1. *Introduction.* Each part opener will summarize the two review papers and the major risks and benefits of intensive youth sports as developed in the workshop.
2. *Recommendations for major issues.* The part opener will summarize the discussions that lead to the development of the major issues during the workshop. This will be followed by recommendations to maximize the benefits and minimize the risks of intensive youth sports.

3. *Review papers*. Each section will present two review papers on intensive youth sports, which will provide the scientific basis for recommendations.

May the reader of this volume learn as much as the workshop participants, and together may we maximize the benefits and minimize the risks of intensive youth sports.

References

Fleck, S.J., & Kraemer, W.J. (1987). *Designing resistance training programs*. Champaign, IL: Human Kinetics.

Selye, H. (1950). *The physiology and pathology of exposure to stress*. Montreal: Acta Medical.

PART I

Psychological Perspectives

Rainer Martens

Sport builds character in our nation's young, argues former U.S. president Gerald Ford. He believes competition and striving to win are essential experiences that prepare our nation's youth to become the leaders of tomorrow.

The celebrated author James Michener also praises the virtues of sport for children, especially the competitive element, as he expressed in *Sports in America*:

> I find competition to be the rule of nature, tension to be the structure of the universe. I believe that normal competition is good for a human being and I am sure that flight from it hastens death. I am prepared to acknowledge every charge against fanatical competition, or senselessly prolonged tension, and I would not foist either upon young people. But I would not wish to avoid reasonable competition, for I like a world in which men and women test themselves against others or against abstract ideals. . . . I do not want to see my nation fall into desuetude because its citizens are unwilling to meet the challenges of our time. (p. 424)

But many critics express grave doubts about the value of intensive sport programs for children. Children's sports are making neurotics of our young because of the relentless pressure to win at all costs, charge some critics. In a recent television documentary, children's sport programs were characterized as a form of organized child abuse.

In Part I we examine the psychological impact of intensive sport participation on young athletes. We begin by considering the risks and benefits that are often thought to be associated with children's participation in sport. The recommendations of the workshop panel of experts are also presented. Chapters 1 and 2 examine in depth the psychological research on the stress of sport participation and its influence on self-esteem.

Major Psychological Issues

Are sports detrimental or beneficial to the psychological and social development of their young participants? Sports medicine professionals, youth sport administrators, coaches, and most of all parents want to know the answer to this question.

The answer is, of course, that it depends—it depends largely on the nature of the experience. It especially depends on the quality of leadership provided by coaches, parents, and officials, the behaviors of peers, and the personalities and attitudes of the young participants.

In developing recommendations about intensive participation in children's sports, the workshop panel of experts identified eight major issues in the psychological aspects of children's sport participation. For each issue, the potential detriments and benefits of sport participation were identified and discussed. These *potential* negatives and positives are presented next, and recommendations about how to minimize the negatives follow.

Competitive Stress

Negative
The psychological stress of intensive sport participation may be so great that it leads to an unhealthy anxiety disorder and diminishes the fun of participation. Stress sustained over extended periods may lead to burnout, resulting in children's choosing to drop out of sport and thus be denied its benefits. It is the process of clearly identifying winners and losers, which may threaten a young athlete's self-worth, that causes the high levels of stress.

Positive
Competitive sport, and the stress associated with it, may help young people to cope with the competitive, stressful world we live in. Metaphorically, competitive stress in children's sports may serve as an inoculation to build antibodies in children against the more harmful stress viruses they will encounter later in life.

Self-Esteem

Negative
When children repeatedly perceive that they have failed in sport and that this failure is a consequence of their own action, their self-esteem may plummet. Associated with the development of negative self-esteem are increased diffidence and feelings of incompetency. Because sport and physical performance have considerable meaning in the lives of young people, especially with their peers, early failure in sport and corresponding reduction in self-esteem may have long-term adverse consequences.

Positive
Sport enhances children's self-esteem by building confidence in their physical and social skills. The key to a positive sport experience is for adults to help children understand that the important thing is not winning the contest but achieving their own realistic, personal goals. When a child's self-esteem is enhanced through sport participation, it increases the likelihood that the child will continue to be involved in sport and will thus attain the other benefits of sport participation

In addition, it is widely believed that enhanced self-esteem from sport participation provides a child with greater confidence to achieve in other spheres of life.

Motivation

Negative
As a result of repeated failure, young athletes may develop a fear of future failure not only in sport but in other achievement-oriented activities. This fear of failure may adversely affect children's motivation to succeed, especially through a self-fulfilling prophecy: If athletes believe that they should not bother to try because past efforts to achieve have only resulted in failure, then this failure to try, of course, almost certainly assures future failure.

Positive
Success fuels the motivation to achieve more success. But just as winning is not the essential ingredient of success in the enhancement of self-esteem, it is not the essential element in building the motive to achieve success. It is athletes' perceptions that they have obtained their personal goals that fuel the desire to undertake new challenges, to pursue reasonable risks, and to not fear failure.

Moreover, many children fail to commit themselves to excellence because in many of society's institutions, especially education, they are not sufficiently stimulated or challenged. Sport, by its nature, provides a tremendous challenge that motivates young people to develop the attributes to become excellent. Sport can help children learn to make an intense commitment to obtain goals that are difficult to achieve and valued highly. Learning this lesson through sport has potential carryover to other achievement endeavors.

Competitiveness

Negative
Children's sport programs may produce young people who are irrationally competitive, a by-product of the adult-induced pressure to win at all costs. The consequence is that children fail to learn when cooperative strategies are more appropriate than competitive strategies.

Positive
Sport provides an excellent opportunity for children to learn when cooperative and competitive behaviors are appropriate in different situations and to learn how cooperative and competitive they should be. Sport especially helps children learn when to cooperate within a competitive context, a behavioral skill essential for success in life.

Moral Development

Negative
It is sometimes charged that children's sport programs retard moral development because they expose children to unsportsmanlike behavior. When children

observe adults and other children cheating, behaving violently, and using intimidation to achieve desired goals in sport, and when these actions are successful, the positive moral development of children can be undermined.

Positive

By observing positive role models and experiencing reinforcement of appropriate behaviors, children can learn socially approved moral behaviors through participation in sport. Through the sport experience, in which rules are frequently tested, children can learn not only to obey the rules but to understand the reasons for rules and their value to fair play. Children especially can learn moral behaviors in a context in which the outcome has great significance for them, which further enhances the impact of these lessons on moral development.

Unhealthy Attitudes

Negative

Children may develop unhealthy attitudes about sport, exercise, and physical fitness because of negative experiences in sport. Repeated failure; constant criticism from coaches, parents, or peers; and the experience of physical activity as a form of punishment are the frequent villains that may create unhealthy attitudes in children. These unhealthy attitudes are of concern because they predispose children to reduce or eliminate further involvement in sport and physical activity, perhaps for the rest of their lives.

Positive

Successful sport experiences are likely to lead children to appreciate sport and physical activity. With adult counsel, children can learn that sport and physical activity contribute to healthy bodies, and healthy bodies permit them to enjoy sport throughout their lives.

Development of Responsibility

Negative

Sport participation may lead children to acquire a personality disposition in which they do not accept responsibility for their own actions but instead perceive that outside forces determine what happens to them. Young athletes develop this perception, referred to as being externally controlled, when adults deny them the opportunity to make decisions for themselves and fail to reinforce self-responsibility. Externally controlled athletes fail to take responsibility for their actions, both positive and negative, because they believe, based on past experience, that the outcome of their actions is determined by external factors, not by the actions themselves. The consequence of developing such a perception is that children do not mature into independent, socially responsible adults.

Positive

When adults allow children to share in decision making in sport, children can learn to become increasingly responsible and independent. As children become more responsible, they develop the healthy personality attribute of being internally controlled. That is, they perceive that they are the origin of their own behaviors and thus are responsible for the outcomes of their actions.

Social Development

Negative

Because of the extensive time commitment to intensive participation in sport programs, children may fail to develop well-rounded, wholesome personalities and may impede their academic, social, and artistic development. Two common criticisms of very intensive participation in sport are that children fail to develop a full array of interpersonal skills and become extremely self-centered.

Positive

Sport provides young people with numerous opportunities to interact with other children and adults, which helps them develop interpersonal skills. Sport also provides excellent opportunities for young people to develop leadership skills as they work within a team to pursue excellence. And sport can help young people develop emotional maturity and psychological skills in order to reach their full potential.

Stress and Self-Esteem

The psychology of children's sport has many dimensions, but probably the two most prominent issues in the past 40 years have been concern about the psychological stress of intensive participation and the impact of the win-loss, competitive environment on children's self-esteem. The two chapters that follow review these issues in depth.

The first chapter, written by Daniel Gould, examines the extensive research literature on competitive stress and its impact on children participating in intensive competitive sports. Gould explains that stress is more a process than a product and draws attention to the importance of perception as the critical factor in determining what causes sport experiences to be stressful. Based on the available evidence, Gould concludes that sport for most children is not overly stressful.

Gould then examines whether intensive participation in sport leads to "burnout." After conceptualizing burnout, Gould examines its causes and prominence among young athletes. He then closes his thorough review with a look at ways to manage stress in young athletes and offers recommendations for professional practice and further research.

Chapter 2 provides an in-depth look at the impact of intensive sport participation on children's self-esteem and motivation. This comprehensive review, written by Maureen Weiss, begins by examining how self-esteem develops, especially within the sport context. Next, Weiss looks at the development of motivation among young athletes, considering factors that influence children's initial decisions to participate, their continued participation, and their decisions to leave sport.

Weiss then presents a series of recommendations for professional practice with regard to enhancing self-esteem and motivation, or at least avoiding their impairment. The thought-provoking chapter closes with opinions about future research directions.

Recommendations

Next the recommendations of the workshop panel of experts are presented with regard to the eight issues discussed previously. The recommendations are more extensive for the issues of competitive stress and self-esteem; these are followed by briefer comments on the other six issues. These recommendations are based on the panel's review of the research literature as presented by Gould and Weiss and on the consensus process followed by the panel of experts.

Competitive Stress

The stress arising from participation in children's sports is not excessive for the vast majority of children. However, a small but significant minority do experience excessive stress, caused primarily by children evaluating their self-worth on the basis of winning or losing.

Coaches, parents, and sports health care professionals need to acquire the skill to identify children who are at risk of excessive stress. Children most susceptible to perceiving the sport environment as threatening are those who have low self-esteem, which often is caused by frequent failure in the past, unrealistic expectations about their abilities, and frequent criticism from others.

Once identified, at-risk children need assistance to reduce their perception of the sport environment as overly threatening. Coaches and parents may especially reduce competitive stress by communicating to at-risk children that their worth is not related to whether they win or lose the game but rather to their striving to achieve personal goals that are within their reach.

When competitive stress becomes inordinate and is not reduced by adult efforts to dissociate self-worth with the outcome of the contest, then professional help may be beneficial. Some young athletes need to learn coping strategies in order to manage their predisposition to perceive excessive stress. Such coping strategies should be taught by a competent sport psychologist or by another sport health care professional who has equal training.

Self-Esteem

Sport has the potential to greatly enhance children's perceptions of self-worth, about both their physical and social selves. However, sport has an equal potential to adversely affect children's emerging perceptions of self. The primary determinant of whether the sport experience enhances or impairs self-esteem is the behavior of adults who are significant to the child, primarily coaches and parents.

Adults must recognize that it is far more important for children to develop realistic and positive views of themselves than for them to defeat their opponents. Coaching to enhance self-esteem first and to win the contest second requires teaching values for most coaches and parents.

A separate book merits writing on the many steps that can be taken to enhance self-esteem and avoid damaging it in sport, but within the space limits here the panel of experts offer these recommendations.

1. Those children with "fragile" egos, who show signs of diffidence and overconfidence, and who appear to be unrealistic about their abilities are especially at risk of sport's adversely affecting their self-esteem. Coaches and parents should provide these youngsters with special care.
2. It is especially valuable for coaches and parents to minimize the importance of winning as a measure of self-worth while emphasizing the merit of achieving personal goals that are realistic for the child.
3. Children, with or without adult influence, may develop unrealistic expectations of their abilities. Coaches and parents must help children keep their expectations realistic so that they have a reasonable chance to experience success.
4. Coaches and parents should provide specific feedback on performance— telling the child what was done incorrectly and how to correct an error— rather than generalized praise. Children perceive generalized praise as meaningless, but with instructive feedback and the resultant improvement in skill, children find that their deeds merit enhanced self-perception.
5. Self-esteem is more likely to be enhanced when children compete with other children of similar ability. Competing against players of much higher ability is likely to impair the self-esteem of low-ability children.
6. Programs should eliminate such practices as an "open draft" selection system and "cutting" players from children's sports teams; this will reduce the threat to self-esteem for those selected last or cut from the team.

Motivation

The panel of experts agreed that success does indeed fuel the motive to achieve more success. Thus sport should be organized so that every athlete will experience success. To achieve this lofty objective, we must redefine success to mean not the winning of the contest but rather the achieving of each athlete's personal goals.

Striving to win the contest is a worthy short-term objective for young athletes. As mentioned earlier, children's learning to make an intense commitment to be excellent by achieving a difficult and valued goal is a benefit of sport participation that adults should encourage. But this objective should not be obtained at the expense of the total development of the child.

Thus, it is recommended that coaches and parents encourage children to try to win the contest, but at the same time adults must teach young athletes to judge their self-worth not on the basis of the outcome of the contest but on the attainment of their own performance goals.

Competitiveness

Sport provides young people an opportunity to learn how to compete and how to cooperate with teammates and opponents. Sport especially provides children an opportunity to learn how to cooperate within a competitive context. That is, to be successful in sport, young players must learn how to cooperate not only with teammates but with the opposing players and the rule structure of the contest, in order for the competition to be optimal. Sport is most challenging when children understand that competitors are not the enemy but are individuals who provide an opportunity for children to challenge themselves in striving to become excellent.

Moral Development

Sport, with its rules that define appropriate behavior, officials to judge these behaviors, and the unambiguous scoring of action, provides a wonderful opportunity to socialize children about appropriate moral behaviors. This opportunity, however, can only be realized when the adults who guide children through the sport experience model and reinforce appropriate moral behavior. Children are more likely to be good sports when adults are good sports.

Administrators of children's sport programs not only must encourage children to be good sports but must prepare coaches to be good models of such behavior and must require coaches and parents to comply with codes of conduct.

Attitudes

The panel of experts recommends that adults manage the sport experience so that children gain an appreciation for physical activity and the health benefits it provides. Adults can achieve this by not using physical activity as punishment and by keeping sport fun rather than turning it into work; coaches in particular can contribute by demonstrating good personal health habits.

Children are much more influenced by what adults do than what they say. Thus, adults who smoke, consume alcohol, and are obese fail to provide positive role models for children. Good adult role models should show children that not only is it important to be fit to play sport but that playing sport will help keep them fit the rest of their lives.

Development of Responsibility

It is highly recommended that adults help children learn to accept responsibility for themselves through their participation in sport. Children cannot learn to become responsible for themselves if coaches and parents make all the decisions for them.

Children should be given opportunities to make decisions, within their developmental capacities, about their participation. Adults must be prepared for children to err in their decision making and must provide wise counsel to help children learn how to make better judgments.

Social Development

Although sport may emphasize the physical and motor skill development of children, adults who guide children's sport experiences should not neglect development of important social skills. These skills include interpersonal skills, such as effective communication and leadership behaviors.

Young athletes may develop social skills within and outside of sport. Sport provides many opportunities for social development, but if sport consumes too much of the athlete's time, development of social skills in other contexts besides sports may be neglected. The panel of experts recommends that youth sport participation not be so extensive that sport skills are developed at the expense of social, academic, and other personal skills.

The panel recommends that prepubescent athletes not be separated from their families for months at a time to attend specialized training camps. The panel of experts also advises against prepubescent athletes specializing in one sport and training for it exclusively year-round. Instead prepubescent children should be encouraged to participate in many sports, choosing to specialize only after they have had the opportunity to participate in several.

Conclusion

Sport is like a double-edged sword. Swung in the right direction the sword can have tremendously positive effects, but swung in the wrong direction it can be devastating. That sword is held by adults who supervise children's sports. Whether sport is constructive or destructive in the psychological development of young children greatly depends upon the values, education, and skills of those adults. Coaches especially are enormously influential in determining if children's sport experiences are positive or negative.

Thus, the workshop panel of experts loudly reinforces the call for coaches to be more than well-intentioned volunteers; coaches must be educated and properly prepared to assume the significant leadership role of coach. Sport is an important institution in our society for the psychological development of young people, and coaches first must be committed to helping young people develop psychologically and socially through sport and second must know how to obtain these benefits.

Chapter 1

Intensive Sport Participation and the Prepubescent Athlete: Competitive Stress and Burnout

Daniel Gould

Children's sport has a long and rich history in North America, dating back to the turn of the century. Since this time concerns about competitive stress and burnout have been voiced (Wiggins, 1987). In fact, competitive stress and burnout were fundamental issues in educators' and physicians' decisions to withdraw their support for competitive youth sport programs in the 1930s, 1940s, 1950s, and 1960s (Berryman, 1988).

Although competitive sport for children has flourished during the 20th century, the controversy concerning stress and burnout has not abated. Writers have discussed this topic by employing terms such as ''psychological trauma'' (Smilkstein, 1980) and ''child abuse'' (Tutko & Burns, 1978) and by asking ''how much does victory cost?'' (Nash, 1987). Hence, stress and burnout effects are two of the most significant issues to be examined by pediatric sport scientists. Moreover, professionals in youth sports have identified these issues as topics on which research is badly needed (Gould, 1990).

Fortunately, pediatric sport psychology researchers have begun to conduct systematic research on these areas, and theoretically derived data has begun to evolve to guide professional practice. This review is designed to examine intensive sport participation for children, by summarizing this literature with particular emphasis on competitive stress and burnout effects. Intensive participation in sport is operationally defined as sport participation in which children attend scheduled competitions and organized practices under the supervision of an adult leader. In addition, these programs involve physical activity dosages in excess of those experienced by nonathletic children taking part in free-play activities or physical education classes. This review will focus on the prepubescent athlete, although extrapolations from literature examining older children must be made because of the dearth of information available on younger children. Finally, it must be noted that research on burnout on elite young athletes—children involved in highly competitive sport environments—is especially lacking.

Understanding Stress and the Stress Process

There is little doubt that those involved in children's sports are concerned with the competitive stress placed on the young athlete. Problems arise when we attempt to discuss this issue, however, because stress is defined differently by different people. At times stress is defined as an environmental variable (e.g., ''the crowd stress was excessive''), whereas at other times it is viewed as an emotional response to a specific situation (e.g., ''the young athlete became highly stressed after the loss''). Smith and Smoll (1982) indicated that these two definitions of stress are not synonymous. Young athletes will vary greatly in their interpretations of how stressful they perceive certain environments. Specifically, one young gymnast may perceive competing in front of a large crowd as very stressful, whereas another may not. A distinction must therefore be made between potential stressors in the environment and the young athlete's perception of stress.

Not only has stress been defined both as an environmental variable affecting the young athlete and as a psychological reaction to environmental events, but it has often been labeled as having positive or negative effects. Youth sports critics suggest that stress is always bad for the child, whereas proponents of competitive youth sports view stress more favorably. These value-ladened definitions are inappropriate because stress researchers have shown that stress can have both positive and negative effects (Selye, 1974).

Because of the difficulties that have arisen in defining stress, many youth sport researchers have adopted process oriented definitions. Moreover, one of the most widely accepted process oriented definitions of stress is that of social psychologist Joseph McGrath (1970). McGrath (1970) defined stress as a process or sequence of steps whereby ''a substantial imbalance [occurs] between [environmental] demand and response capability, under conditions where failure to meet the demand had important consequences'' (p. 20). Moreover, the stress process is subdivided into four interrelated stages:

- The environmental situation in which the child is placed in, or in which demand is placed on the child
- The child's perception of the environmental demand
- The child's physical and psychological response
- The child's behavior as a result of that response

Each of these will be outlined next.

The first stage in the stress process occurs when a set of environmental circumstances places a demand on the young athlete (e.g., a young baseball player must face an outstanding opposing pitcher). However, not all children perceive environmental circumstances as a demand. Therefore, the second stage of the process focuses on the child's perceptions of the situation and whether the child appraises it as threatening. Moreover, Martens (1977) indicated that threat occurs when individuals perceive an imbalance between the perceived demands placed on them and their response capabilities (e.g., the young baseball player feels threatened because he or she has doubts about getting a hit).

The third stage in McGrath's model focuses on the individual's physiological response, actual decision making, and response selection to the perceived demand placed on him or her (e.g., the athlete becomes nervous, tightens up, and strikes out). The fourth stage focuses on the actual behavior or outcome of the process (e.g., the child does not get a hit and receives negative feedback from teammates).

Viewing stress in this fashion has several advantages. First, stress is viewed as a cycle of interrelated stages that can be individually examined. Second, McGrath's definition of stress emphasizes the individual's perception of the objective environment and not the environment alone. This is necessary because all young athletes do not perceive all events identically. Finally, viewing stress as a process means that we do not view stress in an emotional context, automatically assuming that it is good or bad. Rather, stress is defined as a sequence of events that lead to certain reactions and behaviors which may, at times, be positive, negative, or neutral.

Several other terms must be defined before the stress process and its ramifications can be fully understood. These include *state* and *trait anxiety*. State anxiety, which is often a by-product of the stress process, is defined as ''an existing or current emotional state characterized by feelings of apprehension and tension and associated with activation of the organism'' (Martens, 1977, p. 9).

In essence, state anxiety is a negative feeling experienced at a particular moment. It is a feeling that everyone has had at some time, whether it be the butterflies that an athlete feels a few minutes before a competition or that queasy feeling in the stomach that another person feels before giving a public speech for the first time.

Closely associated with the state anxiety is trait anxiety. Unlike state anxiety, trait anxiety is considered to be an enduring attribute, part of one's personality. Trait anxiety is defined as ''a predisposition to perceive certain environmental stimuli as threatening or nonthreatening and to respond to these stimuli with varying levels of state anxiety'' (Martens, 1977, p. 9).

Trait anxiety is important because it has been consistently shown to influence one's level of state anxiety. Specifically, a high-trait-anxious young athlete tends to perceive evaluative environments, like competitions, as very threatening and in so doing experiences increases in state anxiety. In contrast, a low-trait-anxious young athlete placed in the same competitive environment does not perceive the environment to be as threatening and does not experience marked increases in state anxiety. Thus the level of state anxiety a child experiences in evaluative environments is directly related to his or her level of trait anxiety.

In summary, a young athlete's level of trait anxiety affects the second stage of McGrath's stress process by influencing perception of the demands of the environment. High- as compared to low-trait-anxious children tend to perceive competition as threatening, and this results in increased state anxiety responses.

Moreover, increases in state anxiety have been found to be associated with performance variations, perceived satisfaction, and the amount of fun experienced.

Stress Research in Youth Sports

Using process definitions of stress, a number of investigators have begun to examine stress in children's sport. Major questions that have received greatest attention in this line of research include

- an examination of the levels of state anxiety experienced by young athletes in competitive settings,
- levels of trait anxiety in young athletes,
- factors related to state and trait anxiety in young athletes, and
- consequences of anxiety in young athletes.

The research examining each of these questions will now be discussed.

Levels of State Anxiety Experienced by Young Athletes

A fundamental question concerning the controversy surrounding competitive sport participation for the prepubescent athlete focuses on the level of state anxiety the child experiences while participating in sport. Critics of youth sports have suggested that sport negatively affects the mental health of the child athlete, comparing levels of stress experienced by these children to that of soldiers in combat (Martens, 1978). In contrast, proponents of competitive sport for children have argued that the critics are overreacting, in that sport competition does not create unhealthy levels of state anxiety and that the anxiety which is experienced is beneficial because children learn how to successfully cope with stress through sport participation. Hence, one of the most popular areas studied by pediatric sport psychologists is the assessment of state anxiety experienced by young athletes.

The studies that have examined state anxiety experienced by young athletes can be classified into three types: survey assessments of state anxiety and anxiety-related symptoms associated with athletic competition; psychophysiological assessments of state anxiety experienced before, during, and after athletic competition; and assessments of state anxiety before, during, and after competition that use validated self-report state anxiety inventories. The research in each of these categories is summarized next.

Survey Research Findings. A number of investigators (Feltz & Albrecht, 1986; Gould, Horn, & Spreemann, 1983; Hale, 1961; McPherson, Marteniuk, Tihanyi, & Clark, 1980; Purdy, Haufler, & Eitzen, 1981; Ralio, 1982; Skubic, 1955; Tierney, 1988) have asked those involved in competitive sport for children (typically the young athlete, but sometimes parents of young athletes) to rate the degree of state anxiety–related symptoms that the athlete experienced during or as a result of athletic competition. In most cases, one or two questions on anxiety were posed as part of a larger youth sports survey project. For example, in the earliest study on this issue, Skubic (1955) found that about a third of the Little League baseball players she interviewed reported sleeping difficulties related to contests, whereas 33% of the male and 56% of the female youth swimmers surveyed by McPherson et al. (1980) reported experiencing some emotional stress. Hale (1961), however, reported that 97% of the fathers of Little League baseball participants he surveyed indicated that their sons were not affected by participation, whereas Feltz and Albrecht (1986) reported that 41% of their sample of elite young distance runners reported becoming nervous and worried in races, with 50% of these children indicating that this nervousness helped their performances. Because almost all of these studies used nonvalidated instruments and employed only superficial levels of assessment, this literature is most difficult to assess. However, it tends to show that although some young athletes report high levels of competitive state anxiety and state anxiety–related symptoms, this is typically less than one-half of the children involved.

Psychophysiological Assessment Research Findings. Several investigators (Hanson, 1967; Lowe & McGrath, 1971; Skubic, 1955) have used physiological stress measures such as heart rate to examine levels of state anxiety experienced by young athletes. Skubic (1955), for instance, used a Galvanic skin response measure to assess physiological stress in boys, ages 9 to 15 years, who participated in Little League baseball games and physical education class softball competitions. Results revealed few differences between the groups, and the author concluded that the state anxiety experienced during competitive youth baseball was not greater than that experienced in a physical education class competition.

Hanson (1967) continuously monitored the heart rates of 9- to 12-year-old baseball players before a game, in the field during the game, when players were at bat, and after the game. Results revealed that mean heart rates increased from 95 beats per minute (bpm) before the game to a maximum of 167 bpm while a player was at bat. Mean heart rates in the field were 127 bpm, and rates returned to 100 bpm following the game. Considerable variability was also found; the highest reported heart rate at bat was 204 bpm and the lowest 145 bpm. Hanson concluded that the stress of batting was high but short-lived. Moreover, Dishman (1989) cited evidence showing that the elevated physiological state anxiety as assessed by heart rate during youth sport competition does not appear to differ from that occurring during recreational play or bicycle ergometer tests. Hence, although the Hanson study showed that young athletes experience high levels of physiological state anxiety, these effects appear to be short-lived and may not result solely from psychological factors (but from increased physical activation as well). Indeed, in the Hanson (1967) investigation, most of the players did not report the ''stress'' of batting as negative.

In another youth baseball study, Lowe and McGrath (1971) measured respiration and heart rate prior to batting, specifically under conditions of varying game importance (e.g., based on league standings, win-loss records) and situation criticality (e.g., score, number of outs, position of runners on base). The results revealed that physiological state anxiety was positively related to game importance and increased situation criticality. Unfortunately, the authors did not assess nonevaluative or other forms of competition.

In summary, studies examining elevations in physiological state anxiety associated with youth sport competition show that either few differences exist between youth sports and other competitive environments (physical education class competitions) or that high but short-lived elevations in state anxiety occur during events. Interestingly, heightened state anxiety during events has been related to increased game importance and criticality.

Validated State Anxiety Measures. A number of investigators (Gould, Eklund, Petlichkoff, Peterson, & Bump, 1991; Scanlan & Passer, 1978, 1979; Simon & Martens, 1979) have used validated self-report state anxiety instruments to assess levels of state anxiety that children have experienced before, during, and after competitive youth sports events. Simon and Martens (1979) conducted the most extensive study of amounts of state anxiety experienced in competitive and noncompetitive sport settings. In particular, the state anxiety levels of boys ages 9 to 14 years were assessed in practice settings and just before competitions using the Competitive State Anxiety Inventory for Children (CSAI-C) (Martens, 1977). Simon and Martens (1979) examined differences between practice and competitive state anxiety levels and compared band solo performers, band group performers, boys taking an academic test, boys taking part in a physical education competition, and boys competing in baseball, basketball, tackle football, gymnastics, ice hockey, swimming, and wrestling competitions. The results revealed that state anxiety was higher during competition than during practice, although the overall change was not excessive. For example, the mean precompetitive state anxiety score for the entire sample was 16.87. Given that the scoring of the CSAI-C ranges from 10 to 30, the precompetitive state anxiety levels did not seem excessive. The authors noted, however, that substantial individual differences existed, with some boys exhibiting extremely high state anxiety levels.

Of particular interest in the Simon and Martens (1979) study was the comparison of state anxiety levels of boys participating in sports and boys participating in other competitive activities. Comparisons across the specific activities revealed that band soloists exhibited the greatest state anxiety ($M = 21.48$) followed by individual sport participants (M wrestling = 19.52, M gymnastics = 18.52), with the physical education participants showing the lowest levels of anxiety ($M = 14.47$). Of all sport participants, wrestlers exhibited the highest precompetitive state anxiety levels. Once again, however, these levels were not excessive.

In another investigation, Gould et al. (1991) examined state anxiety levels of young athletes by administering the CSAI-C to 13- and 14-year-old boys prior to competitive tournament wrestling matches. The findings revealed that for the 112 participants, prematch state anxiety levels averaged 18.9 (out of a possible 30). Moreover, when the percentages of children falling in each quarter of state anxiety scale were examined, the authors found that only 9% had scores in the upper quartile ($\geq$25), scores that are considered extremely high (Gould &

Petlichkoff, 1988b). These and other studies (Scanlan & Passer, 1978, 1979) conducted in this area reveal, then, that the majority of children participating in competitive youth sports are not experiencing excessive levels of state anxiety.

Investigations that have examined levels of state anxiety and state anxiety–related symptoms in young athletes from these three different research perspectives have shown that the vast majority of children involved in competitive sport do not experience high levels of stress. It appears that the critics of organized competitive sport programs for children are incorrect in their claims about excessive levels of stress placed on young athletes. Concerns about excessive stress should, therefore, not prevent parents from encouraging their prepubescent children to participate in sport. This conclusion does not mean, however, that some children involved in sport do not experience excessive or unhealthy levels of stress. The evidence shows that a small but significant number of young athletes experience high levels of stress that may be manifested in such symptoms as insomnia and a loss of appetite. Moreover, if only 5 to 10% of the estimated 25 million children involved in North American sport experience stress, this would involve 1.25 to 2.5 million youngsters, many of whom would be prepubescents. Thus we need to identify what prepubescent athletes are susceptible to heightened state anxiety and what youth sport situations are related to heightened anxiety states in young athletes.

Levels of Trait Anxiety in Young Athletes

Although the research on state anxiety experienced by young athletes shows that most children do not experience excessive levels, the question still remains as to how competitive sport participation influences a child's trait anxiety. It is important that we examine trait anxiety, because it is a component of child's personality. Hence, if competitive sport influences a child's trait anxiety negatively, the change is much more enduring and stable.

Unfortunately, little research has examined the trait anxiety levels of youth sport participants and nonparticipants. In one of the few studies conducted with children, Magill and Ash (1979) found no competitive trait anxiety differences between fourth-grade youth sport participants and nonparticipants. Nonparticipant fifth graders, however, were higher in trait anxiety than were fifth-grade participants. Similarly, Feltz and Albrecht (1986) found that 28 elite youth distance runners, ages 10 to 15 years, had competitive trait anxiety levels that were slightly higher than norms for comparable age and gender groups. Finally, a 1-year longitudinal study conducted by Raviv (1981) in Israel revealed that 37 children from sports clubs and 37 matched control nonparticipant children did not significantly differ in their competitive trait anxiety levels.

The equivocal and limited nature of the trait anxiety–sport participation research prevents one from drawing definitive conclusions regarding effects of competitive youth sport participation on child trait anxiety. However, the research that has been conducted suggests that at most participants have only slightly elevated levels of trait anxiety compared to nonparticipants, and in half the studies no differences were evident. More longitudinal studies are needed before definitive conclusions can be derived. Finally, potential moderator variables (e.g., extent of involvement, success level) mediating the relationship between participation status and competitive trait anxiety must be assessed.

Factors Related to State and Trait Anxiety in Young Athletes

Given the conclusion that as a group most young athletes do not experience excessive anxiety, but a substantial minority do, it is important that we identify the personal and situational factors associated with competitive state and trait anxiety. Fortunately, youth sport researchers have examined factors related to competitive state anxiety (Gould et al., 1991; Scanlan & Lewthwaite, 1984; Scanlan & Passer, 1978, 1979) and trait anxiety (Brustad, 1988; Brustad & Weiss, 1987; Passer, 1983) in young athletes. The results of these investigations are summarized next.

Factors Associated With State Anxiety in Young Athletes. This type of research typically consists of assessment of state anxiety levels in young athletes immediately before and after a competition. At a prior nonstressful time, such as a practice, the children complete extensive surveys that assess various personality factors such as self-esteem and provide demographic information such as years of experience in sport. Researchers then use this background information to predict their levels of pre- and postmatch state anxiety. Scanlan (1986) summarized this research and identified a number of personal and situational factors associated with competitive state anxiety. These include high competitive trait anxiety, low self-esteem, lower levels of fun, inability to derive satisfaction, low personal performance expectancies, and worries about failure and adult evaluation.

To reiterate, trait anxiety is a personality disposition that is part of a young athlete's personal makeup. This disposition predisposes the young athlete to perceive evaluative and competitive environments as threatening. Thus, when young athletes are high trait anxious, they respond to potentially stressful situations, like competition, with nervousness or high state anxiety levels. High-trait-anxious children, then, generally experience high levels of state anxiety.

The lower the young athlete's self-esteem, the higher the state anxiety level experienced. Closely associated with self-esteem are team performance expectancies. The lower the child's confidence relative to his or her team's ability to perform well, the more state anxiety he or she experiences.

It has been found that fun is related to state anxiety. When winning and losing are controlled, the more fun the child perceives and the less state anxiety is experienced. The less fun the child has, the more state anxiety is experienced.

Similarly, when winning and losing are factored out, postgame state anxiety has been found to be related to the amount of satisfaction the child perceives. The more satisfaction the child perceives from participating in the game, the less state anxiety is experienced. The less satisfaction the child perceives, the more state anxiety experienced.

Low personal performance expectancies are also related to state anxiety. The lower the child's expectancy relative to his personal ability to perform, the greater the state anxiety he experiences.

Finally, worries about failure and adult expectations and social evaluation are associated with elevations in state anxiety. Findings indicate that the more the child worries, the greater the state anxiety experienced. An interesting finding from an investigation conducted by Scanlan and Lewthwaite (1984) suggested that increased parental pressure to participate was associated with increased levels of state anxiety in children. That is, young wrestlers who perceived that their participation was important to their parents experienced more state anxiety than athletes who did not perceive as much parental pressure to participate.

Turning to situational factors that have been associated with heightened state anxiety in young athletes, two are most readily apparent. The first is victory versus defeat; children who win games experience less state anxiety than children who lose (Scanlan & Passer, 1979). Second, as the Lowe and McGrath youth baseball data (1971) showed, the greater the importance placed on a particular event, the more stressful it is for the child (Martens, Vealey, & Burton, 1990).

In summary then, the research on pre- and postgame state anxiety and factors associated with it provides a useful profile of personal and situational factors that are related to that minority of children who experience heightened state anxiety in competitive sport. Knowledge of this profile can help physicians, parents, and adult leaders identify children who experience high levels of state anxiety in sport and, in turn, take steps to reduce this stress.

Factors Associated With Trait Anxiety in Young Athletes. Several investigators (Brustad, 1988; Brustad & Weiss, 1987; Passer, 1983) have begun to study factors associated with high competitive trait anxiety in young athletes. This is an important area of study because the personality disposition of high competitive trait anxiety has been one of the factors most consistently related to elevated levels of high state anxiety in young athletes. A better understanding of the prepubescent high-trait-anxious young athlete and factors related to his or her high trait anxiety should assist youth sport leaders in helping "at-risk" children cope with the stress of athletic competition.

Passer (1983) was the first investigator to study the high-competitive-trait-anxious young athlete. He compared 163 high- and low-competitive-trait-anxious youth soccer players, ages 10 to 15 years, on self-esteem, performance expectancies, criticism for failure expectations, performance- and evaluation-related worries, and perceived competence. Results revealed that the high- as compared to low-anxious players worried more frequently about losing, about not playing well, and about coach, parent, and teammate evaluations. The author concluded that high-competitive-trait-anxious young athletes perceive evaluation and failure as major threats.

In a follow-up investigation, Brustad and Weiss (1987) studied 55 male baseball players and 55 female softball players, ages 9 to 13. Results revealed that high-as compared to low-competitive-trait-anxious boys reported lower levels of self-esteem and more performance worries. No significant differences were found for the girls.

Finally, Brustad (1988) studied 207 youth basketball players and found that high-competitive-trait-anxious children, both boys and girls, demonstrated lower levels of self-esteem. High competitive-trait-anxious athletes also demonstrated more frequent evaluation- and performance-related worries.

These results show that the high-trait-anxious child athlete is likely to perceive failure or negative evaluation from significant others as emotionally very aversive (Brustad, 1988). Hence, adult leaders need to reduce the degree these children are openly evaluated, ensure their success, and enhance their self-esteem.

Consequences of Athletic Stress

Stress is a major concern to those involved in competitive youth sports because it is thought to have important effects on the young athlete. Stress has been linked, for example, to sport withdrawal in young athletes (Gould & Petlichkoff, 1988a), health effects such as loss of sleep (Skubic, 1955; State of Michigan, 1978) and appetite (Skubic, 1955), decreased fun and satisfaction (Scanlan & Lewthwaite, 1984; Scanlan & Passer, 1978, 1979), physical injury (Smith, Smoll, & Ptacek, 1990), and deteriorated performance (Gould et al., 1991; Scanlan, Lewthwaite, & Jackson, 1984). Smoll and Smith (1989) provided an excellent review of this literature; therefore, the literature will not be reviewed in depth here.

Although links have been established between competitive stress, performance, participation, health, and enjoyment in young athletes, at this time few conclusions can be reached with any degree of certainty. In most cases too few studies have been conducted; moreover, lines of systematic research (as have been conducted regarding elevated levels of state anxiety in young athletes) are needed. Last, longitudinal investigations that examine long-term effects of competitive athletic stress on children are warranted.

Given the stress consequence research, we can conclude that competitive-athletic stress can have important physical and behavioral consequences on the child. Unfortunately, the long-term ramifications of such stress and the number of children afflicted with negative consequences are unknown.

Equally important, but to date never studied, are positive consequences of stress. Martens (1978), for instance, suggested that competitive stress may act like a vaccine. That is, when the child athlete receives stress in the appropriate dosage it will allow her or him to learn stress-coping skills (build up antibodies) that can be transferred to other life settings. Yet too much stress will result in severe negative consequences (disease).

Investigations are needed to examine whether Martens's (1978) vaccine stress consequence hypothesis is correct and, if so, what optimal dosages of stress are appropriate, because this issue has never been empirically examined. Similarly, increased state anxiety is often assumed to negatively influence the performance of the young athlete. However, research with adult athletes (see Gould & Krane, 1992, for a review of this research) has shown that increased state anxiety does not always lead to inferior performance and may at times enhance performance. Thus, there is a need to examine both negative and positive consequences of athletic stress for the prepubescent athlete.

Burnout in Young Athletes

> Sally is a 12-year-old age-group swimmer who shows considerable promise in her sport. Her times have improved steadily the last few seasons, and people are starting to discuss her as our next U.S. Olympic hope. However, Sally has decided to stop swimming. Although she still loves the feeling of learning how to swim faster and enjoys the social atmosphere of the pool, she has become tired of the year-round, twice daily, 4,000-m workouts. Sally also feels emotionally drained from her attempts to live up to her parents', coaches', and teammates' expectations that she win races and set records every time she competes. In short, Sally is a youth sports burnout!

Because of scenarios such as Sally's, youth sport leaders and researchers have become increasingly interested in burnout resulting from the physical and psychological demands of sport participation. Questions are being raised as to the number of children burning out of sport, the causes of youth sport burnout, types of sports associated with high incidences of burnout, and ways to prevent burnout. Unfortunately, the questions being posed in this area far outnumber scientific answers.

Although questions far outweigh our knowledge in this area, progress is being made. Since the 1970s the youth sport literature has given increased attention to the topic (Feigley, 1984; Greenspan, 1983; Hellstedt, 1988; Juba, 1986; Nash, 1987; J. Smith, 1986; Tierney, 1988; Tutko & Burns, 1978). Moreover, R.E. Smith (1986) developed an excellent conceptual model of athletic burnout that has done much to define and establish parameters of study for this phenomena and has outlined future research directions.

One of R.E. Smith's (1986) most important contributions to the burnout literature has been to conceptually clarify when and why burnout occurs and when and why it does not. For example, some authors (e.g., Gilbert, 1988) have indicated that burnout is the reason why 80 to 90% of children drop out of organized sport by age 15. R.E. Smith (1986) cogently argues, however, that most children's decisions to drop out of organized sport are not due to burnout. In particular, reviews of youth sport attrition research (Gould, 1987; Gould & Petlichkoff, 1988a; Weiss, chapter 2) show that most children do not discontinue sport involvement because of excessive competitive stress or burnout. Rather, conflicts of interest and interest in other activities are the most consistently cited motives for sport withdrawal. Moreover, many children who discontinue participation in one sport or program elect to participate in another. Hence, all children who drop out of a sport are not necessarily burning out!

In contrast to what may be labeled as the "normal" process of sport selection and attrition, R.E. Smith (1986) indicated that burnout is a special form of sport withdrawal. It is a response to "chronic stress" in which a young athlete ceases to participate in a previously enjoyable activity. That is, the child withdraws from sport physically, psychologically, or emotionally because she or he perceives that it is not possible to meet the physical and psychological demands of sport. For this reason, it is best to view burnout as a special type of youth sports withdrawal.

Not only did R.E. Smith (1986) better delineate burnout, but based on burnout literature in helping professions and his own stress research he developed a conceptual model explaining athletic burnout. This model parallels the relationship between stress stages and stages in burnout. In Stage 1, the young athlete is placed in a situation that involves varying demands (e.g., high training workloads or excessive parent expectations), and in Stage 2 the child perceives those demands as excessive (e.g., he or she perceives few meaningful consequences or feels these demands cannot be controlled or achieved). In Stage 3 the child experiences varying physiological responses (e.g., tension, state anxiety, or insomnia), which in Stage 4 leads to varying burnout consequences (e.g., decreased performance or withdrawal). Hence, the model is significant because those interested in studying burnout can examine the various stages of the model, whereas practitioners can intervene at the varying stages to prevent burnout.

Sport sociologist Jay Coakley (1990) offered an alternative to R.E. Smith's (1986) stress-based model of burnout. Coakley's conceptualization is actually better viewed as an addition to the Smith view, because Coakley did not question Smith's predicted relationship between stress and burnout. Instead Coakley identified two "causes" of stress and subsequent burnout in the adolescent athlete. In particular, based on extensive interviews with 15 adolescent athletes who had burned out of sports in which they had been intensively training, Coakley found that these children were characterized by unidimensional self-conceptualizations (they saw themselves and were viewed by others only in terms of their specialized athletic roles—e.g., tennis prodigy), and he found that they participated in power relationships with others (e.g., coaches, parents) that seriously restricted their control of their own destinies, both in and out of sport. Coakley argued, then, that stress is best viewed as a correlate of burnout in young athletes, whereas the development of unidimensional self-conceptualizations and a lack of control on the part of the young athlete are the causes of stress and ultimately burnout. Hence, if adult leaders help young athletes view sport as only one part of their lives, providing opportunities for developing other nonsport identities and giving athletes more responsibility for making decisions, the likelihood of athletic burnout in the adolescent years will be lessened.

Although it is frustrating that little research exists on burnout and no tests of R.E. Smith's (1986) burnout model and Coakley's (1990) revision of it have been conducted to date, several authors have discussed burnout and suggested possible factors contributing to it. Tierney (1988) in discussing age-group swimmers, for instance, indicated that stress results from strenuous physical activity loads beyond some optimal level, psychological expectations of others, self-imposed expectations, and win-at-all-cost attitudes. Similarly, Juba (1986) identified excessive training workloads, parental pressure, and the repetitive nature of the sport as major burnout sources for young swimmers. J. Smith (1986), in discussing age-group tennis stress from a parent's perspective, cited inconsistent coaching practices, overuse injuries from excessive practice, and excessive time demands as major burnout sources. International travel demands, constant pressure resulting from intense competition, and significant-other love distributed on the basis of event outcome were burnout causes identified by Nash (1987). Finally, Feigley (1984) indicated that elite young gymnasts who are most susceptible to burnout are energetic perfectionists who lack assertive personal skills and are strongly influenced by others. These athletes also see smaller performance improvements due to declining returns and plateaus, and when they reach adolescence they struggle with their needs for self-determination, autonomy, and independence and become increasingly aware of the physical, competitive, and social consequences of participation.

These reports verify J. Smith's (1986) contentions that burnout results from chronic stress, which in turn results from a complex interaction between the personality of the young athlete and sport environment. These reports also provide some support for Coakley's (1990) view that a lack of personal control and unidimensional self-conceptualizations are associated with burnout in young athletes. General environmental characteristics that appear to be related to increased burnout in young athletes include extremely high training volumes and time demands, demanding performance expectations that are either self-imposed or significant-other imposed, constant intense competition, inconsistent coaching practices, and little personal control in sport decision making. Personal factors likely to be associated with young athletes susceptible to burnout include perfectionism, a need to please others, nonassertiveness, and unidimensional self-conceptualizations focusing only on one's athletic involvement. Although the issue is not examined, the burnout literature also seems to imply that those high-trait-anxious, low self-esteem children previously identified in this review as being especially susceptible to heightened competitive state anxiety are prone to burnout under these environmental circumstances. Last, it is very important to recognize that burnout results from prolonged chronic stress and not isolated elevated levels of state anxiety.

Stress Management and the Young Athlete

Although understanding stress levels, sources, and consequences in prepubescent athletes is important, the ultimate objective of most coaches, parents, and physicians is to help young athletes manage stress productively. This involves identifying child athletes who are at risk for experiencing high levels of stress and implementing any number of stress management strategies. These areas are discussed next.

Identifying At-Risk Child Athletes

The literature examined in this review provides evidence, as opposed to specula-tion, relative to the nature and extent of competitive stress and burnout in youth sports. Researchers have found that most children do not experience excessive stress in competitive sport and are not prematurely burning out. However, a significant minority of young athletes do experience high levels of competitive state anxiety and burn out of sport. Adults involved with youth sports need then to identify these at-risk children and help them cope with competitive stress.

The first step in helping at-risk prepubescent athletes cope with competitive stress is to identify these children. This may be much easier said than accom-plished, however. Research with adult collegiate populations (Gould, Krane, & Finch, 1990; Hanson & Gould, 1988) has shown that coaches are not very skilled at predicting their athletes' trait and state anxiety levels. Coaches are in fact very poor predictors of when their athletes are anxious or not anxious; it was found that only one of four coaches is reasonably accurate. Similarly, in a study of 11- and 12-year-old swimmers, Purdy, Haufler, and Eitzen (1981) found that parents underestimated the anxiety experienced by their children, whereas coaches overes-timated the swimmers' anxieties.

These findings signify that talking about assisting at-risk young athletes cope with stress and having good intentions are not enough; youth sport leaders and parents must work at this complex process. Fortunately, research (Gould et al., 1990) has shown that coaches who are more empathetic and who have had training in sport psychology are better able to identify their at-risk, anxious athletes. Hence, youth sport coaching education programs must specifically ad-dress these issues. Empathy training as that suggested by Martens (1987) would be especially useful.

Stress Management Strategies

Although little research has been conducted on stress management training with prepubescent athletes, much has been written on this topic in the general sport psychology literature (see Gould, 1990, for a review). Moreover, evidence shows that children in general can learn to cope with stress (Compas, 1987). Hence, although more research is certainly needed, stress management techniques are available to allow youth sport leaders and parents to help children cope with stress. Two general categories of these stress management strategies are environmental engineering techniques and self-control strategies.

Environmental Engineering Techniques. Because stress involves the complex interplay of environmental demands and personal characteristics of the child, one way to influence the stress process is to manipulate the physical and social environment of the young athletes. Environmental engineering stress management techniques typically focus on reducing uncertainty and the importance of perfor-mance for the athlete (Martens, 1987). For example, a young athlete experiences more state anxiety when she or he perceives there is more uncertainty. A coach waiting to announce the starting lineup is a typical source of uncertainty in the sporting context; players are uncertain about their playing status and therefore become more state anxious. A parent or coach sending vague nonverbal messages to the young athlete will also cause the young athlete to be more uncertain (relative to the parent's or coach's feelings about the sport and the athlete's performance) and in turn will cause more stress. Finally, inconsistent social evaluation, for example if the parent or coach acts as if he or she loves the child one moment and dislikes the child the next, can create uncertainty and more state anxiety. To reduce uncertainty, the coach could announce starting lineups as early as possible and parents, administrators, and coaches could send clearer messages to the young athlete.

Event importance is another environmental factor related to heightened anxiety. Sometimes event importance is heightened by what significant others say to young athletes. For example, a coach attempting to mentally prepare his or her team by giving an emotional pep talk and telling athletes how important the game is may increase their anxiety. In some highly competitive youth sport programs, increased media coverage can also increase state anxiety. Last, when parents and coaches place so much emphasis on sport involvement that the child is not allowed to develop other nonsport competencies, stress is likely to be increased.

Sport organizers can reduce event important by curtailing media coverage of youth events. If large crowds attend children's games and add stress that is thought to be inappropriate, the seating or bleachers can be removed to reduce crowd size. Coaches can refrain from giving emotionally charged pregame talks to their teams, and parents can emphasize involvement in nonsport activities.

These environmental engineering techniques can be very useful. Typically, they are the last techniques recognized by coaches, parents, and administrators, but they are some of the most important, especially with young developing athletes.

Self-Control Techniques. Self-control stress management strategies are techniques that the child can employ to combat emotional reactions accompanying the perception of stress. They may also be classified as physical or cognitively based techniques (Martens, 1987). Physical stress management self-control techniques involve such strategies as self-directed relaxation, progressive relaxation, and biofeedback. Progressive relaxation training, for instance, involves having the young athlete systematically tense and relax muscle groups throughout the body and focus on the feelings produced by these states. After considerable practice, the child learns to quickly relax various muscle groups on demand and can then use this conditioned response to relax during stressful portions of competition. Regardless of the type of physical stress management technique employed, the child focuses on learning how to control the physical effects associated with increased stress.

Cognitive self-control stress management techniques include self-talk analysis and modification, thought stopping, and rational thinking. In essence, these techniques focus on managing the seemingly uncontrollable thoughts and worries that children often experience when they become highly state anxious. For instance, rational thinking focuses on teaching the child to recognize self-defeating thoughts that often trigger other negative thoughts and emotional reactions. "I cannot make an error" is an example of this type of statement. It is irrational because at times all athletes make errors, and the child must realize that although it is highly desirable not to make an error, it is unrealistic to say one cannot. In fact, this is an irrational thought that may cause increased anxiety and actually lead to a mistake. A rational substitute thought might be, "I don't want to make a mistake, but all players do sometimes—remember, watch the ball." Hence, by controlling their thoughts via these techniques, young athletes learn to manage their anxiety.

Although evidence supports the utility of these stress management techniques in adult athletes (see Gould, 1990), Vealey (1988) indicated that we need to examine the efficacy of such techniques with child athletes. Can young athletes learn these self-control strategies? At what age should they be introduced? Are all these strategies equally effective in helping children cope with stress? These are questions that need attention from youth sport researchers. Unfortunately, at this time few if any investigators are attempting to examine them.

Conclusions and Recommendations

This review has examined the literature on competitive stress and burnout effects accompanying intensive sport participation for the prepubescent athlete. Specifically, this chapter has discussed the stress process, levels of state and trait anxiety experienced by young athletes, factors related to heightened state and trait anxiety, consequences of athletic stress, youth sport burnout, and stress management techniques for the young athlete. Although the literature in this area is certainly far from complete, it is appropriate to conclude this review with a number of professional practice and future research recommendations.

Professional Practice Recommendations

1. *Adults involved in youth sports must recognize that competitive stress and burnout effects in young athletes result from the complex interplay of environmental factors and personal characteristics inherent in the child.* Adults must therefore consider both types of factors in the youth sport setting and not attribute stress to the child or situation alone.
2. *Children should not be discouraged from participating in competitive sport because of stress and burnout concerns.* The vast majority of prepubescent children engaged in competitive sports do not experience excessive levels of state anxiety and do not appear to differ from their nonathletic counterparts in trait anxiety. Similarly, large numbers of children are not burning out of competitive sport.
3. *Efforts must be made to identify at-risk young athletes who experience high levels of competitive stress.* That is, although most children who participate in sport do not experience extremely high levels of competitive

stress or burn out, a significant minority of participants suffer from high levels of competitive stress and some are thought to be burning out.

4. *Adult leaders involved in prepubescent sports must be able to identify the profile of the excessively stressed, at-risk child athlete.* Children most likely to experience high levels of state anxiety exhibit high levels of competitive trait anxiety, low self-esteem, and low personal and team performance expectancies; experience less fun and satisfaction; and worry more about failure and adult evaluation. The stress response is most likely to occur when these children are placed in environments characterized by uncertainty about others' expectations, their ability to perform, and social evaluation. These environments are also characterized by the importance placed on competitive performance and contest outcome.

5. *Although little research has been conducted on the topic, parents, coaches, and physicians must recognize that children susceptible to burnout are reported to experience extremely high training volumes and time demands, high self-imposed or significant other–imposed performance expectations, little control over sport and nonsport decisions, constant intense competition, and inconsistent coaching practices.* These at-risk children are also thought to be perfectionists, to have sport-specific unidimensional identities, and to be other-oriented, nonassertive, and high competitive trait anxious. Finally, adult leaders must understand that burnout results from prolonged chronic stress and not from isolated elevated levels of state anxiety.

6. *Empathy and sport psychology training are necessary to ensure that parents and coaches accurately identify at-risk children who are especially susceptible to heightened anxiety and burnout.* Concerted efforts must be made to identify these children.

7. *Young athletes must be taught stress management strategies.* Competitive stress in children's sports can be effectively managed through a variety of environmental engineering and self-control stress management strategies.

Future Research Recommendations

1. *Studies examining heightened state anxiety, trait anxiety, and burnout in prepubescent athletes involved in intensive competition are badly needed.* Researchers must use prospective longitudinal designs to examine long-term ramifications of participation.

2. *Longitudinal investigations that examine long-term effects of competitive athletic stress on children are warranted.* Not only should researchers examine the negative consequences but also positive consequences such as Martens's (1978) vaccine stress consequence hypothesis.

3. *We must identify the number of children who burn out versus withdraw from competitive sport each year.*

4. *Because parents and coaches are inaccurate predictors of state and trait anxiety in young athletes, both parents and coaches must be taught to identify at-risk children.*

5. *Intervention studies designed to alleviate stress and burnout effects in young athletes are warranted.* Such studies will be most beneficial if they are based upon existing conceptual frameworks of stress and burnout, like those of McGrath (1970) and Smith (1986).

Notes

Portions of this manuscript are based on an address titled "Stress and Stress Management in Sport: Sport Science Implications for Guiding Practice," delivered at the International Association for Physical Education in Higher Education World Conference at the Loughborough University, England (July, 1990) as well as the previously published work of Gould and Petlichkoff (1988b). The author would also like to thank the personnel at the U.S. Olympic Training Center, Department of Educational Services, for their help in conducting computer-assisted literature searches on stress and burnout in youth sport.

References

Berryman, J.W. (1988). The rise of highly organized sports for preadolescent boys. In F.L. Smoll, R.A. MaGill, & M.J. Ash (Eds.), *Children in sport* (3rd ed., pp. 3-16). Champaign, IL: Human Kinetics.

Brustad, R.J. (1988). Affective outcomes in competitive youth sport: The influence of intrapersonal and socialization factors. *Journal of Sport and Exercise Psychology*, **10**, 307-321.

Brustad, R.J., & Weiss, M.R. (1987). Competence perceptions and sources of worry in high, medium, and low competitive trait-anxious young athletes. *Journal of Sport Psychology*, **9**, 97-105.

Coakley, J. (1990). *A sociological alternative to stress-based models of burnout among adolescent athletes.* Unpublished manuscript, University of Colorado, Colorado Springs.

Compas, B.E. (1987). Coping with stress during childhood and adolescence. *Psychological Bulletin*, **101**, 393-403.

Dishman, R.K. (1989). Exercise and sport psychology in youth 6 to 18 years of age. In C.V. Gisolfi & D.R. Lamb (Eds.), *Perspectives in exercise and sports medicine: Vol. 2. Youth exercise and sport* (pp. 47-97). Indianapolis: Benchmark Press.

Feigley, D.S. (1984). Psychological burnout in high-level athletes. *The Physician and Sportsmedicine*, **12**(10), 109-112, 115-119.

Feltz, D.L., & Albrecht, R.R. (1986). Psychological implications of competitive running. In M.R. Weiss & D. Gould (Eds.), *Sports for children and youth* (pp. 225-230). Champaign, IL: Human Kinetics.

Gilbert, R. (1988). Player burnout: How to prevent it. *Soccer Journal*, **33**(3), 32.

Gould, D. (1987). Understanding attrition in children's sport. In D. Gould & M.R. Weiss (Eds.), *Advances in pediatric sport sciences* (pp. 61-86). Champaign, IL: Human Kinetics.

Gould, D. (1990, July). *Stress and stress management in sport: Sport science implications for guiding practice.* Presentation made at the International Association for Physical Education in Higher Education World Conference, Loughborough, England.

Gould, D., Eklund, R., Petlichkoff, L., Peterson, K., & Bump, L. (1991). Psychological predictors of state anxiety and performance in age-group wrestlers. *Pediatric Exercise Science*, **3**, 198-208.

Gould, D., Horn, T., & Spreemann, J. (1983). Sources of stress in junior elite wrestlers. *Journal of Sport Psychology*, **5**, 159-171.

Gould, D. & Krane, V. (1992). The arousal-athletic performance relationship: Current status and future directions. In T.S. Horn (Ed.), *Advances in sport psychology* (pp. 119-141). Champaign, IL: Human Kinetics.

Gould, D., Krane, V., & Finch, L. (1990). *Factors influencing coaches' ability to predict multidimensional state and trait anxiety levels in their athletes.* Unpublished manuscript, University of North Carolina at Greensboro.

Gould, D., & Petlichkoff, L. (1988a). Participation motivation and attrition in young athletes. In F.L. Smoll, R.A. MaGill, & M.J. Ash (Eds.), *Children in sport* (3rd ed., pp. 161-178). Champaign, IL: Human Kinetics.

Gould, D., & Petlichkoff, L. (1988b). Psychological stress and the age-group wrestler. In E.W. Brown & C.F. Branta (Eds.), *Competitive sports for children and youth* (pp. 63-73). Champaign, IL: Human Kinetics.

Greenspan, E. (1983). Burnout. *Women's Sports*, **5**(10), 50-53, 74.

Hanson, D.L. (1967). Cardiac response to participation in Little League baseball competition as determined by telemetry. *Research Quarterly*, **38**, 384-388.

Hanson, T.W., & Gould, D. (1988). Factors affecting the ability of coaches to estimate their athletes' trait and state anxiety levels. *The Sport Psychologist*, **4**, 298-313.

Hale, C.J. (1961). Injuries among 771,810 Little League baseball players. *Journal of Sports Medicine and Physical Fitness*, **1**, 3-7.

Hellstedt, J.C. (1988). Kids, parents and sports: Some questions and answers. *The Physician and Sportsmedicine*, **16**(4), 59-62, 69-71.

Juba, N. (1986). The requirements of competitive swimming—the effect on children: A coach's perspective. In G. Gleeson (Ed.), *The growing child in competitive sport* (pp. 173-178). London: Hodder & Stoughton.

Lowe, R., & McGrath, J.E. (1971). *Stress, arousal and performance: Some findings calling for a new theory* (Report No. AF1161-67). Washington, DC: Air Force Office of Strategic Research.

Magill, R.A., & Ash, M.J. (1979). Academic, psycho-social and motor characteristics of participants and nonparticipants in children's sports. *Research Quarterly*, **50**, 230-240.

Martens, R. (1977). *Sports competition anxiety test.* Champaign, IL: Human Kinetics.

Martens, R. (1978). *Joy and sadness in children's sports.* Champaign, IL: Human Kinetics.

Martens, R. (1987). *Coaches guide to sport psychology.* Champaign, IL: Human Kinetics.

Martens, R., Vealey, R.S., & Burton, D. (1990). *Competitive anxiety in sport.* Champaign, IL: Human Kinetics.

McGrath, J.E. (1970). A conceptual formulation for research on stress. In J.E. McGrath (Ed.), *Social and psychological factors in stress* (pp. 19-49). New York: Holt, Rinehart & Winston.

McPherson, B., Marteniuk, R., Tihanyi, J., & Clark, W. (1980). The social system of age group swimmers, parents and coaches. *Canadian Journal of Applied Sport Sciences*, **4**, 142-145.

Nash, H.L. (1987). Elite child-athletes: How much does victory cost? *The Physician and Sportsmedicine*, **15**(8), 129-133.

Passer, M.W. (1983). Fear of failure, fear of evaluation, perceived competence and self-esteem in competitive-trait anxious children. *Journal of Sport Psychology*, **5**, 172-188.

Purdy, D.A., Haufler, S.E., & Eitzen, D.S. (1981). Stress among child athletes: Perceptions by parents, coaches and athletes. *Journal of Sport Behavior*, **4**, 32-44.

Ralio, W.S. (1982). The relationship of sport in childhood and adolescence to mental and social health. *Scandinavian Journal of Sports Medicine*, **29**(Suppl.), 135-145.

Raviv, S. (1981). Reactions to frustration, level of anxiety and loss of control of children participating in competitive sports. In E. Geron, A. Mashiach, N. Dunkelman, S. Raviv, Z. Levin, & E. Nakash (Eds.), *Children in sport: Psychosociological characteristics* (pp. 72-94). Netanya, Israel: Wingate Institute.

Scanlan, T. (1986). Competitive stress in children. In M.R. Weiss & D. Gould (Eds.), *Sport for children and youth* (pp. 113-118). Champaign, IL: Human Kinetics.

Scanlan, T.K., & Lewthwaite, R. (1984). Social psychological aspects of competition for male youth sport participants: I. Predictors of competitive stress. *Journal of Sport Psychology,* **6**, 208-227.

Scanlan, T.K., Lewthwaite, R., & Jackson, B.L. (1984). Social psychological aspects of competition for male youth sport participants: II. Predictors of performance outcomes. *Journal of Sport Psychology,* **6**, 422-429.

Scanlan, T.K., & Passer, M. (1978). Factors related to competitive stress among male youth sports participants. *Medicine and Science in Sports,* **10**, 103-108.

Scanlan, T.K., & Passer, M. (1979). Sources of competitive stress in young female athletes. *Journal of Sport Psychology,* **1**, 151-159.

Selye, H. (1974). *Stress without distress.* New York: New American Library.

Simon, J., & Martens, R. (1979). Children's anxiety in sport and nonsport evaluative activities. *Journal of Sport Psychology,* **1**, 160-169.

Skubic, E. (1955). Emotional responses of boys to Little League and Middle League competitive baseball. *Research Quarterly,* **26**, 342-352.

Smilkstein, G. (1980). Psychological trauma in children and youth in competitive sport. *The Journal of Family Practice,* **10**(4), 737-739.

Smith, J. (1986). My son used to enjoy tennis . . . A concerned parent's perspective. In G. Gleeson (Ed.), *The growing child in competitive sport* (pp. 179-183). London: Hodder & Stoughton.

Smith, R.E. (1986). Toward a cognitive-affective model of athletic burnout. *Journal of Sport Psychology,* **8**, 36-50.

Smith, R.E., & Smoll, F.L. (1982). Psychological stress: A conceptual model and some intervention strategies in youth sports. In R.A. Magill, M.J. Ash, & F.L. Smoll (Eds.), *Children in sport* (2nd ed., pp. 178-195). Champaign, IL: Human Kinetics.

Smith, R.E., Smoll, F.L., & Ptacek, J.T. (1990). Conjunctive moderator variables in vulnerability and resiliency research: Life stress, social support and coping skills, and adolescent sport injuries. *Journal of Personality and Social Psychology,* **58**, 360-370.

Smoll, F.L., & Smith, R.E. (1989). Competitive stress and young athletes. In C.O. Teitz (Ed.), *Scientific foundation of sports medicine* (pp. 375-390). Toronto: Decker.

State of Michigan. (1978). *Joint legislative study on youth sports programs: Phase II, agency sponsored sports.* East Lansing, MI: Author.

Tierney, J. (1988). Stress in age-group swimmers. *Swimming Technique,* **24**(4), 9-14.

Tutko, T., & Burns, W. (1978, March). The child superstar: A curse or a blessing. *Tennis USA,* pp. 40-48, 56.

Vealey, R.S. (1988). Future directions in psychological skills training. *The Sport Psychologist,* **4**, 318-336.

Wiggins, D.K. (1987). A history of organized play and highly competitive sport for American children. In D. Gould & M.R. Weiss (Eds.), *Advances in pediatric sport sciences: Vol. 2. Behavioral issues* (pp. 1-24). Champaign, IL: Human Kinetics.

Chapter 2

Psychological Effects of Intensive Sport Participation on Children and Youth: Self-Esteem and Motivation

Maureen R. Weiss

The psychological benefits of competitive sport participation for children and adolescents have been debated since the turn of the century (Wiggins, 1987). Among the positive psychosocial outcomes advocated as natural consequences of active sport participation have been self-esteem, perceptions of physical ability, interpersonal skills with peers and adults, positive attitudes toward the value of physical activity, and "character" or sportspersonship (Gould & Weiss, 1987; Martens, 1978; Smith, Smoll, & Smith, 1989; Weiss & Gould, 1986). Despite these intuitive and widely held beliefs, little evidence exists to substantiate that intensive sport participation *causes* positive changes in psychological and social characteristics of youth.

The majority of studies examining the relationship between participation in competitive youth sports and social psychological development have been correlational in nature. Thus, rather than saying that sport participation causes changes in psychosocial development, we can more accurately say that there is an association between participating in organized sport activities and self-esteem, motivational, and personality changes. Although these study designs limit the extent to which we can make statements about the effects of sport participation on psychological development, these studies nevertheless provide us with a wealth of information about consistent relationships among participation, sport achievement, and selected psychological characteristics. Moreover, in the early 1990s, several lines of research investigations systematically produced findings demonstrating how self-esteem and motivation are associated with sport participation. Therefore, rather than a series of isolated research findings so prevalent in the early 1980s (Gould, 1982), there is now a solid knowledge base on youth sport psychological development.

This chapter provides an overview of two major areas of psychological development through intensive sport participation: self-esteem and motivation. The development of self-esteem is one of the most popular topics in the pediatric sport psychology and anecdotal literatures. Researchers, parents, coaches, and physicians all show an interest in and concern for the child's self-esteem development as a consequence of intense competitive sport involvement. Intimately related to self-esteem is motivation, and more specifically children's desires to remain active in sport and physical activity. In fact, it is difficult to talk about self-esteem without also alluding to subsequent changes in motivation. Research has consistently shown that self-esteem, and more specifically perceptions of physical ability, are predictive of achievement behavior (e.g., physical skill development), intrinsic motivation, and positive affect (see Fox, 1988; Weiss, 1987a; Weiss & Chaumeton, 1992). Thus, a child's self-perceptions have a powerful influence on sustained participation in sport and the subsequent skill mastery benefits that occur.

Although this chapter addresses perhaps two of the most popular, significant, and far-reaching psychological constructs affecting children's achievement in sport, several other psychosocial benefits are available through sport participation. One of the hottest topics in recent years in the youth sport literature is moral development or sportspersonship (Bredemeier & Shields, 1985; Weiss, 1987b; Weiss & Bredemeier, 1990). Physical and verbal aggression toward opponents and teammates (e.g., intent to injure, name calling), unfair play (e.g., cheating), and unequal opportunities (e.g., only the best athletes play) have occurred more frequently and intensely in recent years. These actions can be attributed, at least in part, to an overemphasis on winning by either the competitive program itself or the significant others that comprise the sport environment (i.e., coaches, parents, and peers). Thus, researchers and practitioners advocate that the sport setting be structured to maximize sportspersonship and minimize undesirable conduct among young athletes (Weiss, 1987b; Weiss & Bredemeier, 1986, 1990). Due to page limitations, this important research literature will not be covered here. However, for in-depth discussions of the theory, research, and implications of moral development in sport, readers are directed to several major review papers (Bredemeier & Shields, 1987; Weiss & Bredemeier, 1986, 1990).

The remainder of this chapter is divided into three sections. First, the development of self-esteem and the research to date investigating this development in sport will be discussed. Self-esteem development will be reviewed in relation to several related issues: influence from significant others, its multidimensional nature, the strong link to affective experiences, and its motivational influence on participation behavior. Second, the development of motivation and the contemporary research in sport psychology will be reviewed. Subsections include factors influencing children's initial participation in sport, their continued participation, and attrition from competitive sport. Finally, this paper will offer professional practice recommendations as well as future research directions on the psychological effects of youth sport participation on self-esteem and motivation.

Youth Sport Participation and Self-Esteem Development

The maintenance and enhancement of one's overall self-evaluation as a person, as well as more specific self-evaluations such as physical ability, physical appearance, physical fitness, interpersonal skills, and morality, have played a pervasive role in the study of psychological development of children and adolescents. In fact, in the late 1980s California Governor George Dukmajian organized a task force on self-esteem because he strongly believed that frequent societal problems such as juvenile delinquency, teenage pregnancies, and adolescent suicides are ultimately grounded in issues of self-esteem. Thus, self-esteem is viewed as a personality characteristic that is strongly tied to subsequent attitudes and behaviors relevant to one's social roles and expectations.

Traditionally, all sorts of *self* words have appeared in the literature and this has been a source of definitional confusion. Such terms have included *self-concept, self-worth, self-esteem, self-image, self-confidence*, and *self-perceptions*. Although each of these terms may be defined somewhat uniquely, they will be used interchangeably in this paper to refer to the description of, evaluation of, and affect toward one's competencies. Specifically, Coopersmith's (1967) definition of self-esteem has been particularly relevant to physical activity and sport. According to Coopersmith, self-esteem is

> the evaluation which the individual makes and customarily maintains with regard to himself: It expresses an attitude of approval or disapproval and indicates the extent to which an individual believes himself to be capable, significant, successful and worthy. In short, self-esteem is a personal judgment of worthiness that is expressed in the attitudes the individual conveys to others by verbal reports and other expressive behavior. (p. 5)

What is most attractive about Coopersmith's definition is that it highlights the extent to which a person "believes" himself or herself to be competent and successful, and that these beliefs are conveyed through both verbal and nonverbal behaviors. Thus, it is the individual's cognitions and perceptions of her or his ability, not objective ability estimates per se, that are most revealing with regard to attitudes and behavior in a particular achievement domain. Moreover, Coopersmith's definition also suggests that indicants of a child's self-esteem may be identified through his or her communication, such as attributions for success and failure, as well as through nonverbal behaviors, such as participation in or avoidance of physical activity, effort or lack thereof, and persistence or lack of persistence when learning new skills.

One of the critical questions surrounding an understanding of self-esteem is, How is it developed? That is, how are self-evaluations formed, from what or whom is information obtained, and what implications do high and low levels of self-esteem have for motivation to participate in sport? A number of theories by social psychologists and philosophers have addressed the nature of self-esteem development and its subsequent influence on behavior (see Weiss, 1987a, for a description of these theories). The numerous self-esteem theories can be translated into several common themes that have particular relevance for the competitive youth sport setting, and substantial research supports these themes in the sport domain.

Self-Esteem Is a Product of Social Interactions

Powerful sources of self-esteem development emanate from the reflected appraisals by and social comparisons to significant others in the child's life, such as parents, friends, coaches, and siblings. Reflected appraisals refer to verbal (e.g., "Good job!" or "What is the matter with you?") and nonverbal (e.g., a smile or frown) communications from these significant others regarding approval or disapproval of physical and social behaviors. Social comparison refers to the child's interest in evaluating his or her skills in comparison to other similar (or dissimilar) children. These appraisals and comparisons have a significant impact on the development of a child's self-esteem.

Research by Horn (Horn & Hasbrook, 1986, 1987; Horn & Weiss, 1991) suggests that the sources of information children and adolescents use to estimate their physical competence vary developmentally. Younger children (ages 8 and 9) tend to rely upon game outcome and parental feedback and evaluation as primary informational sources, whereas older children (ages 10 to 14) depend more heavily on social comparison to and evaluation by peers. Thus, although children are capable of engaging in social comparison processes as young as 6 or 7 (Scanlan, 1988), they appear to prefer evaluation from significant adults during middle childhood and switch to peer comparison and evaluation at later childhood and early adolescent stages. Moreover, Horn and Weiss (1991) found that children became more accurate about their physical competence with age: children 10 to 14 years of age were significantly more accurate about physical competencies than 8- to 9-year-old children (determined by correlations between measures of perceived competence and teachers' ratings of competence). These age differences in accuracy were related, in part, to the sources of information children used to evaluate ability. Younger children preferred feedback and evaluation from parents and teachers, whereas older children were more likely to use peer comparison and evaluation. In sum, the use of reflected appraisals by and comparison to significant others is influenced by cognitive-developmental factors.

This line of research has also revealed that preference for particular sources of information is related to self-perception and motivation-related characteristics. For example, Horn and Hasbrook (1987) found that for 10- to 14-year-old children, preference for external sources of information such as parental feedback and evaluation was higher in children who were low in perceived physical ability and high in external locus of control. Conversely, children high in perceived competence and internal locus of control were more likely to identify internal sources of criteria to judge competence, such as degree of improvement in skills, ease in learning new skills, and effort exerted. Moreover, Weiss and Horn (1990) found that children who underestimated their abilities (i.e., their perceptions of competence were much lower than teachers' ratings of their actual competence) demonstrated lower levels of intrinsic motivation, higher trait anxiety, and higher perceptions of external and unknown loci of control than children who were either accurate estimators or overestimators of their abilities. In sum, the line of research by Horn, Weiss, and colleagues suggests that children have several sources of information for evaluating their competence, but significant adults and peers occupy a central role. These social influences appear to be age related, and they affect the accuracy with which children judge their physical abilities. Finally, accuracy of perceived physical ability was found to be related to self-perceptions and achievement-related constructs such as intrinsic motivation and locus of control.

Only a handful of studies have examined the influence of coaches' attitudes and behaviors on children's self-esteem and perceived physical competence. The classic series of studies conducted by Smith, Smoll, and their colleagues at the University of Washington (see Smoll & Smith, 1989, for an overview of their entire research program and findings) revealed that coaches can significantly contribute to children's self-esteem and ability perceptions in the sport domain. These positive changes in self-perceptions, in turn, were found to be strongly related to motivational characteristics that ensure future sport involvement. Specifically, male baseball and basketball players whose coaches used more frequent encouragement, positive reinforcement, and corrective feedback had significantly higher self-esteem ratings from pre- to postseason in comparison to children whose coaches used these techniques less frequently. More importantly, the children who started the season with the lowest self-esteem ratings seemed to be influenced by the "positive-approach" coaches considerably more than were their moderate- and high-self-esteem peers (Smith, Smoll, & Curtis, 1979). That is, low-self-esteem kids evaluated their coaches more positively than did children with higher self-esteems who played for "positive-approach" coaches. This systematic series of investigations, which proceeded from psychometric development of observational ratings, to correlational analyses of athletes' ratings and observed coaching behaviors, to experimental intervention techniques, is regarded as one of the best in the youth sport literature. In fact, the intervention study (Smith et al., 1979), in which coaches were trained to use a more positive approach style of frequent and contingent positive reinforcement and skill-relevant performance feedback, is one of the few studies that have determined the direct influence of coaches' behaviors on the psychosocial development of children and adolescents.

Horn (1985) also examined the influence of observed coaching behaviors on the self-esteem and perceived competence of youth. Her sample consisted of female junior high school softball players ranging in age from 13 to 15 years. Coaches' reinforcement patterns in both practice and competitive settings were analyzed in relation to players' self-perceptions of ability across the entire season. Although skill improvement was the primary contributor to positive changes in self-perceptions of ability, certain coaching behaviors also significantly influenced physical self-esteem during practice situations only. Specifically, players who received more frequent positive reinforcement or no reinforcement in response to desirable performances scored lower in perceived physical competence, and players who received more criticism in response to performance errors had higher perceptions of competence. Although these results appear to contradict common-sense interpretations of the roles of positive and negative reinforcement, Horn was able to attribute these reinforcement findings to their contingency and appropriateness to player behaviors.

Looking more closely at the data, Horn (1985) found that the positive reinforcement statements given by the coaches were often unconditional to players' skill behaviors. That is, these statements were not responses to desirable skill techniques and behaviors, per se, but rather were more general (e.g., "good job, Sally" rather than "good job, Sally, on using two hands to catch the ball"). The coaches' use of criticism, however, was often associated with a direct response to a skill error and usually contained skill-relevant information on how to improve (e.g., "That's not the way to hit a ball, Jill! Put both hands together and keep your elbows away from your body"). These results demonstrate that the quantity of reinforcement and the mere use of positive statements are not sufficient to effect changes in self-esteem. Rather, the quality of coaches' behaviors, specifically the contingency to athletes' behavior and the appropriateness of the information given, is crucial to children's cognitions about the meaning of these messages.

Accordingly, Horn (1986, 1987) has provided guidelines for coaches with regard to the effective instructional behaviors that will maximize positive psychosocial development. These guidelines include (a) the contingency and quality of praise and criticism in response to children's performance successes and failures; (b) the frequency and quality of performance-relevant information provided to children during their performance attempts; and (c) the direct or implicit attributions contained in the evaluative feedback given to children. It is clear, however, that more research is essential if we are to understand the way that coaches' attitudes and behaviors in the sport setting directly and indirectly influence children's psychological and social development.

Surprisingly few studies have systematically examined parental influences on the formation of children's self-perceptions about physical ability. A review paper by Pickering and Weiss (1990) about parental influences on children's self-perceptions and motivation in youth sport revealed that this sparse knowledge base can be classified into three categories: general socialization influences (see Lewko & Greendorfer, 1988), self-perceptions of ability (McElroy & Kirkendall, 1981), and parental pressure (Brustad, 1988; Scanlan & Lewthwaite, 1984). Another category, achievement motivation in the academic domain (e.g., Parsons, Adler, & Kaczala, 1982), represents a significant amount of research about children's perceptions of their academic abilities. For example, Parsons et al. (1982) found a significant relationship between parental expectancies and beliefs about a child's academic ability and the child's own beliefs and attitudes. Also, Harter (1988), a developmental psychologist, reported that children's perceptions of social support by parents and classmates were strongly predictive of self-worth, which in turn significantly predicted affect and motivation. Replication and extension of research examining social support by parents, classmates, close friends, and teachers in the competitive sport domain await future attention. Of special interest is the relationship of parental expectations, beliefs, and reinforcement patterns with children's cognitions and expectations of their own abilities in the physical domain. Brustad (1992), in a thoughtful synthesis of the educational psychology research that has examined parental influences on competence perceptions and goal orientations, communicated how cognitive-developmental theory can be employed to test similar relationships in the physical domain.

Another salient significant-other group is a child's peers, including close friends, teammates, and classmates. However, despite numerous references to the contribution of sport involvement to the development of friendships, peer acceptance, and interpersonal competence, this area of research has been literally neglected (Evans & Roberts, 1987). This is very surprising given the attention that peer relations, social competence, and friendship formation receive in the general educational and psychology literature. For example, popular adolescents (especially males) are often characterized as those who are socially and physically competent (Coie, Dodge, & Kupersmidt, 1991; Coleman, 1961; Eitzen, 1976).

Recent studies in the sport domain have demonstrated a significant relationship between physical competence, interpersonal skills, and peer acceptance (Evans & Roberts, 1987; Weiss & Duncan, 1992). For example, Weiss and Duncan found a strong relationship between physical competence and peer acceptance. Specifically, boys and girls who believed they were physically competent were actually competent as rated by their teachers, and children who predicted successful performance in future sport situations were also those who perceived themselves to be accepted by their peers, were interpersonally competent as rated by their teachers, and expected to be successful in future interpersonal situations. Thus, given the importance of social comparison and peer evaluation in competitive sport situations, the area of peer relations, friendships, and social competence within the physical activity domain is one that must be pursued with more vigor.

Self-Esteem Is Multidimensional

Traditional discussion about self-esteem has centered around a general sense of self-worth or a global self-esteem. This general self-perception is characterized by an evaluation of how much an individual likes and values himself or herself as a human being (Fox, 1988; Fox & Corbin, 1989; Weiss, 1987a). Moreover, global self-esteem may also represent an individual's own personal definition of "worthiness," which may be related to abilities, attitudes, or behaviors. Finally, a global sense of self-worth is usually defined independently of specific situations or domains of competence. Rather, it is an overall evaluation that cuts across achievement and nonachievement situations.

More contemporary views of self-esteem, however, acknowledge not only an overall sense of self-worth, but situation- or domain-specific self-esteems as well (Harter, 1981b, 1986, 1988; Marsh, 1986; Marsh & Shavelson, 1985). That is, people form unique self-evaluations depending on the domain serving as the reference for their judgments (i.e., academic, social, physical). In addition, these domains may be differentiated at more specific levels, such as physical self-esteem branching out to perceived sport ability, perceived physical condition, perceived strength, and perceived physical attractiveness (Fox & Corbin, 1989). Thus, self-esteem can be viewed from a multidimensional perspective, and situation-specific or more general domain-specific measures of self-evaluation may be obtained.

The multidimensionality of self-esteem has been readily accepted and applied in the youth sport psychological literature (Fox, 1988; Fox & Corbin, 1989; Marsh & Peart, 1988; Weiss, 1987a). In fact, the majority of research exploring the influence of youth sport participation on self-perceptions has taken either a multidimensional approach by assessing perceived physical, social, or cognitive competence (e.g., Horn, 1985; Marsh & Peart, 1988; Weiss, McAuley, Ebbeck, & Wiese, 1990) or a more situation-specific approach by examining perceptions of specific sport competence (e.g., soccer, gymnastics) or physical self-efficacy (i.e., confidence in this situation) as determinants of competitive sport involvement and performance (e.g., Feltz & Brown, 1984; Ulrich, 1987; Weiss, Bredemeier, & Shewchuk, 1986; Weiss, Wiese, & Klint, 1989). These studies showed that specific measures of physical self-esteem have been more accurate and reliable than measures of global self-worth in predicting sport participation. For example, Weiss et al. (1986) found that activity-specific self-perceptions (e.g., gymnastics, swimming) were significantly predictive of achievement in that specific sport but not in other sports.

Given the consistent finding that specific aspects of self-esteem such as perceived physical competence and physical self-efficacy are more suitable than general self-esteem aspects for understanding sport participation, it appears that many of the earlier studies on self-esteem development through sport participation have been plagued by methodological problems. These include problems of definition (e.g., general vs. specific self-esteem), measurement (global self-worth measures with questionable validity and reliability), and design (e.g., study length, lack of control group). As an example, Gruber's (1986) meta-analysis of physical activity and self-esteem development in children resulted in only 27 out of 84 studies having sufficient data to calculate effect sizes. Of these 27 studies, only 6 related to competitive sport participation. It is apparent that the literature needs considerably more quality research on self-esteem effects of youth sport participation.

Affect Is a Determinant and Consequence of Self-Esteem Development

''The thrill of victory'' and ''the agony of defeat'' are phrases often used in the anecdotal literature. Indeed, emotional involvement characterizes sport participation and ensuing psychological development accurately: Children experience pride, joy, and excitement when they perceive their experiences to be successful, and similarly shame, disappointment, and anxiety when they believe that they have not done very well. These positive and negative affects are intimately related to self-esteem and future motivated behavior. In fact, Harter (1981a) said that "affect should be given center stage" when it comes to the study of motivated behavior (p. 5).

Most studies of affect in children's sport have centered around anxiety and stress in competitive settings (see Gould, chapter 1). Not until the late 1980s were empirical investigations of positive affect initiated, especially that of enjoyment (Brustad, 1988; Klint, 1988; Scanlan & Lewthwaite, 1986; Scanlan, Stein, & Ravizza, 1989; Wankel & Sefton, 1989). Scanlan and Lewthwaite found that 9- to 14-year-old wrestlers who perceived themselves higher in ability, had greater parental and coach satisfaction, and had less maternal pressure and evaluation experienced more enjoyment during the season than their counterparts. Brustad (1988) also found that low perceived parental pressure, as well as an intrinsic motivational orientation, predicted season-long enjoyment for 9- to 13-year-old basketball players. In a retrospective study of former elite figure skaters, Scanlan et al. (1989) found perceived competence to be a major source of enjoyment in competitive participation, and this perceived competence was characterized by experience of mastery processes and outcomes, competitive and performance achievement, and demonstration of athletic ability. These findings illuminate the relationship among affective experiences, self-perceptions, and motivated behavior. When young athletes enjoy their activity involvement and experience the "thrill" of victory, however defined by each child, higher levels of self-esteem and participation motivation are inevitable.

Self-Esteem Has a Motivational Influence on Behavior

As alluded to throughout this section, self-esteem is a primary construct determining motivation to participate and sustain involvement over time. The basic motivational elements associated with self-esteem have been self-enhancement and self-maintenance. Self-enhancement emphasizes growth and expansion of one's self-esteem, whereas self-maintenance refers to the preservation of one's existing self-esteem (Weiss, 1987a). More specifically, a self-consistency viewpoint of self-esteem contends that individuals interpret experiences and behave in ways that are consistent with or confirm their beliefs of themselves. These cognitions and behaviors, in turn, preserve the integrity of one's self-judgments. For example, a child who is low in self-esteem but who experiences success may look to "discount" what he or she sees as inconsistent with past behavior by making dysfunctional attributions such as "I was lucky" or "anybody can do that" (Harter, 1986; Weiss, 1987a). In response to an unsuccessful outcome, however, a low-self-esteem child may accept responsibility by attributing the outcome to her or his lack of physical ability. A high-self-esteem child, in contrast, would make attributions for success that are internal ("I'm good at sports"), stable ("I can do this well again in the future"), and personally controllable ("I am responsible for my success, not others' lack of ability or low task difficulty").

A high-self-esteem child will see failures as temporary setbacks and will seek to adopt new strategies, try harder, or problem solve to change future outcomes.

Several studies of youth sport participation have shown a consistent relationship between self-esteem and motivational variables that support a self-consistency viewpoint (see Weiss, 1987a; Weiss & Chaumeton, 1992). For example, Klint and Weiss (1987) found that children high in perceived physical competence rated skill-development as a more important reason for participation than did their low-perceived-competence peers. Similarly, children high in perceived peer acceptance rated affiliation-related motives more importantly than did children low in perceived peer acceptance. Thus, children appeared to be motivated by opportunities to demonstrate their competence in the competitive sport setting.

Similarly, Weiss, McAuley, Ebbeck, and Wiese (1990) also supported the self-consistency stance of self-esteem by finding a strong relationship between self-perception constructs such as perceived competence and perceived success with causal attributions. Specifically, children who were higher in physical competence perceptions made causal attributions for perceived success that were more internal, stable, and personally controllable than did low-self-esteem children. Moreover, children in the upper and lower quartiles of perceived physical competence could be discriminated fairly accurately on measures of perceived success, future success expectations, and stability attributions. In all cases, the differences were in the predicted directions as suggested by a self-consistency viewpoint. Thus, children who have low self-perceptions of ability may be considered at risk for persisting in sport and physical activity, as well as receiving the physical and psychosocial benefits of such participation.

Weiss and Horn (1990) investigated accuracy of children's physical estimates by comparing children's ability perceptions to sport teachers' assessments of actual competence. That is, quantity of perceived competence was not the focus per se, but whether children were underestimators, accurate estimators, or overestimators of their physical abilities. Findings from this study suggested that an "illusion of incompetence" (coined by Langer, 1979) in the sport domain may occur when children are both low and inaccurate in their ability perceptions. Results showed that the accuracy with which children rated their perceived competence in relation to actual competence was associated with motivation and achievement behavior. Specifically, 8- to 13-year-old children participating in a sport program were classified as underestimators, accurate estimators, or overestimators based on lower and upper quartiles of accuracy scores (computed by subtracting one's perceived competence from a coach's rating of actual competence). It was found that girls who seriously underestimated their physical competence recorded lower intrinsic motivation and higher trait anxiety and external locus of control scores than their accurate or overestimating peers. Underestimating boys only showed a higher unknown locus of control score than accurate and overestimating peers. This illusion of incompetence in the physical domain may seriously limit a child's success and may increase the likelihood of discontinued sport participation.

Another study from a self-consistency perspective was conducted by Weiss, Bredemeier, and Shewchuk (1986), who used causal modeling procedures to examine the relationships among perceived competence, perceived performance control, physical achievement, and motivation. Results revealed that children high in perceived competence and low in unknown locus of control demonstrated higher achievement scores and a more intrinsic motivational orientation than children low on these self-perception characteristics. That is, children who believed that they were competent and who understood the contingencies under which performance occurs (internal or external locus of control) preferred optimal challenges and recorded higher sport performance scores than children who scored lower on these self-perception variables. The results of the studies discussed in this section suggest that children with high levels of physical self-esteem follow a pattern of functional achievement behaviors reflected by success perceptions, appropriate causal attributions for success and failure, an intrinsic motivational orientation, and positive affective outcomes. Conversely, children who inaccurately perceive their physical abilities as low may enter a spiral of self-doubts and misperceptions about ability, and this may be reflected by their inappropriate attributions, low confidence ratings, and lack of effort and persistence at sport skills. Remember the definition of self-esteem by Coopersmith? It appears that the verbal and nonverbal indicants of attitudes and perceptions about oneself have been shown clearly in the youth sport psychological literature.

The findings of a significant relationship between self-perceptions of ability and motivation are perhaps some of the most robust in the pediatric sport psychology literature. The consistent findings that high-self-esteem children are characterized by positive achievement behaviors and sustained motivation, and that low-self-esteem children are characterized by dysfunctional achievement cognitions and behaviors, suggest that self-esteem is a powerful variable that drives children's motivation in youth sports. In turn, children who evidence higher levels of intrinsic motivation and continue to participate in sport are more likely to become more competent by learning and improving skills, which ultimately feeds into even higher levels of self-esteem. The discussion about the self-esteem/motivation relationship in competitive youth sports leads naturally to another area of psychological development: the motivation to initiate, continue, and discontinue intensive participation in sport.

Motivation to Initiate, Continue, and Discontinue Intensive Sport Participation

Since the 1980s, one of the most popular topics in the pediatric sport psychology literature has been participation motivation, a general topic that addresses the factors that influence why children and adolescents initiate, sustain, and withdraw from involvement in physical activity. This topic is a salient one with regard to mental and physical health because participation patterns and the quality of physical activity experiences during childhood are believed to have profound effects upon adult participation choices, patterns of adherence, and overall active lifestyles (Seefeldt, 1986).

Understanding children's motives for participating in sport and reasons for discontinuing involvement have been cited as two priorities of pediatric sport psychology researchers (Gould, 1982, 1987; Gould & Petlichkoff, 1988). Initial participation motives may vary for children and adolescents depending on a number of socialization influences (Coakley, 1987; McPherson & Brown, 1988). Once children are involved, their motivation to continue or discontinue participation will depend on a number of personal and contextual factors such as perceived ability, locus of control, coaching style, and social support from significant others such as parents, coaches, and teammates (Gould & Petlichkoff, 1988; Weiss, 1987a; Weiss & Petlichkoff, 1989). This portion of the chapter will focus on the personal and environmental factors that influence children's initial sport involvement, sustained participation, and withdrawal from a particular sport or sport program, or from sport altogether.

Initial Sport Participation Influences

Children's entry into organized, competitive sport programs generally evolves from three interacting factors (Coakley, 1987; Lewko & Greendorfer, 1988; McPherson & Brown, 1988): (a) modeling and reinforcement from significant others such as parents, teachers, and peers; (b) available opportunities for becoming involved and demonstrating skill competencies; and (c) attributes that are ascribed (e.g., sex, race, social class) and achieved (e.g., perceived ability, value toward sport). Thus, a child's initial involvement in intensive sport participation depends on both personal and situational factors.

A substantial amount of research has shown that children who have supportive parents, peers, siblings, teachers, and coaches are more likely to initiate and continue their participation in sport than individuals for whom this support is much lower (Lewko & Greendorfer, 1988; McPherson & Brown, 1988). Thus, individuals who comprise the sport environment of the child have a powerful influence over participation motivation. For example, Brown (1985) found that social support from parents, teammates, and friends was positively related to adolescent female swimmers' participation status. Specifically, current swimmers reported significantly more positive reinforcement and encouragement for their involvement in swimming than did former swimmers. In a follow-up study, Brown, Frankel, and Fennell (1989) found that the degree to which adolescent females maintained physical activity involvement was positively related to both the amount and type of influence received from mothers, fathers, and male and female peers.

The large majority of sport socialization studies have focused on white middle- to upper-middle-class males (Lewko & Greendorfer, 1988; McPherson & Brown, 1988). This is surprising given that sociocultural factors such as race, socioeconomic status, ethnicity, gender, and religion are known to play a large role in the available opportunities to become actively involved in sport, the extent to which parents encourage or discourage children to participate, and the value placed on sport as a salient achievement area. Only a few studies have investigated the relationship between race or ethnicity and sport socialization factors (Duda, 1985; Greendorfer & Ewing, 1981). Given the diversity of the population of the United States, and the fact that sport involvement is not exclusive to the white mainstream, it is imperative that future research pay more attention to cross-cultural differences in socialization influences and participation motivation (Duda & Allison, 1990).

Reasons for Continued Participation in Sport

Research on participation motives for continued involvement has been primarily descriptive (Gould & Petlichkoff, 1988; Weiss & Chaumeton, 1992). In essence, these research efforts were designed to develop a database so researchers could identify motives among several subgroups (e.g., participants, nonparticipants, former participants) as well as develop a theory or theories of sport-specific motivation. More recently, several theoretically based studies have supplemented the initial descriptive studies to contribute to a richer understanding of why children participate in sport (Gould & Petlichkoff, 1988; Weiss & Chaumeton, 1992). Both the descriptive and theoretical knowledge bases of children's motives for continued participation in sport are critical to an understanding of this phenomenon.

Descriptive Studies of Participation Motivation. The descriptive research on participation motivation has examined why children participate in sport in general (Gill, Gross, & Huddleston, 1983; Longhurst & Spink, 1987; Wankel & Kreisel, 1985), or in specific sports, such as swimming (Brodkin & Weiss, 1990; Gould, Feltz, & Weiss, 1985; McPherson, Marteniuk, Tihanyi, & Clark, 1980), gymnastics (Klint & Weiss, 1986), and ice hockey (Ewing, Feltz, Schultz, & Albrecht, 1988; McClements, Fry, & Sefton, 1982). A summary of these studies of young athletes reveals several common themes. First, the reasons children and adolescents give for participating in sport fall into several major categories: competence (e.g., to learn and improve skills, to achieve personal goals); affiliation (e.g., to be with or make new friends); team aspects (e.g., to be part of a group or team); competition (e.g., to win, to be successful); and fun (e.g., for excitement, challenge, action).

A second common finding of these descriptive studies is that children and adolescents typically indicate that several of these motivation categories are salient as reasons for continued participation. That is, children are likely to cite multiple motives, such as skill improvement, friendships, and competition aspects, as important reasons for staying involved in a particular sport or program. The final common theme is that to date, minimal age, gender, experience level, and sport type differences in participation motives have emerged. One of the possible reasons for this finding is the relative infancy of this area of research; only a few studies have examined differences among levels in these categories. Another possible reason for this finding is that reasons for enjoying participation and remaining involved may be universal, and participation occurs regardless of any number of individual difference or contextual factors.

Typical of early descriptive research conducted in participation motivation was a study by Sapp and Haubenstricker (1978). As part of a larger study for the state of Michigan, they examined reasons for nonschool sport participation for more than 1,000 boys and girls ranging in age from 11 to 18 years. Results revealed that major motives cited for participation were fun, skill improvement, physical fitness gains, to be with friends, and the desire to make new friends.

Gill, Gross, and Huddleston (1983) made the next significant step in this line of research by tapping a large number of youth participants across a wide variety of sports. Boys and girls ($N = 1138$) participating in university summer athletic camps were administered the Participation Motivation Questionnaire (PMQ). The most important reasons emerging for both boys and girls were to improve skills, to have fun, to learn new skills, to be challenged, and to be physically fit. Similarly, Gould, Feltz, and Weiss (1985) administered the PMQ to 365 age-group and school team swimmers and found that the most important participation motives were fun, fitness, and skill improvement. Finally, Klint and Weiss (1986) found that competitive, recreational, and former competitive gymnasts all cited competence- and fitness-related motives as important for their participation. However, the recreational and former athletes also indicated that fun was a very important motive for their continued gymnastic involvement.

Descriptive research conducted in England, Australia, and Canada has reported similar sport participation motives in children (Longhurst & Spink, 1987; Robertson, 1981; Wankel & Kreisel, 1985; Wankel & Sefton, 1990; White & Coakley, 1986). For example, Longhurst and Spink (1987) examined the motives of 621 Australian children involved in nonschool sport programs and reported that improving skills, being physically fit, enjoying the challenge, and the excitement of competition were among the most important reasons for participation. Similarly, Wankel and Kreisel (1985) studied the motives of 822 Canadian youth participating in ice hockey, soccer, and baseball. The four items rated as most important for this group were skill improvement, testing one's abilities against others', personal accomplishments, and excitement of the game. The motives rated as least important were winning, getting rewards, and pleasing others.

In summary, the large descriptive database on participation motivation provides important information about children's needs and desires in sport programs. These motives are multidimensional in nature (e.g., skill and affiliation), similar for boys and girls, and similar across sport types (e.g., gymnastics and swimming). Over the last few years, however, an increasing number of theoretically based studies have emerged (see Gould & Petlichkoff, 1988; Weiss & Chaumeton, 1992). These studies offer additional salient information, because theoretical research has the potential to not only describe but also explain and predict participation behavior in sport settings. Theoretical studies go beyond mere description by contributing to an understanding of how children's cognitions and perceptions, as well as factors within the competitive situation, influence decisions of whether to remain involved in sport or withdraw from sport (Gould & Petlich-koff, 1988; Weiss & Chaumeton, 1992; Weiss & Petlichkoff, 1989).

Theory-Based Studies of Participation Motivation. Several psychological theories or models of motivation have been used as frameworks for designing sport participation motivation studies (Deci & Ryan, 1985; Harter, 1978, 1981a, 1981b; Maehr & Nicholls, 1980; Nicholls, 1984; Thibaut & Kelley, 1959). All of these theories have received some support when applied to the sport domain; however, Harter's (1978, 1981a, 1981b) competence motivation theory has been tested the most frequently and has gleaned the most support with regard to factors influencing participation motivation (Weiss & Chaumeton, 1992). According to competence motivation theory, children are motivated to demonstrate competence and do so by engaging in mastery attempts (i.e., learning and demonstrating sport skills). If successful, these mastery experiences result in perceptions of enhanced competence and internal control, positive affect, and continued motivation to participate in sport.

Central to competence motivation theory are the constructs of perceived competence and perceived performance control as they contribute to affective outcomes and motivation. According to Harter, individuals who have higher perceptions of competence and internal control will demonstrate higher levels of intrinsic motivation, functional attributions for performance outcomes, higher performance scores, and will experience more enjoyment and less anxiety than individuals lower in these characteristics. Several empirical studies support these competence motivation predictions (Feltz & Petlichkoff, 1983; Klint, 1985, 1988; Klint & Weiss, 1987; Roberts, Kleiber, & Duda, 1981; Weiss, Bredemeier, & Shewchuk, 1986; Weiss, McAuley, Ebbeck, & Wiese, 1990).

Similar to competence motivation theory, achievement goal orientation theories (Maehr & Nicholls, 1980; Nicholls, 1984) and cognitive evaluation theory (Deci & Ryan, 1985) also emphasize the role of perceived competence and perceptions of success as predictors of sustained motivation in achievement settings. These theories are supported by sport-related studies designed to test these theories from the standpoint that self-perceptions of ability are strongly related to participation behavior and intrinsic motivation (Burton & Martens, 1986; Duda, 1987; Ewing, 1981; Petlichkoff, 1988; Ryan, Vallerand, & Deci, 1984).

Most of the participation motivation research that has been conducted from a theoretical perspective has also been designed to compare several subgroups on reasons for continued participation in sport. For the purposes of discussion here, these studies are classified according to particular areas of knowledge development. These include participant status (current participants, nonparticipants, former participants); playing status (starters, nonstarters, bench players); age-related differences; and level of intensity (elite, competitive, recreational athletes). The following section presents findings to date regarding comparative group differences on participation motives from both theoretical and descriptive perspectives and highlights topical areas in need of more participation motivation research.

Participant Status. Early studies examined differences on a number of perceived ability constructs among participants, nonparticipants, or former participants of a program. It was hypothesized that currently active participants would have higher perceptions of competence than either nonparticipants or dropouts. For example, Roberts, Kleiber, and Duda (1981) compared school sport participants and nonparticipants (defined as children who did not participate in that particular program) on perceptions of competence, general self-worth, and success expectations. Participants scored significantly higher on perceived cognitive and physical competence, general self-worth, and expectations for future success than did nonparticipants. Feltz and Petlichkoff (1983) reported similar findings for interscholastic participants versus dropouts across a variety of sports, as did Burton and Martens (1986) for current versus former youth wrestlers.

However, Klint (1985) did not find such a pattern of results in her study of current (mean age = 12.4 years.) and former (mean age = 16.7 years.) elite gymnasts. Rather, the former gymnasts reported higher perceptions of both physical competence and peer acceptance than did current gymnasts, and there were no differences in perceived gymnastic competence. These findings, which contradict previous studies, seem to have two reasonable explanations. First, in light of the specific training nature of high-level gymnastics, children who had dropped out of gymnastics were able to pursue other sport skills and social opportunities. Thus, their perceived competence scores may characterize a successful transition from a narrow focus on competitive gymnastics (mean practice time was 24 hr per week) to a broader focus on physical and social skill development. Second, it also appears that classifying children as participants, nonparticipants, and dropouts, as they were in previous studies, poses some problems. A nonparticipant or former participant in a particular program may, in fact, be actively involved in another sport type or program (Gould et al. 1982; Klint & Weiss, 1986).

The difficulties associated with defining participant classifications prompted Klint and Weiss (1987) to examine the relationship between perceptions of competence and particular motives for participation. More specifically, current elite gymnasts ($N = 67$) were categorized as either high or low in perceived physical competence, and high or low in perceived peer acceptance. Results supported competence motivation predictions, according to which children high in perceived competence should be motivated to demonstrate their abilities in that particular domain of competence. When compared to their low-perceived-competence peers children high in perceived physical competence were more motivated by skill development reasons, whereas gymnasts high in perceived peer acceptance were more highly motivated by the affiliation aspects of sport. These findings may explain, at least in part, the discrepant results previously reported relevant to perceived competence and participant status. That is, it is not enough to label an athlete as a participant or dropout; rather researchers must develop specific hypotheses based on sound theoretical bases.

Playing Status. Several subcategories of participation status exist even for children and adolescents who can be labeled as active or current athletes of a program. Three studies have examined differences in perceived competence and motivation-related characteristics among starters, nonstarters or primary substitutes, and survivors or secondary substitutes (Frazer, 1989; Petlichkoff, 1988; Robinson & Carron, 1982). Starters were defined as players who started the majority of their teams' games and played frequently; nonstarters or primary substitutes were defined as athletes who did not start the game but played frequently and were among the first athletes to be substituted; and survivors or secondary substitutes were defined as those athletes who played infrequently or were substituted into the game only when the outcome had been decided.

All three studies consistently revealed that players who "rode the bench" perceived their sport experiences much differently than did their peers who received significantly more playing time and thus more opportunities to learn and improve upon sport skills. Robinson and Carron (1982) found that starters in youth football displayed significantly more positive attitudes and socialization influences than did either survivors or dropouts from the program. Moreover, survivors perceived their coaches' behaviors to be more autocratic (or controlling) than did starters and nonstarters. Similarly, Petlichkoff (1988) found that interscholastic participants of several sports who were starters had significantly higher ability perceptions in comparison to nonstarters, survivors, dropouts, and players who were cut from their teams. Starters and nonstarters had higher levels of satisfaction than did these other groups, and, interestingly, survivors had lower satisfaction levels than did dropouts. Perhaps those athletes who were motivated to "hang on" despite their minimal playing opportunities were willing to put up with higher levels of dissatisfaction than those who voluntarily withdrew from the program. The survivors may have been motivated for external reasons such as social status or pleasing others, and this may have influenced their decisions to stay, despite their reports of low ability and dissatisfaction associated with being on the team.

Finally, Frazer (1989) also found that amount of playing time was significantly related to self-perceptions and motivation in adolescent female basketball players. Specifically, starters and primary substitutes, in comparison to secondary substitutes, showed significantly higher perceptions of basketball success, physical competence, peer acceptance, and enjoyment at pre-, middle-, and end-of-season assessments. Thus, athletes who enjoyed higher participation status and competition playing times had higher self-perceptions of competence and success and perceived their involvement as more enjoyable than did those who had substantially less playing time. Moreover, these findings were robust across an entire sport season. Taken together, the findings from these three studies suggest that considerable differences in self-perceptions and participation motivation exist among athletes who vary in playing time. In short, players who "ride the pine" don't perceive their skills to be improving (and probably they are not, due to lack of playing opportunities), perceive themselves as less competent in physical and interpersonal skills, and don't have as much fun, in comparison to their peers with more opportunities to learn, improve, and demonstrate their sport-specific abilities.

Age-Related Differences. Given that children and adolescents possess markedly different cognitive-developmental capabilities, one would hypothesize that motivation to participate in sport could be distinguished among younger children, older children, and adolescents. However, surprisingly few studies have examined age-related differences in participation motives (Weiss & Petlichkoff, 1989). This information would seem to be imperative as administrators and practitioners seek to design sport programs that maximize physical and psychosocial development in their young athletes.

To date, only three studies have examined age-related differences in reasons for continued motivation in sport. Gould, Feltz, and Weiss (1985) identified some age-difference trends in their study of participation motivation in young swimmers. Their sample was divided into three age groups: 8 to 11, 12 to 14, and 15 to 19 years. The researchers found that the 8- to 11-year-old children were more highly motivated by external factors such as social status, encouragement by parents and friends to participate, liking for the coach, and access to the swimming pool. The two older age groups were motivated by more internal factors such as developing physical fitness and skills, and the excitement and challenge of swimming. Wankel and Kreisel (1985) were also interested in determining whether age differences existed in the participation motives of children participating in ice hockey, soccer, and baseball. Players were divided into four age groups: 7 to 8, 9 to 10, 11 to 12, and 13 to 14 years. Findings revealed that ''pleasing others'' and ''doing the skills of the game'' were more important for the younger participants, whereas the ''excitement of the game'' became more important with age.

Brodkin and Weiss (1990) examined lifespan differences in participation motives for competitive swimming. Age groups were selected based on underlying cognitive criteria identified in the research literature: young children (6 to 9 years), older children (10 to 14 years), high school/college age individuals (15 to 22 years), younger adults (23 to 39 years), middle adults (40 to 59 years), and older adults (60 to 74 years). Results revealed that the younger and older children rated motives related to competition (team aspects, excitement and action, enjoyment of meets), liking the coaches, and pleasing significant others (family and friends) as more important than did the other age groups. Social status motives (to be popular with others, to feel important) were rated highest by the high school/college age group, followed by the younger children. Health and fitness reasons were rated as most important by young and middle adults, whereas younger and older children, and older adults rated health and fitness motives lowest. Finally, fun motives (enjoyment of swimming in the pool, and having fun) were rated as most important by older adults and younger children.

In sum, these findings by Brodkin and Weiss revealed that reasons for participating in competitive sport varied by age group and included differences in intrinsic (e.g., fun, fitness) and extrinsic (e.g., competition, social status) motives. These differences provide insights pertaining to cognitive-developmental variations and reveal important implications for coaching strategies and program emphases. Thus, considerably more research is needed before we can determine whether age-related differences exist for other sports or different intensity levels of participation.

Level of Intensity. Another factor to consider in the area of participation motivation is the intensity level of sport involvement. Children and adolescents are involved at elite, subelite, and recreational levels of organized sport, yet little research has addressed possible differences in motivation at these levels of participation intensity. This is quite surprising given the anecdotal literature recounting the detrimental effects of intensive sports participation on stress and burnout in young athletes (see Gould, chapter 1). Only one study to date has compared differences in participation motives among elite, recreational, and former elite athletes (Klint & Weiss, 1986). The elite gymnasts in this study practiced their sport for an average of 23.9 hr per week ($SD = 8.9$ hr), whereas the former elite gymnasts had averaged 31.43 hr per week ($SD = 11.9$ hr). The recreational gymnasts practiced for an average of 2.38 hr per week ($SD = .64$ hr). All three groups cited competence, fitness, and challenge as motives that were equally important for their competitive involvement. However, fun was the factor distinguishing the former from the current elite gymnasts. It is possible that the prohibitive number of hours spent in the gym (about 31 hr per week) turned an activity that was once fun into work and may have been a factor in these athletes' decision to leave high-level gymnastics.

Ewing, Feltz, Schultz, and Albrecht (1988) examined participation motivation and perceived ability differences among 15- to 19-year-old male midget, midget elite, and junior national ice hockey players. The junior national group represented the highest competitive intensity and skill level, whereas the midgets represented the lowest intensity level. Athletes at all three participation levels rated the desire to go on to a higher level as their most important reason for participating. However, the two lower competitive intensity levels identified skill improvement as their second most important reason, whereas the junior nationals identified winning as their second choice.

In summary, very little research is available on the psychological development of elite young athletes as a result of their sport participation, and even less is available from a motivational perspective (Feltz & Ewing, 1987). Moreover, little is known about how elite young athletes differ from those at subelite and less competitive levels. If researchers and policymakers are to understand the role of sports participation in developing young athletes who participate at varying levels of intensity, more studies of a comparative nature are essential.

Why Children and Youth Discontinue Competitive Sport Participation

The literature on motives for attrition from sport has paralleled that of participation motives. Specifically, a descriptive knowledge base is slowly evolving into a more theoretically oriented one (Gould, 1987; Weiss & Chaumeton, 1992). The first studies of attrition were conducted by Orlick (1973, 1974), with interviews of 60 former Canadian sport participants ranging in age from 7 to 18 years. The majority of these youth indicated that they would not participate the following year because of negative experiences such as lack of playing time, the competitive emphasis of the program (including an overemphasis on winning), and dislike for the coach. Orlick also found age differences in discontinuation motives, with children under 10 years of age reporting lack of playing time and lack of successful experiences, and children older than 10 reporting conflicts of interest such as other extracurricular activities or interest in other sports.

These discouraging findings were not replicated in a large-scale study conducted by the Michigan Youth Sports Institute (Sapp & Haubenstricker, 1978). Youths between the ages of 11 and 18 years ($N = 1,183$), and parents of children 6 to 10 years of age ($N = 418$) were administered questionnaires about their future participation patterns. The percentages of children who reported that they would not continue with their sport the following year were alarmingly high, with 37% of older children and 24% of younger children being identified as potential dropouts. However, the types of negative sport experiences identified by Orlick accounted for less than 15% of the reasons cited for sport withdrawal in the Michigan study. The most frequent reasons given were "other interests" by the younger children and "work" by the older children.

Further insight about attrition from youth sport was provided in a large-scale study of age-group swimmers ($N = 1,880$) conducted by McPherson et al. (1980), who found that a majority of the respondents identified at least one friend who had quit swimming the previous year. The reasons cited for their friends' withdrawal were too much pressure, lack of progress, lack of fun, failure to win, belief that swimming was too time consuming, and conflict with the coach. Moreover, 48% of the swimmers stated that they wanted to quit at some time during their career. Their reasons included boredom, dislike for the coach, interest in other activities, and belief that swimming was too time consuming.

Guppy (cited in McPherson, Guppy, & McKay, 1976) presented a different viewpoint to the attrition percentage rate problem by suggesting that many dropouts from competitive sport programs continue their sport involvement at a different level of intensity. His conclusions were based on the finding that over 50% of the dropouts he studied continued sport at the intramural level of intensity. He proposed that the high attrition rate may be a reflection of shifting interests and involvement from a more highly competitive level of organized sport to a less competitive level.

Following these early studies, a number of investigations were conducted to determine the extent of attrition from youth sports (Feltz & Petlichkoff, 1983; Gould et al., 1982; Klint & Weiss, 1986). Although approximately 35% of subjects were identified as dropouts across various programs, the negative reasons so prevalent in the Orlick studies did not emerge. Generally, "conflicts of interest" and "other things to do" have been the predominant reasons cited (Gould, 1987). Moreover, the only two studies that followed up on athletes who had withdrawn from sport programs found that withdrawal was only temporary (Gould et al., 1982; Klint & Weiss, 1986). Klint and Weiss found that 95% of the former competitive gymnasts they interviewed were either participating in another sport or were still participating in gymnastics but at lower levels of intensity. Similarly, Gould et al. found that 68% of the youth swimming dropouts they interviewed were participating in other sports and 80% stated that they planned to reenter swimming the following year. These two studies, therefore, were consistent with Guppy's view of shifting interests and involvement.

Definitional Problems. A complete understanding of reasons for attrition from sport has been hindered by problems of defining participant groups. Specifically, the terms *participant, nonparticipant,* and *dropout* have been used inconsistently from study to study. A majority of the studies have defined a sport participant as an athlete who is currently involved in a particular sport program. A nonpartici-pant is subsequently defined as one who is not involved in that particular program, a definition that does not preclude those who may have transferred to another sport program. Moreover, it appears that research has defined two types of sport dropouts: children who leave one program and transfer to another sport program (Gould et al., 1982; Klint & Weiss, 1986), and children who leave a sport program with no intention of becoming involved in sports again (McPherson et al., 1980; Orlick, 1974).

Another consideration in the definition of the sport dropout is whether the athlete had a clear choice in the decision to drop out or whether situational factors warranted leaving the program. As a result of extensive interviews, Klint and Weiss (1986) were able to classify their gymnasts into three types of dropouts. "Reluctant dropout" described the athlete who was forced to discontinue because of an injury or the prohibitive cost of participating in such an elite program. The "voluntary dropout" was interested in sampling other sports and extracurricular activities. This person was not unhappy with his or her current sport situation but wanted to experience other aspects of "normal" adolescent lifestyle. Finally, the "resistant dropout" still valued gymnastics but was genuinely unhappy in the competitive situation. The decision to leave gymnastics was difficult for this person, even though the situation was not satisfying. The stigma of being a quitter was often a deterrent to making the final decision to leave. Two of the gymnasts, for example, disclosed that they had caused their own injuries in order to have an acceptable reason for leaving the program!

This resistant dropout should be the center of our concerns when we discuss sport attrition. Specifically, it is not that children and adolescents withdraw from sport but rather why they withdraw that deserves further attention. The resistant dropout wants to remain part of the competitive sport environment but the cost of remaining involved (lack of fun, frustration, anxiety) may exceed the benefits (skill development, affiliation). The reluctant and voluntary dropouts, however, are a different story. They still associate sport with positive affect, but due to factors beyond their control (e.g., injury, cost) or their own choices to try new and different activities, they are no longer involved in that particular sport or program.

The inappropriateness of the label *dropout* as reflective of all participants who are no longer involved in a program was highlighted in an in-depth, qualitative study of English subjects ages 13 to 23 years (White & Coakley, 1986). These subjects were initially identified as participants and nonparticipants of youth clubs. However, White and Coakley concluded that *dropout* and *nonparticipant* were inappropriate descriptions of young people who decide not to participate in organized sport activities. Through the use of extensive structured interviews, the researchers discovered that for most of the subjects, changes in participation patterns and leisure activity priorities were normal and that discontinuation from sport was often a constructive decision based on age-related norms and social roles.

Thus, it is apparent that definitional problems have plagued this important topic in the pediatric sport psychology literature. The phenomenon of attrition from sport ranges on a continuum from sport transfer (e.g., discontinuing one sport to try another sport, or trying the same sport at a different level of intensity) to total withdrawal from sport with no intention of reentering. The reasons for temporary or total withdrawal may be based on practical, developmental, or negative reasons (Gould, 1987; Gould & Petlichkoff, 1988; Weiss & Chaumeton, 1992). Children withdrawing for negative reasons such as overemphasis on winning, controlling coaching styles, and lack of fun should be a priority matter for both researchers and practitioners. The absolute percentage of children withdrawing from sport is not the enemy; rather, the research strongly suggests that our main concern is those children who have negative sport experiences that may have dramatic implications for psychological development and future sport involvement.

Conclusions and Recommendations

This chapter has reviewed the literature related to self-esteem and motivational effects of intensive youth sport participation. Self-esteem was discussed in terms of the influential factors related to the process whereby children formulate judgments about their competence. This included reflected appraisals by and social comparisons to significant others such as parents, coaches, and peers; affective determinants and consequences; and motivational concomitants of high- and low-self-esteem children. Moreover, the multidimensionality of self-esteem revealed that children differentiate judgments about their competence according to the reference domain or situation at hand. Participation motivation was extensively reviewed from the standpoint of factors related to children's initiation into sport, their continued involvement, and attrition from sport. Both descriptive and theory-based literature revealed that this area has been extensively researched over the past decade and many insightful findings have been uncovered. The knowledge bases in self-esteem and motivation, therefore, provide practical information for youth sport professionals, and highlight areas requiring further research.

Professional Practice Recommendations

1. *Adults involved in youth sport programs must ensure high* quality *in the interactions children have with significant others such as parents, peers, and coaches.* For example, the contingency of praise in response to desirable performances and criticism in response to performance errors, and the frequency and quality of skill-relevant feedback, are significant sources of information children use to evaluate their physical competence. Thus, it is imperative that adults become aware of the different sources of

information children may use to judge competence and how these judgments, in turn, relate to participation behavior. Parents and coaches, especially, need to understand the influential roles they play in the self-esteem development of youngsters and should structure their performance feedback and general communication styles to enhance children's self-esteem.

2. *Adults must assess specific self-esteem dimensions, as well as their importance, such as physical, academic, and social competence.* These general dimensions include more domain-specific self-perceptions; physical competence, for example, can be divided into sport ability, physical appearance, physical fitness, strength, and peer acceptance. These domains can be further broken down to specific sports and situations. Thus, to best understand sport participation effects on self-esteem, adults must assess the dimension that is most relevant for the situation as well as the salience that the child places on particular dimensions. Knowing what is most important to an individual child will help practitioners understand how a child defines his or her self-esteem, which in turn helps predict participation behavior in sports or other activities. For example, an adolescent participating in weight training may value strength and physical attractiveness more than sport ability, whereas a youngster participating in an age-group competitive tennis program may place more importance on sport ability and peer relationships than strength or appearance.

3. *Adults must maximize opportunities for enjoyment, development of perceived competence, and intrinsically motivating activities within the physical domain.* Children with high self-perceptions report higher levels of enjoyment, a greater liking for their sports and coaches, and higher intrinsic motivation in the form of effort and persistence than do children low in self-esteem. Thus, practitioners must make the youth sport experience a positive one in terms of affect, perceptions of competence, and motivation, in order to maximize self-esteem development. For example, adults can make sport experiences more enjoyable by keeping practices and competitions fun as well as achievement oriented, and by matching the difficulty of sport skills and goals to the developmental capabilities of the participants. Coaches and parents can enhance perceptions of competence by appropriately using feedback and reinforcement and by focusing on individualized goals and challenges. Finally, adults can make sport intrinsically motivating by maximizing the involvement of all participants during practices and by providing opportunities for developing and enhancing friendships.

4. *Practitioners must identify children who seriously underestimate their physical abilities and thus may be at risk for discontinuing their sport involvement.* These are children whose perceptions of ability are much lower than actual estimates of their skilled behavior; they are inaccurate estimators of their own potential achievement behavior. Thus, adult leaders must identify children who underestimate their competence, by noting their verbal (e.g., attributions for performance outcomes) and nonverbal (e.g., effort, persistence) behaviors. Instructional interventions such as goal

setting, attribution retraining, and appropriate and contingent feedback may help to reverse this spiral of negative evaluations and ensuing unmotivated behavior.

5. *Adults must provide opportunities for satisfying children's multiple reasons for participating in sport.* The major reasons cited are related to competence, affiliation, team membership, fun and excitement, and physical fitness. Therefore, programs should emphasize these objectives and provide opportunities for children to benefit in all of these areas. Meeting these needs will enhance levels of positive affect, motivation, and self-esteem.

6. *Practitioners must consider the variety of personal and contextual factors that may influence children's motivated behavior in sport.* These factors include but are not limited to cognitive maturity, physical maturity, gender, playing status, and program intensity level. Therefore, practitioners need to consider the quality of the child's experience and the child's cognitions about this experience (e.g., starter vs. bench player, younger vs. older child) in order to understand continued participation in and attrition from sport.

7. *Practitioners must follow children through phases of participation such as initial involvement, maintenance, and withdrawal.* The large percentage of children who withdraw from particular sport programs may do so only temporarily. However, for some children, intense negative experiences may result in their total withdrawal from sport and physical activity or detrimental psychological development. Children should be monitored through all stages of participation, a type of longitudinal evaluation that will help determine physical, psychological, and social developmental effects of children's sport participation and discontinuation (e.g., coach's attitude and behavior, parental expectations, low perceptions of competence).

Future Research Recommendations

1. *More studies are needed that determine the* effects *of sport participation on psychosocial development of young athletes.* Although an extensive number of studies have been conducted on self-perceptions and motivation in youth sport, few have been designed to determine the psychological effects of this participation. Thus, more experimental, naturalistic, and longitudinal research is needed. Experimental studies will allow a direct comparison of children intensively involved versus those less intensively involved in sport. Naturalistic studies will provide for an understanding of the process of sport involvement from the child's perspective. Finally, longitudinal studies will facilitate a more complete understanding of the psychological effects that occur as children initiate, sustain, and discontinue their sport participation.

2. *Children who participate at various levels of intensity of physical activity should be studied in terms of psychological development.* The majority of contemporary research on self-esteem and motivation has examined children who are involved in organized, competitive sport programs. However, very few studies have examined children and adolescents involved at varying levels of intensity, ranging from exercise/fitness programs to elite levels of highly competitive sport. Moreover, studies have not systematically investigated self-esteem and motivational effects of participating in interscholastic versus agency-sponsored competitive programs. The emphasis on performance outcomes and the high expectations placed on young athletes at the elite levels are likely to result in different self-esteem and motivational effects than children receive from less intense programs.

3. *More studies are needed to investigate what characterizes the child who discontinues sport participation.* Qualitative methods such as extensive interviews, open-ended responses, and behavioral observations would embellish the knowledge base about the nature of the decision to drop out (i.e., reluctant, voluntary, resistance dropouts), as well as the benefits and costs involved in deciding to withdraw. Additionally, no research has been conducted on the child who is involuntarily cut from a team. Some anecdotal literature has suggested that the child who is cut is likely to be the kind of child who can benefit most from positive sport experiences, for example, the late-maturing boy, the child with low self-esteem, or those who may need social support. Empirical research is needed, however, to confirm this speculation.

4. *Intervention studies are needed to determine what instructional strategies and coaching behaviors enhance self-esteem and motivation in young sport participants.* Interventions targeted toward low-self-esteem children and those who underestimate their physical abilities might include sport and game modifications, feedback and reinforcement techniques, modeling strategies, and goal setting programs.

5. *More research is needed to determine the extent to which social support by parents, coaches, and peers influence self-esteem, affect, and motivation in youth sport.* This important link has been studied with regard to the academic domain, with results indicating a strong influence from both parents and peers in the psychological development of the child. Given the importance placed on sport by children as well as their parents, and the visibility with which physical competence is publicly demonstrated, this appears to be a critical area of future study. Results related to this area of research might be expected to differ as a function of age, gender, and sociocultural factors.

6. *An integrated sport science approach will help us better understand youth sport participation and the developmental effects on children and adolescents.* For example, researchers should concurrently assess physical, biological, psychological, and social development as a result of intense

participation, where it is feasible and logical to do so. Possible areas are the biological and psychological effects of weight training; the physical, social, and psychological ramifications of an athletic injury; and the physiological and psychological consequences of competitive stress in youth sport. To date, very few studies have taken such a multidisciplinary approach.

Acknowledgments

Portions of this manuscript are based on previously published work by the author (Weiss, 1987a; Weiss & Chaumeton, 1992; Weiss & Petlichkoff, 1989).

The author would like to gratefully acknowledge Tony Pickering for his assistance in compiling the literature search on self-esteem and motivation and Susan Duncan for her thoughtful comments and suggestions on an earlier draft of this paper.

References

Bredemeier, B.J., & Shields, D.L. (1985). Values and violence in sport. *Psychology Today*, **19**, 22-32.

Bredemeier, B.J., & Shields, D.L. (1987). Moral growth through physical activity: An interactional approach. In D. Gould & M. R. Weiss (Eds.), *Advances in pediatric sport sciences: Vol. 2. Behavioral issues* (pp. 145-165). Champaign, IL: Human Kinetics.

Brodkin, P., & Weiss, M.R. (1990). Developmental differences in motivation for participating in competitive swimming. *Journal of Sport and Exercise Psychology*, **12**, 248-263.

Brown, B.A. (1985). Factors influencing the process of withdrawal by female adolescents from the role of competitive age group swimmer. *Sociology of Sport Journal*, **2**, 111-129.

Brown, B.A., Frankel, B.G., & Fennell, M.P. (1989). Hugs or shrugs: Parental and peer influence on continuity of involvement in sport by female adolescents. *Sex Roles*, **20**, 397-412.

Brustad, R.J. (1988). Affective outcomes in competitive youth sport: The influence of intrapersonal and socialization factors. *Journal of Sport and Exercise Psychology*, **10**, 307-321.

Brustad, R.J. (1992). Integrating socialization influences into the study of children's motivation in sport. *Journal of Sport and Exercise Psychology*, **14**, 59-77.

Burton, D., & Martens, R. (1986). Pinned by their own goals: An exploratory investigation into why kids drop out of wrestling. *Journal of Sport Psychology*, **8**, 183-197.

Coakley, J.J. (1987). Children and the sport socialization process. In D. Gould & M.R. Weiss (Eds.), *Advances in pediatric sport sciences: Vol. 2. Behavioral issues* (pp. 43-60). Champaign, IL: Human Kinetics.

Coie, J.D., Dodge, K.A., & Kupersmidt, J. (1991). Peer group behavior and social status. In S.R. Asher & J.D. Coie (Eds.), *Peer rejection in childhood* (pp. 17-59). New York: Cambridge University Press.

Coleman, J.S. (1961). Athletics in high school. *The Annals of the American Academy of Political and Social Science*, **338** (November), 33-43.

Coopersmith, S. (1967). *The antecedents of self-esteem*. San Francisco: Freeman.

Deci, E.L., & Ryan, R.M. (1985). *Intrinsic motivation and self-determination in human behavior*. New York: Plenum.

Duda, J.L. (1985). Goals and achievement orientations of Anglo and Mexican-American adolescents in sport and the classroom. *International Journal of Intercultural Relations*, **9**, 131-155.

Duda, J.L. (1987). Toward a developmental theory of motivation in sport. *Journal of Sport Psychology*, **9**, 130-145.

Duda, J.L., & Allison, M.T. (1990). Cross-cultural analysis in exercise and sport psychology: A void in the field. *Journal of Sport and Exercise Psychology*, **12**, 103-113.

Eitzen, D.S. (1976). Athletics in the status system of male adolescents: A replication of Coleman's, "The Adolescent Society." In A. Yiannakis, T. McIntyre, M. Melnick, & D. Hart (Eds.), *Sport sociology: Contemporary themes*. Dubuque, IA: Kendall-Hunt.

Evans, J.R., & Roberts, G.C. (1987). Physical competence and the development of children's peer relations. *Quest*, **39**, 23-35.

Ewing, M. E. (1981). *Achievement orientations and sport behavior of males and females*. Unpublished doctoral dissertation, University of Illinois at Urbana-Champaign.

Ewing, M.E., Feltz, D.L., Schultz, T.D., & Albrecht, R.R. (1988). Psychological characteristics of competitive young hockey players. In E. W. Brown & C. F. Branta (Eds.), *Competitive sports for children and youth* (pp. 49-61). Champaign, IL: Human Kinetics.

Feltz, D.L., & Brown, E.W. (1984). Perceived competence in soccer skills among youth soccer players. *Journal of Sport Psychology*, **6**, 385-394.

Feltz, D.L., & Ewing, M.E. (1987). Psychological characteristics of elite young athletes. *Medicine and Science in Sports and Exercise*, **19**, 98-105.

Feltz, D.L., & Petlichkoff, L.M. (1983). Perceived competence among interscholastic sport participants and dropouts. *Canadian Journal of Applied Sport Sciences*, **8**, 231-235.

Fox, K.R. (1988). The self-esteem complex and youth fitness. *Quest*, **40**, 230-246.

Fox, K.R., & Corbin, C.B. (1989). The self-perception profile: Development and preliminary validation. *Journal of Sport and Exercise Psychology*, **11**, 408-430.

Frazer, K.M. (1989). *Initial, continued, and sustained motivation in adolescent female athletes: A season-long investigation*. Unpublished master's thesis, University of Oregon, Eugene, Oregon.

Gill, D.L., Gross, J.B., & Huddleston, S. (1983). Participation motivation in youth sports. *International Journal of Sport Psychology*, **14**, 1-14.

Gould, D. (1982). Sport psychology in the 1980's: Status, direction and challenge in youth sports research. *Journal of Sport Psychology*, **4**, 203-218.

Gould, D. (1987). Understanding attrition in youth sport. In D. Gould & M.R. Weiss (Eds.), *Advances in pediatric sport sciences: Vol. 2. Behavioral issues* (pp. 61-85). Champaign, IL: Human Kinetics.

Gould, D., Feltz, D., Horn, T., & Weiss, M. (1982). Reasons for attrition in competitive youth swimming. *Journal of Sport Behavior*, **5**, 155-165.

Gould, D., Feltz, D., & Weiss, M. (1985). Motives for participating in competitive youth swimming. *International Journal of Sport Psychology,* **6**, 126-140.

Gould, D., & Petlichkoff, L. (1988). Participation motivation and attrition in young athletes. In F. Smoll, R. Magill, & M. Ash (Eds.), *Children in sport* (3rd ed.), (pp. 161-178). Champaign, IL: Human Kinetics.

Gould, D., & Weiss, M.R. (1987). *Advances in pediatric sport sciences: Vol. 2. Behavioral issues.* Champaign, IL: Human Kinetics.

Greendorfer, S.L., & Ewing, M.E. (1981). Race and gender differences in children's socialization into sport. *Research Quarterly for Exercise and Sport, 52*, 301-310.

Gruber, J.J. (1986). Physical activity and self-esteem development in children: A meta-analysis. In H. Eckert (Ed.), *Effects of physical activity on children and youth: The academy papers* (pp. 30-48). Champaign, IL: Human Kinetics.

Harter, S. (1978). Effectance motivation reconsidered. *Human Development, 21*, 34-64.

Harter, S. (1981a). The development of competence motivation in the mastery of cognitive and physical skills: Is there still a place for joy? In G.C. Roberts & D.M. Landers (Eds.), *Psychology of motor behavior and sport—1980* (pp. 3-29). Champaign, IL: Human Kinetics.

Harter, S. (1981b). A model of intrinsic mastery motivation in children: Individual differences and developmental change. In W. A. Collins (Ed.), *Minnesota symposium on child psychology* (Vol. 14, pp. 215-255). Hillsdale, NJ: Erlbaum.

Harter, S. (1986). Processes underlying the construction, maintenance, and enhancement of the self-concept in children. In J. Suls & A. Greenwald (Eds.), *Psychological perspectives on the self* (Vol. 3, pp. 137-181). Hillsdale, NJ: Erlbaum.

Harter, S. (1988). Causes, correlates, and the functional role of global self-worth: A life-span perspective. In J. Kolligan & R. Sternberg (Eds.), *Perceptions of competence and incompetence across the life-span.* New Haven, CT: Yale University Press.

Horn, T.S. (1985). Coaches' feedback and changes in children's perceptions of their physical competence. *Journal of Educational Psychology, 77*, 174-186.

Horn, T.S. (1986). The self-fulfilling prophecy theory: When coaches' expectations become reality. In J.M. Williams (Ed.), *Applied sport psychology: Personal growth to peak performance* (pp. 59-73). Palo Alto, CA: Mayfield.

Horn, T.S. (1987). The influence of teacher-coach behavior on the psychological development of children. In D. Gould & M.R. Weiss (Eds.), *Advances in pediatric sport sciences: Vol. 2. Behavioral issues* (pp. 121-142). Champaign, IL: Human Kinetics.

Horn, T.S., & Hasbrook, C.A. (1986). Information components influencing children's perceptions of their physical competence. In M.R. Weiss & D. Gould (Eds.), *Sport for children and youths* (pp. 81-88). Champaign, IL: Human Kinetics.

Horn, T.S., & Hasbrook, C.A. (1987). Psychological characteristics and the criteria children use for self-evaluation. *Journal of Sport Psychology, 9*, 208-221.

Horn, T.S., & Weiss, M.R. (1991). A developmental analysis of children's self-ability judgements in the physical domain. *Pediatric Exercise Science, 3*, 310-326.

Klint, K.A. (1985). *Participation motives and self-perceptions of current and former athletes in youth gymnastics.* Unpublished master's thesis, University of Oregon, Eugene.

Klint, K.A. (1988). *An analysis of the positivistic and naturalistic paradigms for inquiry: Implications for the field of sport psychology.* Unpublished doctoral dissertation, University of Oregon, Eugene.

Klint, K.A., & Weiss, M.R. (1986). Dropping in and dropping out: Participation motives of current and former youth gymnasts. *Canadian Journal of Applied Sport Sciences, 11*, 106-114.

Klint, K.A., & Weiss, M.R. (1987). Perceived competence and motives for participating in youth sports: A test of Harter's competence motivation theory. *Journal of Sport Psychology, 9*, 55-65.

Langer, E.J. (1979). The illusion of incompetence. In L. C. Perlmutter & R. A. Monty (Eds.), *Choice and perceived control*. Hillsdale, NJ: Erlbaum.

Lewko, J.H., & Greendorfer, S.L. (1988). Family influences in sport socialization of children and adolescents. In F. Smoll, R. Magill, & M. Ash (Eds.), *Children in sport* (3rd ed., pp. 287-300). Champaign, IL: Human Kinetics.

Longhurst, K., & Spink, K.S. (1987). Participation motivation of Australian children involved in organized sport. *Canadian Journal of Sport Sciences*, **12**, 24-30.

Maehr, M. L., & Nicholls, J. G. (1980). Culture and achievement motivation: A second look. In N. Warren (Ed.), *Studies in cross-cultural psychology* (Vol. 3, pp. 221-267). New York: Academic Press.

Marsh, H.W. (1986). Global self-esteem: Its relation to specific facets of self-concept and their importance. *Journal of Personality and Social Psychology*, **51**, 1224-1236.

Marsh, H.W., & Peart, N.D. (1988). Competitive and cooperative physical fitness training programs for girls: Effects on physical fitness and multidimensional self-concepts. *Journal of Sport and Exercise Psychology*, **10**, 390-407.

Marsh, H.W., & Shavelson, R. (1985). Self-concept: Its multi-faceted hierarchical structure. *Educational Psychologist*, **20**, 107-123.

Martens, R. (1978). *Joy and sadness in children's sports*. Champaign, IL: Human Kinetics.

McClements, J., Fry, D., & Sefton, J. (1982). A study of hockey participants and drop-outs. In T.D. Orlick, J.T. Partington, & J.H. Salmela (Eds.), *Mental training for coaches and athletes* (pp. 73-74). Ottawa, Ontario: Coaching Association of Canada.

McElroy, M.A., & Kirkendall, D. (1981). Conflict in perceived parent/child sport ability judgments. *Journal of Sport Psychology*, **3**, 244-247.

McPherson, B., & Brown, B.A. (1988). The structure, processes, and consequences of sport for children. In F.L. Smoll, R.A. Magill, & M.J. Ash (Eds.), *Children in sport* (3rd ed., pp. 265-286). Champaign, IL: Human Kinetics.

McPherson, B.D., Guppy, L.N., & McKay, J.P. (1976). The social structure of the game and sport milieu. In J.G. Albinson & G.M. Andrews (Eds.), *Children in sport and physical activity* (pp. 161-200). Baltimore: University Park.

McPherson, B., Marteniuk, R., Tihanyi, J., & Clark, W. (1980). The social system of age group swimmers: The perception of swimmers, parents, and coaches. *Canadian Journal of Applied Sport Sciences*, **5**, 142-145.

Nicholls, J.G. (1984). Achievement motivation: conceptions of ability, subjective experience, task choice, and performance. *Psychological Review*, **91**, 328-346.

Orlick, T.D. (1973, January/February). Children's sport—a revolution is coming. *Canadian Association for Health, Physical Education and Recreation Journal*, pp. 12-14.

Orlick, T.D. (1974, November/December). The athletic dropout: A high price for inefficiency. *Canadian Association for Health, Physical Education and Recreation Journal*, pp. 21-27.

Parsons, J.E., Adler, T.F., & Kaczala, C.M. (1982). Socialization of achievement attitudes and beliefs: Parental influences. *Child Development*, **53**, 310-321.

Petlichkoff, L.M. (1988). *Motivation for sport persistence: An empirical examination of underlying theoretical constructs*. Unpublished doctoral dissertation, University of Illinois at Urbana-Champaign.

Pickering, M.A., & Weiss, M.R. (1990, May). *Parental influence in youth sport: Current status and future research directions*. Paper presented at the annual meeting of the North American Society for the Psychology of Sport and Physical Activity, Houston, TX.

Roberts, G.C., Kleiber, D.A., & Duda, J. L. (1981). An analysis of motivation in children's sport: The role of perceived competence in participation. *Journal of Sport Psychology*, **3**, 206-216.

Robertson, I. (1981). *Children's perceived satisfactions and stresses in sport.* Paper presented at the Australian Conference on Health, Physical Education and Recreation.

Robinson, T., & Carron, A.V. (1982). Personal and situational factors associated with dropping out versus maintaining participation in competitive sport. *Journal of Sport Psychology, 4,* 364-378.

Ryan, R.M., Vallerand, R.J., & Deci, E.L. (1984). Intrinsic motivation in sport: A cognitive evaluation theory interpretation. In W. F. Straub & J. M. Williams (Eds.), *Cognitive sport psychology* (pp. 231-242). Lansing, NY: Sport Science Associates.

Sapp, M., & Haubenstricker, J. (1978, April). *Motivation for joining and reasons for not continuing in youth sport programs in Michigan.* Paper presented at the American Alliance for Health, Physical Education, Recreation and Dance national conference, Kansas City, MO.

Scanlan, T.K. (1988). Social evaluation and the competition process: A developmental perspective. In F.L. Smoll, R.A. Magill, & M.J. Ash (Eds.), *Children in sport* (3rd ed., pp. 135-148). Champaign, IL: Human Kinetics.

Scanlan, T.K., & Lewthwaite, R. (1984). Social psychological aspects of competition for male youth sport participants: I. Predictors of competitive stress. *Journal of Sport Psychology, 6,* 208-226.

Scanlan, T.K., & Lewthwaite, R. (1986). Social psychological aspects of competition for male youth sport participants: IV. Predictors of enjoyment. *Journal of Sport Psychology, 8,* 25-35.

Scanlan, T.K., Stein, G.L., & Ravizza, K. (1988). An in-depth study of former elite figure skaters: II. Sources of enjoyment. *Journal of Sport and Exercise Psychology, 11,* 65-83.

Seefeldt, V.D. (1986). *Physical activity and well-being.* Reston, VA: American Alliance for Health, Physical Education, Recreation and Dance.

Smith, R.E., Smoll, F.L., & Curtis, B. (1979). Coach effectiveness training: A cognitive-behavioral approach to enhancing relationship skills in youth sport coaches. *Journal of Sport Psychology, 1,* 59-75.

Smith, R.E., Smoll, F.L., & Smith, N.J. (1989). *Parents' complete guide to youth sports.* Costa Mesa, CA: HDL Communications.

Smoll, F.L., & Smith, R.E. (1989). Leadership behaviors in sport: A theoretical model and research paradigm. *Journal of Applied Social Psychology, 19,* 1522-1551.

Thibaut, J.W., & Kelley, H.H. (1959). *The social psychology of groups.* New York: Wiley.

Ulrich, B.D. (1987). Perceptions of physical competence, motor competence and participation in organized sport: Their interrelationships in young children. *Research Quarterly for Exercise and Sport, 58,* 57-67.

Wankel, L.M., & Kreisel, S.J. (1985). Factors underlying enjoyment of youth sports: Sport and age group comparisons. *Journal of Sport Psychology, 7,* 52-64.

Wankel, L.M., & Sefton, J.M. (1989). A season-long investigation of fun in youth sports. *Journal of Sport and Exercise Psychology, 11,* 355-366.

Weiss, M.R. (1987a). Self-esteem and achievement in children's sport and physical activity. In D. Gould & M.R. Weiss (Eds.), *Advances in pediatric sport sciences: Vol. 2. Behavioral issues* (pp. 87-119). Champaign, IL: Human Kinetics.

Weiss, M. R. (1987b). Teaching sportsmanship and values. In V. Seefeldt (Ed.), *Handbook for youth sports coaches* (pp. 137-152). Reston, VA: American Alliance for Health, Physical Education, Recreation and Dance.

Weiss, M.R., & Bredemeier, B.J. (1986). Moral development. In V. Seefeldt (Ed.), *Physical activity and well-being* (pp. 373-390). Reston, VA: American Alliance for Health, Physical Education, Recreation and Dance.

Weiss, M.R., & Bredemeier, B.J. (1990). Moral development in sport. In K.B. Pandolf & J.O. Holloszy (Eds.), *Exercise and sport sciences reviews* (Vol. 18) (pp. 331-378). Baltimore: Williams & Wilkins.

Weiss, M.R., Bredemeier, B.J., & Shewchuk, R.M. (1986). The dynamics of perceived competence, perceived control, and motivational orientation in youth sports. In M.R. Weiss & D. Gould (Eds.), *Sport for children and youths* (pp. 89-101). Champaign, IL: Human Kinetics.

Weiss, M.R., & Chaumeton, N. (1992). Motivational orientations in sport. In T.S. Horn (Ed.), *Advances in sport psychology* (pp. 61-99). Champaign, IL: Human Kinetics.

Weiss, M.R., & Duncan, S.C. (1992). The relation between physical competence and peer acceptance in the context of children's sport participation. *Journal of Sport and Exercise Psychology, 14*, 61-99.

Weiss, M.R., & Gould, D. (1986). *Sport for children and youths*. Champaign, IL: Human Kinetics.

Weiss, M.R., & Horn, T.S. (1990). The relation between children's accuracy estimates of their physical competence and achievement-related characteristics. *Research Quarterly for Exercise and Sport, 61*, 250-258.

Weiss, M.R., McAuley, E., Ebbeck, V., & Wiese, D.M. (1990). Self-esteem and causal attributions for children's physical and social competence in sport. *Journal of Sport and Exercise Psychology, 12*, 21-36.

Weiss, M.R., & Petlichkoff, L.M. (1989). Children's motivation for participation in and withdrawal from sport: Identifying the missing links. *Pediatric Exercise Science, 1*, 195-211.

Weiss, M.R., Wiese, D.M., & Klint, K.A. (1989). Head over heels with success: The relationship between self-efficacy and performance in competitive youth gymnastics. *Journal of Sport and Exercise Psychology, 11*, 444-451.

White, A., & Coakley, J. (1986). *Making decisions: The response of young people in the Medway towns to the "Ever thought about sport?" campaign*. London: Sports Council.

Wiggins, D.K. (1987). A history of organized play and highly competitive sport for American children. In D. Gould & M.R. Weiss (Eds.), *Advances in pediatric sport sciences: Vol. 2. Behavioral issues* (pp. 1-24). Champaign, IL: Human Kinetics.

PART II

Sociological Perspectives

Jay Coakley
Peter Donnelly
Greg Landry

The varying consequences of intensive participation in children's sports are usually said to depend on the individual participants. Sociologists disagree with this explanation and point out that sport participation does not occur in a social vacuum. The developmental and social consequences do vary greatly from one child to the next, but these consequences seem to be closely connected to the values and meanings associated with sport in a particular society and the resultant conditions under which participation occurs.

Thus, both the problems and the benefits of intensive sport participation by children are consequences not only of children's personal dispositions, abilities, and immediate relationships (with family, coaches, and fellow participants) but also of the place of sport (and specific sports) in the society. The consequences for a child in a society that places great value on success in sport—and on the need for "hard work," early specialization, ascetic denial (of food, childhood pleasures), and rewards (both immediate and long term) in order to achieve success in sport—will be very different than consequences for a child in a society with a different set of emphases and expectations.

In North America, the emphasis on success in sport, when combined with an understanding of success or failure in primarily individual terms, has a number of unfortunate consequences for participants. Because sport, by its very nature, produces a great many more "losers" than "winners," children who have worked hard, specialized early, and practiced ascetic denial and who are not successful are frequently made to feel inadequate; they may even blame themselves for their lack of success and for the negative consequences associated with that lack of success. Sociologists have identified this as "victim-blaming" behavior and prefer to see the personal troubles of these children as a public issue that warrants a social response.

A typical conclusion from this type of analysis is that the only way to effect change in areas such as sport is to change the entire society, and because such drastic social change appears to be unfeasible, we should simply make the best of the present system. However, human action has clearly produced continuing change in North American society; if everyone had drawn such status quo conclusions there would have been no changes in civil rights or women's rights.

It would be a mistake at this time to think that major changes could be made in the values and meanings of sport in North American society as a whole. However, it is possible to examine in detail and to change the conditions under which sport participation occurs. In Part II we explore the range of experiences available to children who participate intensively in sport. Our goal is to identify the conditions under which positive or negative outcomes occur and to suggest ways to maximize the positive outcomes and minimize the negative ones.

Major Sociological Issues

Sociologists are concerned with how human behavior, social relationships, and individual development are connected to the social and cultural context in which people live. It is generally assumed that what happens in people's lives is tied to the decisions they make. But it is also assumed that people rarely have complete control over the conditions under which they make decisions and that decisions frequently result in unintended consequences. This is especially important to remember when we consider the intensive participation of children in sport.

For the most part, children live under the control of adults. In sport programs, adults not only shape the overall organization of the programs but also control what happens in them daily. The extent to which children in these programs control what happens in their own lives depends on adults. Children usually make the decision to participate intensively in sport, but that decision is closely tied to an awareness of alternatives and rewards shaped by important adults in their lives.

What happens to children once they become intensively involved depends on three major factors: the way sport programs are organized, the way sport experiences are mediated by the important social relationships in a child's life, and the way sport experiences are defined and integrated into the rest of a child's life. One of the reasons why intensive participation is not associated with a single, consistent set of developmental outcomes for children is that sport experiences are, because of these three factors, extremely diverse. Some children clearly benefit from intensive participation whereas far too many experience negative outcomes.

Sociologists are just beginning to identify the conditions under which positive or negative social and developmental outcomes are most likely to occur for child athletes. However, because many researchers tend to focus initially on negative outcomes (with the hope of arriving at some immediate recommendations for urgently needed changes), we have some good ideas about what should be avoided when it comes to intensive participation.

Sociological research suggests that negative outcomes for the overall development of children as human beings are most likely when intensive participation occurs in rigidly organized programs in which children have little or no control over what happens in their lives in and out of sport. Negative outcomes are also likely when child athletes are defined by others, especially significant others, in terms of their potential or actual performances. Finally, negative outcomes are most likely when participation constricts developmental experiences rather than expanding those experiences.

In light of these negative outcomes, the chapters in Part II are concerned with the following general issues:

- How the structure of sport programs may encourage children to make detrimental choices, or may actually deny children the rights they would have in other organizational settings and severely limit the control they have over what happens in their lives
- The connection between intensive participation and important social relationships in the lives of children, especially if children are defined in terms of their performances
- Whether intensive participation in sport provides or denies access to experiences that lead to overall social development for children

The benefits and costs of intensive participation that are discussed include elements of the structure and administration of sport programs, such as

- the positive or negative implications of performance-centered versus child-centered programs,
- the developmental consequences of the social isolation that may accompany participation in certain programs,
- the danger of converting sport activities into work when children have a basic developmental need for unrestrained play,
- the potential loss of rights among children when adults (either parents or program personnel) depend upon them and their performance successes for status and monetary benefits,
- the connection between sport programs and other aspects of a child's life (e.g., does the sport organization work with or against the educational system in order to facilitate or unthinkingly hinder a child's education?), and
- the ways in which political infighting among sport administrators can have a detrimental effect on a child's athletic development.

The dynamics of social relationships are also explored, with attention to

- the connection between sport participation and a child's tendency to either establish independence from family relationships or become overdependent on parents or other adults,
- ways children can use sport participation to learn to deal with peers or how participation may limit needed experiences with peers,
- how children can use sport participation to learn to deal with authority figures or how participation may cause overdependence on a coach,

- the different ways in which coaches can influence the lives of child athletes—as dictators, role models, or advocates, and
- how norms within sport groups can lead to healthy behaviors or to an objectification of the body that leads to unhealthy eating habits, dangerous diets, or the use of performance-enhancing substances or undisclosed injuries.

And finally, access to experiences among young athletes is reviewed, including

- the importance of organizing sport experiences and setting performance expectations in ways that fit the child athlete's stages of social development,
- the ways in which sport participation might restrict needed developmental experiences or expand those experiences, and how we need to recognize developmental issues when considering the implications of skill specialization and travel experiences,
- the control children have over the nature of their own sport experiences and the danger present when adults define those experiences for children in ways that do not give priority to social development, and
- the possibility that young athletes might use excessive behavior as a reaction against overcontrolled and highly restricted experiences.

Social Development and Negative Sport Experiences

Chapter 3, by Jay Coakley, briefly discusses the history of organized youth sport programs and then reviews issues related to social development and intensive sport participation. Using developmental theory, Coakley looks at how sport participation can either facilitate or impede social development at various stages from early childhood to preadolescence. The connection between social development and a child's readiness to participate in sports is also discussed.

Coakley reviews some of his own research in outlining what children look for in their sport experiences, and then he discusses the ways in which adults mediate the sport experiences of children. He closes with a discussion of the different ways coaches may become important in the lives of child athletes. Coaches can be influential as dictators, role models, or advocates, and each of these styles has different developmental implications for young athletes.

Chapter 4, by Peter Donnelly, reports on the results of a number of in-depth interviews with retired high-performance athletes, interviews that concern the athletes' experiences with intensive sport participation during childhood and adolescence. Despite the fact that subjects were selected on the basis of their generally positive careers in high-performance sport, all of the subjects reported high rates of negative experiences resulting from their intensive sport participation.

The experiences of these athletes, both positive and more particularly negative, involve family relationships, educational problems, and relationships with coaches. These experiences are interpreted in terms of the age and gender of the athletes, the rationalization of sport, and the disappearance of childhood. Recommendations made by the subjects are reported, and Donnelly suggests that examination of intensive participation in children's sports as a child labor issue may be welcomed by all involved.

Chapter 3

Social Dimensions of Intensive Training and Participation in Youth Sports

Jay Coakley

Intensive training and participation in competitive sports among preadolescent children comprise a relatively new phenomenon that exists only in societies in which children have large amounts of free time and there are resources to fund facilities, equipment, and other program costs. Facilities and equipment for many sports are not cheap, and unless basic public services are adequately provided in a society, few public or private sponsors are willing to support widespread intensive training and sport programs for children.

A widespread, systematic emphasis on intensive training and sport competition among children is found almost exclusively in industrial societies whose socialization processes emphasize achievement and organization. Children in these societies are taught the importance of setting goals, developing their potential, and becoming successful in terms defined by their families and communities. It is with these orientations in mind that adults in industrial countries, including the U.S., have organized the play activities of their children and have encouraged participation in sport programs that emphasize goal setting, skill development, and the achievement of rewards.

Intensive Training and Youth Sports in the United States

Before the 1930s, organized sport for children in the United States was primarily supervised by physical educators, recreation professionals, and athletic coaches who worked in schools, parks departments, social service programs, and youth organizations. Sport programs for children involved neither intensive training nor heavy competition. During the 1930s some people began to push for change, for more emphasis on intensive training and competition. In response to this shift in emphasis, physical educators and professional recreation leaders withdrew their sponsorship and control of these programs as a way to denounce practices they thought were destructive of overall child development. They were unwilling to supervise programs they believed were elitist and exclusive, overemphasized winning, and placed excessive physical and emotional pressures on children (Berryman, 1988).

The void created by this withdrawal of physical educators and professional recreation leaders was quickly filled by other adults from organizations concerned with the well-being of young people, the development of high-level sport skills, or both. These organizations developed a diversified range of youth sport programs, most of which were staffed with volunteers who lacked formal training in child development and which operated outside the context of schools. Initially, programs were usually funded by parents and local communities, but sponsorship also came from a combination of youth organizations, churches, civic groups, and local businesses. Eventually, these sponsors were joined by national corporations, professional sport organizations, and amateur sport groups, including universities and national sport federations (Berryman, 1988).

This highly diversified mix of sponsors and program organizers led to a wide array of independent and autonomous programs across a wide range of sports. This diversity and decentralization make organized youth sports in the U.S. unique. Program philosophies, game rules, regulations governing the conditions of participation for both athletes and coaches, league structures, playoff systems, and the use of formal rewards for competitive success all vary by program, by community, and by sport. Standardization is rare except in cases where local programs are closely tied to powerful national sport organizations such as the Little League Association or the U.S. Tennis Association, and even in these cases local programs often do things their own ways. No other country's youth sports are characterized by such diversity and decentralization. Furthermore, the strong vested interests in the current decentralized system are so strong that changes on a national level are unlikely. However, it is possible to make changes on the local level through specific programs that sponsor intensive training and competitive sport experiences for children. This is why it is important that we be aware of the benefits and risks of participation.

Programs involving intensive training and competition have continued to grow in size despite warnings from educators, physical educators, and recreation leaders (Berryman, 1988). Parents continue to see programs as sources of valuable experiences for their children. In the face of the continued popularity of youth sport programs, the warnings coming from educators and others, including many sport sociologists, have mellowed considerably. Now there is more concern with making all youth programs, especially those involving intensive training and competition, more responsive to the interests and developmental needs of children. Calls to dismantle the programs have given way to more tempered recommendations for reform. In the meantime, intensive training and competitive programs continue to be made available for more children at younger and younger ages.

These programs are not equally accessible to all children in the U.S. Few publicly funded programs emphasize intensive training, and those that emphasize heavy competition are gradually being cut or scaled down in many communities. The expenses associated with many of these programs are beyond the budgets of most American families. As expenses have increased, parents paying for their children's participation are more likely to see their sponsorship as an ''investment'' in their children's futures. These parents are very concerned about the organization of programs, the qualifications of coaches, and the progress of their children's skill development. Such parents often conclude that their children's sport experiences must be carefully and thoroughly controlled. As this control increases, there have been additional concerns among sport sociologists with the benefits and risks of intensive training and competition for the children involved. This chapter discusses benefits and risks from a social-developmental perspective.

The Effects of Intensive Training and Participation

Between 1950 and 1980 numerous studies set out to identify the social developmental consequences of sport participation among young people. Research subjects in these studies were mostly adolescents, although some studies included preadolescent children, and nearly all the research focused on white boys from middle- and upper middle–income families; information about girls, black children, children from low-income families, or children from specific ethnic groups is scarce. Researchers were eager to explore possible connections between sport participation and general attitudes and behaviors. Studies often tested hypotheses based on popular beliefs about the consequences of sport participation. Researchers hoped that science could shed light on whether participation really built character. However, the beliefs that participation in youth sports produces good citizens, enhances moral development, fosters academic achievement, promotes future occupational success, and builds what we might call ''character'' has received no consistent support in the sport science literature (Coakley, 1990; Coakley & Bredemeier, 1985; Kleiber & Kelly, 1980; McPherson, Curtis, & Loy, 1989). This conclusion is clearly highlighted in a review of dozens of studies on the socialization outcomes of sport participation:

> To date, there is little empirical support for the many beliefs and hypotheses concerning the positive or negative outcomes for character and personality development that are alleged to be derived from involvement in competitive sport. (McPherson & Brown, 1988, p. 274)

This conclusion is important, but it should not be taken to mean that involvement in intensive training and sport competition does not effect the lives of children. It does mean that participation by itself does not seem to offer a unique and consistent set of character- and life-shaping experiences to every child who becomes involved in intensive training and competitive youth sports.

One of the reasons why involvement in intensive training and competitive sports is not associated with a unique and consistent set of developmental outcomes is that sport experiences are extremely diverse, and children are likely to define and integrate them into their lives in many different ways (McCormack & Chalip, 1988). Furthermore, sport experiences may not be especially unique in the lives of children who are also involved in a variety of other activities that certainly impact social development. This is why simple comparisons of children who participate in sport programs with children who do not participate have not done much to increase our understanding of the benefits and risks of sport participation. By itself, participation does not lead to positive or negative developmental outcomes. It is becoming more and more clear that the conditions under which participation occurs set the stage for outcomes. This is why some children seem to grow in positive ways because of their involvement in sport whereas others seem to suffer from retarded social development as a result of their involvement.

Research will never provide an unconditional list of the benefits and risks of sport participation for children. The developmental implications of participation largely depend on the conditions under which participation takes place. At this point, research only offers a basis for hypotheses about the relationships between specific conditions and possible developmental outcomes for children. These conditions and associated hypotheses include the following.

Condition:

The type of organized sport program in which participation takes place

Possible Outcome:

When programs are organized to foster an expansion of a child's developmental experiences, outcomes will be positive; when programs constrain or preclude exposure to normal developmental experiences, outcomes will be negative.

Condition:

The relationships through which sport experiences are mediated in a child's life

Possible Outcome:

When the relationships and interactions occasioned by sport involvement enable a child to effectively deal with developmental challenges, outcomes will be positive; when relationships occasioned by involvement hinder dealing with developmental challenges, outcomes will be negative.

Condition:

The ways in which sport experiences are defined in the general social and cultural context in which participation takes place

Possible Outcome:

When sport involvement opens doors to supportive relationships and opportunities outside of sport participation itself, outcomes will be positive; when involvement undercuts supportive relationships and opportunities outside of sport participation itself, outcomes will be negative.

Thus, the developmental outcomes of intensive training and participation in competitive sports can be positive or negative, outcomes depend on the ways in which participation is connected to the rest of a child's life, and the way participation is connected is mediated by important relationships in the child's life.

Future research on benefits and risks must focus on

- the developmental implications of different types of training regimes and program structures;
- the ways that sport experiences are mediated through relationships with parents, peers, coaches, and others who are significant to children; and
- the ways in which gender, race and ethnicity, social class, and other factors affect children's subjective experiences in sport.

At this point, research provides little basis for definitive conclusions. However, we can develop a better understanding of the developmental implications of sport participation by taking a close look at what we know about the process of social development among young people. Observation of young people provides a basis for assessing possible risks and benefits associated with involvement in intensive training and competitive sport programs.

Social Development and Sport Participation*

Social development is usually described in terms of a series of stages or sequences, movement through which depends on a combination of age (maturation) and experience. The most widely accepted and well-documented theories of social development emphasize the following:

- Each stage in the developmental process involves special challenges or "developmental tasks."
- A young person must accomplish developmental tasks at one stage before addressing the tasks in the next stage; in other words, the learning that is supposed to occur at one stage is a precondition for the learning at the next stage.
- Experiences are most likely to contribute to overall development when they "fit" the young person's age and particular stage of development.
- Social development is distorted when young people are faced with experiences beyond their maturational capacities or with repetition of experiences that do not allow them to address the next level of developmental tasks.
- At the beginning of each successive stage in the social development process, young people are especially willing and able to making up work on developmental tasks left unfinished in previous stages; in other words, it is never too late to get on track developmentally.

---

*This section is adapted from Coakley and Hughes (1992).

During early childhood, ages 2 to 7 years, one of the most important developmental tasks is the mastery of physical control and physical performance. The major tasks for 7- to 10-year-olds are learning how to cope with authority that is not based on personal and emotional ties, and learning how to interact with social equals (i.e., age peers). Between 10 and 13 years of age, children have a strong need to develop close friendships and to share and assess everyday experiences with friends. Research on children in sport should focus on relationships between sport participation and the ways children deal with each of these developmental tasks. At this point we can discuss some of the likely possibilities and emphasize the fact that youth sport experiences are mediated through social relationships in young people's lives.

Physical Mastery and Sport Participation

As small children master basic physical self-care tasks such as getting dressed, and as they establish a certain amount of control over their physical environments, they learn to distinguish the self as an agent, and they begin to see themselves as actors who can control themselves and the world around them. As this happens they experience a great deal of satisfaction. Their accomplishments are often followed with joyful declarations: "Look! I did it!" They are visibly proud of being able to perform new and challenging tasks. This joy in the mastery of physical control and performance is integral to the process of social development. It is closely related to physical abilities and accomplishments in later stages in life, and it is crucial for the development of a healthy self-concept.

Youth sports would seem to be ideal activities in which to help young children achieve physical mastery. Children are eager to learn almost any new physical feat. They experience sheer joy when they master things as simple as performing a headstand, catching a ball, or accurately kicking a ball at a target. Accomplishing physical tasks is intrinsically satisfying to children. They want to learn how to do things for themselves and then say, "Look! I did it." To the extent that sport programs provide opportunities for children to master physical skills, these programs lead to positive developmental outcomes, unless the sense of mastery is minimized by a constant emphasis on long-term performance goals that children view as distant and out of reach. This sense of mastery is most likely to be minimized when parents, coaches, and child athletes focus their attention on ultimate rather than immediate realistic goals.

Development may also be temporarily undermined if sport participation creates fears about learning physical skills or a careless disregard for the physical well-being of oneself or others. Fears, often grounded in the overprotectiveness of parents or other adults, can subvert a child's natural desire to extend skills and self-control. At the other extreme, when children recklessly leap into physical challenges, their behavior is often a response to parental or adult encouragement to take risks and prove they are no longer babies. Some adults may mistakenly identify this recklessness as courage or precociousness, but it is actually a form of behavior that will interfere with realistic assessments of abilities and the consequences of one's behavior for self and others. When this happens, social development is forestalled.

Children are naturally eager to master physical skills and avoid pain in the process. They don't need extrinsic reasons to play and develop skills; motivation to play and develop physical abilities to deal with the environment is simply a part of childhood itself. Becoming an Olympic or professional athlete is irrelevant to the motivational system at work among children, even when adults get them to say all the "right" words about future goals. As they play, children gradually learn to deal with fears of injury and fears of failure. When adults criticize or ridicule children for being afraid, or when they try to motivate children by calling them "babies," the developmental outcomes of sport participation are not likely to be positive.

Sport Participation and Learning to Cope With Authority and Peers

At about age 7 children must learn how to deal with adults who are not their parents or close relatives. This is part of the overall process of making a necessary psychological break from their families. Relationships with these outside adults are unique because they're based on shared interests in accomplishing a task rather than on personal, emotional ties. The classroom teacher, the coach, the gym teacher, the school crossing guard, the Sunday school teacher, the music instructor, and many others contribute to childhood socialization primarily because they provide children opportunities to experience a new type of authority figure. This is why participation in organized sports, like many other activities, can be a useful developmental experience, but only if adults understand the developmental limitations characteristic of this stage of development (as outlined in the following section on social development and a child's readiness to participate in sports).

During this stage, children not only must learn how to react to and deal with authority but they must also learn how to get along with their social equals, their peers. When it comes to handling relationships with peers, 7- to 10-year-olds learn important things during play and games, such as how to stand up for themselves, how to compromise for the sake of getting along, and how to cooperate and compete with equals. If children don't learn these interactional skills, they may run into difficulties when addressing developmental tasks in subsequent stages. This is why adults must avoid overcontrolling a child's life in sport. When parents or coaches control involvement and all the decisions associated with involvement, children do not have opportunities to meet developmental challenges through their relationships with peers.

Games and group activities become increasingly important during childhood as the need for peers and for experiences with peers continues to emerge as an important part of the developmental process. Peers provide the means for children to separate their identities from the identities of parents and other family members. Parents and other family members cannot replace peers in the developmental process, nor can parents directly teach their children how to interact with peers.

Peers are often unknown to parents, and peer-group dynamics are so spontaneous that adults find it difficult to anticipate what children will face with peers. Unless children have opportunities to explore and deal with these relationships, social development will be forestalled.

Organized games are especially valuable because they provide children a context for learning how to react to and deal with authority and how to get along with peers all at the same time. In fact, it may be that positive memories of past developmental experiences in these games lead many adults to emphasize the connection between sport participation and social development.

Sport Participation and the Development of Friendship

Preadolescence (10 to 13 years of age) is the stage of best friends and same-sex peer groups. For boys, peer groups are often called gangs; for girls, they are often called cliques. The major developmental tasks for preadolescents are to discover how they are similar to and different from others and to develop a sense of themselves as individuals distinct from others. Taking on these tasks creates a strong emotional need among young people to develop close friendships and share and assess experiences with these friends. As this happens they gradually learn more about right and wrong, good and bad, and what other people are like. They discover how they are similar to and different from others, and this, in turn, provides a foundation for the origins of insight and empathy, both of which will be developed more fully in early adolescence.

Organized sport programs can provide an excellent context for fostering the achievement of these developmental tasks. As children learn and perform physical tasks, they have numerous opportunities to compare themselves to others and discover their own uniqueness. All young people want to be recognized as competent, and if they learn that they can display competence in many different ways, the outcomes of participation for confidence and self-esteem are likely to be positive. Furthermore, when a young athlete's uniqueness is recognized, the athlete is motivated to extend existing skills and develop new ones. Motivation also depends on the athlete's knowing that somewhere there will always be someone who is better at an activity, and that this doesn't detract from her or his own worth or achievements. Unless the goal of being the best at something is carefully qualified, it will eventually backfire and destroy children's motivation.

Organized sport programs can also provide excellent contexts for developing and maintaining friendships. However, when parents or coaches define loyalty to friends as defiance, and the concern for what friends think as a lack of character, they may jeopardize the relationships that are crucial for a child's positive social development. At age 12, being like one's friends, fitting in, and having friends reaffirm and validate feelings about oneself are absolutely crucial. Of course, being able to critically evaluate what friendships mean and knowing how to positively influence friends are also crucial. Whether a child learns this during sport participation heavily depends on the social relationships through which sport experiences are mediated. Simply telling children to avoid peer pressure and not to listen to peers is a mistake that parents and other adults frequently make. A child's awareness of how he or she is perceived by others can only be gained through experiences with peers. The developmental challenge is not to avoid so-called peer pressure but to be able to influence friends and to recognize when friends are being insensitive to others. Children need guidance combined with freedom to develop these abilities.

Relationships and the Mediation of Youth Sport Experiences

Children's sport experiences are mediated through relationships, especially relationships with significant others. Information from peers, parents, and coaches significantly impacts the meanings that children assign to sport participation in general and individual experiences in particular. This is why the consequences of participation, even among children in the same program and on the same teams, are often so different. Children construct definitions of success and failure primarily through social interaction during or after practices or games. It is in conversations with coaches, parents, and peers that a good play or a mistake takes on meaning and is integrated into a child's life.

Unfortunately, these relationships and what happens in them has been overlooked in nearly all the research on children in sport. This leaves a large void in our knowledge about the risks and the benefits of intensive training and participation in youth sports.

Social Development and Children's Readiness to Participate in Sport*

Physical movement and physical activities should be encouraged among all children, even infants and toddlers. But at what stage of social development are children ready to participate in organized sports? Parents and coaches often ask this question; the answer is somewhat complicated but is directly related to social development issues.

Before age 12 most young people do not have the social abilities to fully understand the meaning of competition or conceptually grasp competitive strategies. Anyone who has ever watched two teams of 8-year-old soccer players probably understands this statement. Eight-year-olds usually play what might be called "beehive soccer." In other words, shortly after the opening kick there are 20 bodies and 40 legs within 5 to 10 yd of the ball. And throughout the game, the players continue to follow the ball like a swarm of bees following the queen bee. Everyone is out of position and adults usually spend much of the game shouting directions about where the young players should be positioned on the field.

---

*This section is adapted from Coakley (1986).

Staying in position is a real challenge for children, because they are not developmentally ready to handle the cognitive operations used to determine positions on a team. For example, understanding the whole idea of positions on a soccer team demands that players do two complex cognitive operations:

1. Mentally visualize the overall spatial relationships between their 10 teammates and 11 opponents in relation to the placement of the ball
2. Assess their own position responsibilities in relation to the actual positions of the other 21 players and the ball

But the ability to conceptualize a complex system of social relationships in this manner is seldom developed before age 12. There may be individual exceptions to this rule, but no coach of a group of 11-year-olds can expect that even the majority of players will be cognitively capable of fully understanding positions and the relationships between positions on a team. This makes it very difficult to teach things like zone defenses and complex offensive plays. In fact, any complex strategy, even in a tennis match, will be tough for an 11-year-old to really understand and consistently apply.

This is clearly illustrated by the case of a coach trying to teach a team of 11-year-old baseball players what to do defensively when the other team has one out, runners are on first and second, and the batter hits a line drive that falls between the right and center fielders. Everyone has a responsibility tied to the responsibilities of all the other players. But getting a group of children under 12 to respond to this situation with true tactical understanding is impossible. Eleven-year-old left fielders will not on their own conclude that they should run and back up third base for a possible overthrow from the cutoff person in short right center field when the batter tries to stretch a double into a triple. Such a conclusion is beyond the developmental capabilities of all but a few developmentally advanced 11-year-olds, and coaches usually put them at shortstop, not in left field!

When I've been told of exceptions to this developmental rule, I've usually discovered that the young players who seemingly have a full grasp of strategy are simply highly talented athletes and efficient imitators. They have watched so many highly skilled older players that they have picked up a ''sense'' of strategy. But this sense is based on their advanced physical skills and their abilities to imitate, not on their cognitive understanding of game strategies. Imitation is an ability developed during infancy and early childhood, and it is carried forward to subsequent stages of social development. Some children become expert imitators.

The inability of most children to conceptualize and understand a complex system of social relationships causes considerable frustration among parents and coaches. Without knowing why children cannot understand and conform to team strategies, many adults accuse children of not trying hard enough or having bad attitudes. This is frustrating to the children because most of them are thinking and trying hard. Adults who continue to accuse them of a lack of effort often lose credibility with children.

Some coaches have tried to avoid beehive soccer and its equivalents in other sports by carefully and tediously conditioning their young players to respond in precise ways to various game situations that might occur. They do this by creating various game situations during practices and then having each player rehearse the correct individual responses to each situation. But doing this with every player across even a few situations makes practices long and boring. When coaches use this approach, they may successfully condition their players to do the right things more often, and they may even win some games because of it, but they are also likely to destroy much of the action and personal involvement that children value in their sport experiences. When this happens, players will not want to come to practices, and when they do show up, they will spend much of their time "horsing around." When players are cognitively and socially unable to grasp the notion of strategies, much less apply them within the spontaneous action of a game, it is better for coaches to accept a little chaos and emphasize the learning of basic physical skills than to tediously condition players to perform certain moves.

Although the ability to mentally visualize complex sets of social relationships obviously affects children's performances in most team sports, it also has implications for what can be expected from children under the age of 12 when they are involved in any organized competitive games. According to theories and research on social development, children are not born with the ability to compete or cooperate but must learn how to handle competitive and cooperative relationships. This learning is based on experience, but it is also governed by the gradual development of abstract thinking abilities.

As abstract thinking abilities develop, children move from a stage in which they can see the world from only their own limited viewpoints to a stage in which they can see the world from a more objective, third-party perspective. This third-party perspective involves more than the child's own egocentric view of the world and more than the view of any single other person, such as a parent or teacher. Instead, it is based on a recollection and summary of the different perspectives used by many people that the child encounters.

A person needs this third-party perspective to fully engage in any complex group interaction. And because it is not usually developed before the age of 12, a young person experiences competitive relationships quite differently from how adults do. As long as adults realize this and adjust their expectations accordingly, participation in sport provides children valuable exposure to the social relationships and experiences they will encounter in the course of normal social development.

But many adults do not appreciate the differences between their views of competition and the views held by children. For this reason, many coaches and parents have unrealistic expectations for children in organized sport programs. Realistically, any sport program for children under the age of 8 should emphasize physical skill development almost exclusively. Competition is generally irrelevant to children under this age, although they can imitate the concerns of the adults around them. For children between 8 and 12, an emphasis on individual physical skill development should be balanced with a gradually increased emphasis on tactics and strategies. High-performance programs involving competition for significant rewards and requiring an extreme degree of personal commitment should wait until young people are at least 13 or 14 years old.

In summary, children under the age of 8 are not socially developed enough to grasp the dynamics of organized competitive sports; they don't have the requisite social and cognitive abilities. Between 8 and 12, children gradually develop these abilities, although at different rates among different children. Adults must realize that only a handful of children under 12 will be developmentally ready to fully grasp the idea that a team consists of an interrelated set of positions that shift in response to one another, in response to opponents, and in response to the placement of a ball or some other object. Therefore, adults need to modify their expectations to avoid creating frustration for themselves and child athletes.

Expectations should also be modified when working with children in individual sports. Children under age 12 may be able to learn complex physical skills in a sport such as gymnastics, but the learning process often involves the formation of a dependency relationship with an adult (coach) who has extensive control over the young athlete's life. The control may lead to early competition success, but child athletes do not have the social and cognitive abilities to separate their skills and successes from their relationships with the adults who control their lives. As these children get older, this dependency often impedes future social development.

What Children Look for in the Sport Experience

When dealing with children in intensive training and competitive programs, adults often forget that children see sport experiences in their own unique ways. Knowing what children look for in the sport experience is very important, because when children do not find what they are looking for, their motivation will wane and skill development will suffer. One way to discover what children look for in their sport experiences is to ask children themselves; another way is to watch how children organize their own free-time activities. Research using these approaches has discovered that children are interested in four things when they play sports (Coakley, 1983, 1990):

- Action
- Personal involvement in the action
- Close scores and challenges matching their skills
- Opportunities to reaffirm their friendships

Whenever children create their own games, they put much effort into setting up rules promoting action. Most of the activity during their games occurs around the scoring area, and scores are so frequent that it's usually impossible to keep track of any personal performance statistics. When children are asked what is most fun in their informal sport experiences, they emphasize action-related events like hitting, catching, shooting, scoring, and so forth. Furthermore, children seldom sit on the bench during informal games.

During informal games, children often develop and use rule qualifications and handicap systems to sustain satisfying action and maximize the personal involvement of all participants. "Do-overs," interference calls, and other special rules may be used to help less skilled players maintain their involvement at satisfying levels. Children are also quick to realize that close scores make games exciting and lopsided scores make them boring, and their games usually reflect this realization. Children often construct or modify teams to keep game scores close enough to make the games interesting and challenging, even if individual players must accept handicaps (such as batting left-handed in a pick-up baseball game).

Finally, children use games to reaffirm friendships, a desire reflected in the makeup of teams and the strategies they use during games. In fact, children may sometimes even sacrifice close scores in order to use games to reaffirm friendships.

When we talk to children about their sport involvement and watch them play informal games, it is clear they are not interested in building character or achieving long-term goals. Generally, they are interested in developing and displaying competence and having some degree of control over what they do. They want to learn new things about themselves, develop and display new abilities, and have their abilities recognized by others. Their informal games are usually organized so these things happen regularly.

Unfortunately, many youth sport programs are organized in ways that discourage action, limit personal involvement (especially among those who need it the most), permit lopsided scores, and assign teams without any concern for friendships. Fortunately, it is relatively easy to create or revise programs in ways that emphasize what children look for in their sport experiences. This happens when the adults who control those programs define game models as arbitrary and changeable and respect the subjective interests of children.

Coaches as Significant Others in the Social Development Process*

The idea that coaches build character among athletes of all ages probably originated when school administrators tried to justify the use of educational funds to support interscholastic sport programs. Because many people believed that enjoyment and development of physical skills were not reasons enough to justify school-funded interscholastic sports, administrators argued that organized competitive sport participation was itself a character-building experience. As this argument was made, coaches quickly came to be defined as character builders because they organized and supervised sport experiences.

---

*This section is adapted from Coakley and Hughes (1992).

The image of coaches as character builders has been perpetuated by athletes who claim their lives have been greatly influenced by former coaches. When athletes make such claims, they do not always mean that the influence is benign. Claims of influence could mean one or more of the following:

1. They could mean that some coaches had such total control over the lives of athletes that a dependency relationship developed. In this way, coaches influenced the lives of athletes in the same way dictators influence the lives of their people or drill sergeants influence the lives of recruits in basic training. The impact of these coaches was certainly great, but it is unlikely that their influence led to the development of self-control and independence (unless, of course, the athletes rebelled or the coach eventually provided opportunities to make decisions).

2. Such claims could mean that coaches either set good examples for athletes to follow or share personal information to such an extent that athletes were able to use coaches as models for making their own choices for the rest of their lives.

3. These claims could mean that coaches acted as advisers or advocates for athletes, helping them explore alternatives, meet challenges, make choices, and deal with the consequences of successes and failures. In this sense, coaches served as ''adult allies'' who used their connections and influence to keep athletes out of trouble and in control of their lives.

In other words, coaches can become significant in the lives of athletes in different ways. They can make athletes dependent on them, serve as exemplars or role models, or act as advisers and advocates. Each of these types of influence is explained further to outline the ways in which coaches impact young athletes' lives.

Coaches as Dictators

Judging from the number of athletes who use ''love-hate'' to describe former coaches, I suspect that many coaches become important in the lives of athletes because they use extreme command-style methods. Rigid systems of control often lead to dependency relationships, and the dependent people in these relationships often use love-hate terms to describe those who have power over them.

The dynamics of rigid control systems have been vividly described in studies of abused children and spouses. Abused children and spouses often make excuses for those who control and abuse them and may even go so far as to say they deserve the inhumane treatment they receive from the people who so rigidly control their lives. The reason for this is that people who lack power in rigid systems of social control often protect themselves by learning as much as they can about the people who control them. This learning involves putting themselves in the positions of the controllers and trying to see things from the controllers' perspectives. Sociologists call this process ''taking the role of the other.'' This process of taking the role of the other gives powerless people the "inside informa-tion" they need to exert at least some degree of control over their controllers; they please them to avoid pain. If powerless people know their controllers well enough, they can try to behave in ways that please the controllers on their own terms. However, when this tactic is used for an extended time these powerless people sometimes begin to identify with their controllers. This phenomenon is sometimes described as "identification with the aggressor." When this type of identification occurs, controllers become significant and influential in the lives of the people they control. In fact, the powerless people who experience this type of dependency relationship will generally talk about the dramatic impact these controlling people have had on their lives.

This description of the dynamics of extreme dependency relationships is not given to equate controlling coaches with abusive spouses and parents; it is given to illustrate how some coaches may use control to become significant in the lives of athletes. This description also explains why athletes who have experienced extended relationships with overcontrolling coaches may for the rest of their lives describe those coaches as important and influential in their lives.

When coaches create extreme dependency relationships, they often do impact the lives of athletes. The impact, however, does not contribute to overall growth and development or provide athletes with appropriate models to use in their own relationships. But it may be so strong that athletes refer to it long after they have retired from competitive sport. Fortunately, there are other ways to exert influence, ways that are positive and that lead athletes to develop responsibility and concern for others. Serving as role models and serving as advocates are much preferred alternatives.

Coaches as Role Models

"Role model" has become a buzzword in many circles and is used by different people to mean different things. This variety of uses has created confusion about what role models are, even among sociologists who developed the term.

Role modeling is actually a complex process that goes beyond simply setting a good example for others to follow. Becoming a role model is most likely when a person shares information about her or his own life within the context of a relationship characterized by some degree of emotional connection. The sharing and the emotional connection provide the other person with the necessary informa-tion to use the first person as a model.

Being a model requires that others get to know the model well and then experience situations similar to the ones in which they have seen that person. This is why it is often unrealistic to expect coaches to be role models in a true sense. Athletes don't have enough information to pattern their lives after the lives of their coaches. Coaches do not make enough personal self-disclosures, nor do athletes observe the personal lives of coaches often enough for any true role modeling to occur. Furthermore, coach-athlete relationships are not often characterized by the emotional ties required for anything beyond a superficial form of role modeling. Finally, because many coaches are different than their athletes, as far as race, ethnic background, or gender, it makes little sense to expect coaches to be lifetime role models.

Another problem is that after the age of about 8 years, young people seldom depend on a single model in their lives. Young people between the ages of 8 and 13 gradually develop the ability to think abstractly about expectations for their behavior. As this ability develops they are less and less likely to base behavior on imitation of others. Instead, they choose from the guidelines and lessons they've learned in many different relationships, and then develop their own sense of what is right and wrong and how they should behave in different situations.

Because development occurs in this way, it is probably unrealistic to expect coaches to be true role models. Research suggests that few athletes use coaches as general role models in their lives. However, research also shows that coaches do have a direct and important impact on team norms and on the behavior of young people as they interact with team members (Fine, 1987). Therefore, it is more realistic to expect that coaches can set some good examples for young people of how to handle themselves in sport situations.

Coaches as Advocates

The importance of an advocate in the life of a young person is illustrated through this statement of a junior high school coach who recalled his relationship with his former high school coach:

> My high school coach was short, white, and out of shape—different than me. But he cared about me even though I wasn't the best player on our team. And it's a good thing too. Because nobody else was looking out for me then, and I needed his help more than once. (Coakley, 1990, p. 160)

This quote shows that coaches can be important in the lives of athletes, even when they are different from their athletes. Coaches are most likely to impact the lives of athletes when they act as advisers or advocates. An *adviser* gives information, offers opinions, and consults with another person. An *advocate* is someone in a position of power and influence who directly supports or defends others or pleads a case in time of need—someone who keeps us out of trouble or gets us out when we've made a mistake. All young people need advisers and advocates because all young people make mistakes as they learn about how the world works, who they are, and how they fit into that world.

Adults set the course of young people's lives, not simply because they teach lessons, set down rules, and enforce those rules, but primarily because they are sources of information and opportunities. They control resources that can limit and restrict young people or open up opportunities for achievement. In other words, they can subvert or promote growth and development. Adults are gatekeepers in the lives of young people, and as gatekeepers they exert significant influence.

One of the easiest and most effective ways to be an advocate is to privately single out young people, call attention to their "specialness," and assist them in building on that specialness for their own benefit or the benefit of a team. All children need to be noticed and defined by others as valuable and worthwhile. When someone as important as a coach does this, young people almost always feel good about themselves.

Summary

Intensive training and youth sport participation occur primarily in industrial societies where children have much free time and where resources are available for facilities, equipment, and program costs. Organized youth sport programs in the U.S. are numerous and are unique in that they are highly decentralized and diverse. These programs are an established part of the social landscape; they will continue to grow in the future.

The consequences of participation in youth sports are difficult to pin down; research evidence is confusing and contradictory. However, if we evaluate participation in terms of the developmental tasks faced by children between the ages of 5 and 12, we see that children may benefit from participation by gaining an increased sense of physical self-mastery, increased abilities to deal with authority and peers, and increased opportunities to develop friendships crucial to social development. Social development may be impeded when the social context in which participation takes place restricts experiences, interferes with peer relationships, and limits opportunities outside of sport.

The benefits and risks associated with participation largely depend on the structure of the sport programs themselves; the ways in which sport experiences are mediated through relationships children have with peers, parents, and coaches; and the ways in which sport participation is defined in the overall social context in which participation occurs.

A child's readiness to participate in organized sports depends on social as well as physical development. Before the age of 12 children do not have the social and cognitive skills needed to fully grasp and participate in organized competitive games. This does not mean they should not participate, but it does mean that game structures and adult expectations for performance should be revised to meet the developmental capabilities of children.

Research shows that when children participate in sports, they look for a combination of action, personal involvement, challenges that match their skills, and opportunities to reaffirm friendships. Although organized sport programs provide satisfying experiences to many children, programs can be revised to increase enjoyment by emphasizing these factors.

Coaches may also significantly impact the lives of child athletes; however, that impact may not always be constructive. Coaches may exert influence by making young athletes dependent on them, by serving as exemplars, or by being advocates. When influence is based on control that leads to dependency relationships, it is likely that coaches will have a negative impact on the overall development of children. When influence is based on example and guidance, it is likely that the overall impact will be positive.

The developmental outcomes of participation in intensive training and competitive sport are problematic. However, when adults are sensitive to the developmental needs of children there is a greater likelihood that programs and relationships with children will be structured to maximize benefits and minimize risks. Given the demands of high-performance programs, the greatest threat to children's social development is that adults will overcontrol the lives of child athletes for the sake of achievements in sport. Overcontrol, more than any other dimension of the sport experience, can undermine the ways in which participation can help children meet the developmental challenges of childhood.

References

Berryman, J. (1988). The rise of highly organized sports for preadolescent boys. In F. Smoll, R.A. Magill, and M.J. Ash (Eds.), *Children in sport* (3rd ed., pp. 3-16). Champaign, IL: Human Kinetics.

Coakley, J. (1983). Play, games and sports: Developmental implications for young people. In J. Harris & R. Park (Eds.), *Play, games and sports in cultural contexts* (pp. 431-450). Champaign, IL: Human Kinetics.

Coakley, J. (1986). When should children begin competing? A sociological perspective. In M.R. Weiss & D. Gould (Eds.), *Sport for children and youths* (pp. 59-63). Champaign, IL: Human Kinetics.

Coakley, J. (1990). Sport in society: Issues and controversies (4th ed.). St. Louis: Times Mirror/Mosby.

Coakley, J., & Bredemeier, B. (1985). *Youth sports: Development of ethical practices.* Paper presented at the Ethics and Athletics Conference, Baton Rouge, LA.

Coakley, J., & Hughes, R. (1992). *Social issues for coaches.* Unpublished manuscript.

Fine, G.A. (1987). *With the boys: Little League baseball and preadolescent culture.* Chicago: The University of Chicago Press.

Kleiber, D., & Kelly, J. (1980). Leisure, socialization and the life cycle. In S. Iso-Ahola (Ed.), *Social psychological perspectives on leisure and recreation* (pp. 91-137). Springfield, IL: Charles C Thomas.

McCormack, J.B., & Chalip, L. (1988). Sport as socialization: A critique of methodological premises. *The Social Science Journal, 25*(1), 83-92.

McPherson, B.D., & Brown, B. (1988). The structure, processes, and consequences of sport for children. In F.L. Smoll, R.A. Magill, and M.J. Ash (Eds.), *Children in sport* (pp. 265-286). Champaign, IL: Human Kinetics.

McPherson, B.D., Curtis, J., & Loy, J. (1989). *The social significance of sport.* Champaign, IL: Human Kinetics.

Chapter 4

Problems Associated With Youth Involvement in High-Performance Sport

Peter Donnelly

With the Assistance of
Erika Caspersen
Laura Sergeant
Brenda Steenhof

I suppose that the chief thing about being a child is being in the power of grown-ups. Everything comes from them—food, love, treats and punishments. They have the power to give and to withhold. Some of them make up the rules as they go along to suit their convenience and the child, who would like the chance to make up a few rules himself, knows it. (Vittachi, 1989, p. 1)

In adult-organized sport programs for children,[1] the control that adults have over children, as in the preceding quotation, is extended from parenting and education to children's play. The problems associated with this have been recognized for some time and have been a significant area of interest in the fields of sport sociology and psychology. Concerns have been expressed about competitive stress and anxiety, increased aggression, parental pressure, high dropout rates, and tendencies of coaches to treat children as "miniadults."

Early research tended to idealize unstructured children's play in comparison to adult-organized sport (e.g., Devereux, 1976).[2] Subsequent work, such as Martens on competitive anxiety, Orlick on dropouts, and Smith and Smoll on coaching behavior, has been instrumental in improving children's sport programs. The development of participation-oriented house leagues for age-group sports, and the growth of movement education, cooperative games, and the play movement, may be seen as responses to the academic critique of highly competitive organized sport programs. The establishment of coach-education programs (e.g., the Rookie Coaches Course by the Coaching Certification Program by the Coaching Association of Canada and the American Coaching Effectiveness Program) is also an attempt to ensure that the volunteer coaches of children's sports will have at least minimal competence and will be conscious of some of the issues associated with children's sport involvement.

Developments in this area were so rapid that in the 3-year period between the appearance of the first and second editions of the book *Children in Sport*, McPherson was able to note the establishment of three centers for the study of youth sport; two major studies of youth sport; numerous books, pamphlets, and manuals for use by volunteer coaches and leaders; and a rapidly developing academic interest in the field (McPherson, 1982). Increasing requirements for coaching certification and increasing parental and media awareness of the potential negative effects of competitive sport programs for children may ensure that the climate in children's sport, at least at the recreational and minor competitive levels, will continue to improve.

However, the climate at the elite level appears to be worsening. As children encounter opportunities for increasingly lucrative careers as professional athletes, parents are tempted to encourage their children to become heavily involved in preprofessional sports at early ages. As evidenced by increasing demands for international success in sport as a justification for government and corporate spending on elite participation, and by a variety of attempts to establish schemes for the early identification of athletic talent, there is an obvious trend toward earlier and more intensive athletic involvement for younger and younger children.

Our interest in this area derives from two specific sources, the first being personal encounters with and media accounts of retired high-performance athletes who attribute subsequent life problems directly to their childhood experiences in competitive sport. For example, a retired figure skater has drawn a direct link between her childhood athletic experiences and her recent divorce; a former world-class diver says he "thought a lot about suicide" in the year after he quit; and two former international swimmers look back on their competitive careers as "hell," one claiming that it took nearly 15 years to get over the ill effects.

The second source is work by researchers such as Beamish and Borowy (1988), Cantelon (1981), Geldbach (1977), Grupe (1985), and Ulrich (1976) concerning "child athletic workers" and the possibility of protecting young high-performance athletes under the law. Children do not instigate their own involvement in such activity:

Children would never think on their own accord of subjecting themselves to an organized form of sport aimed for long-term performance, and to organization of their daily, weekly and yearly schedules as is required by the preparation to achieve top performance. (Grupe, 1985, p. 10)

Under adult guidance and supervision large numbers of children are training and competing under highly worklike conditions for long hours and in many cases for immediate or potential remuneration.

These children are involved in an increasing number of competitions (some 10-year-old hockey players have played 90 games in a season) and increasing training time (young figure skaters have trained 60 hr/week when preparing for national competition). Children are also, in some cases, suffering from deteriorating coach and parent behavior, and anecdotes abound concerning the notorious behavior of many of these young athletes and their abusive parents and coaches. They concern assaultive hockey players, the pampered and battered students of elite tennis schools, and the parents and coaches who use a variety of punishments from denial of affection to outright beatings in order to extract maximum performance from their charges.

The principle concerns were summarized by Grupe (1985, pp. 10-11), who wrote that these children

- are not permitted to be children,
- are denied important social contacts and experiences,
- are victims of disrupted family life,
- are exposed to excessive psychological and physiological stress,
- may experience impaired intellectual development,
- may become so involved with the sport that they become detached from the larger society, and
- face a type of abandonment on completion of their athletic careers.

When we consider these concerns in light of the recently adopted United Nations Convention on the Rights of the Child (1989), it appears that there are significant problems in the area of high-performance sport for children and there is a serious need for action.

Unfortunately, the evidence upon which to base any action is fragmented and frequently anecdotal. The study on which this chapter is based[3] represents a systematic attempt to document athletes' concerns about intensive involvement during childhood and to suggest some directions for future action.

Research Procedures of High-Performance Youth Sports

The research involved in-depth interviews with 45 recently retired Canadian high-performance athletes and was supplemented by a number of documentary and informal sources of data.

The Subjects

At the outset of this study a number of criteria and rationales were established for subject selection:

1. The research should involve male and female subjects representing a range of sports. The available fragments of evidence concern single sports, and this

study is an attempt to determine if problems are common to a variety of sports and if there are problems common to both girls and boys. The particular sampling procedure resulted in an unequal number of male and female subjects but with no apparent effect on the results. Also, the sampling criteria generated a disproportionate number of individual-sport athletes, but because these athletes tend to be more involved in intensive training and competition at younger ages (often because their sports are less seasonally based) and tend to be mentioned more frequently in the anecdotal evidence, the sample was considered to be appropriate.

2. Subjects should have competed at high levels in their sports, preferably at early ages (e.g., national team, nationally ranked). This is the level of sport that is of most concern in terms of "child athletic labor." All of the sample met this criterion, although this limitation resulted in rejection of a number of potential subjects and the lack of representation of a number of sports, especially team sports (because the particular nature of some sports tends to preclude high-level involvement at younger ages).

3. Subjects should have been involved for 25 hr or more per week of practice/ competition for a period of time during their childhood. Again, because of the nature of certain sports, we were obliged to reduce this criterion somewhat by including subjects who had been involved fewer than 25 hr a week. However, we were assured of the intensive high-performance involvement of the subjects.

4. Subjects should be "recently" retired from their sports. We specifically felt that three types of athlete/former-athlete should be excluded. First were those who had had unsuccessful careers in high-performance sport and who might be embittered as a consequence. We felt that these subjects would necessarily have had negative experiences and may use the study as a forum to vindicate themselves regarding their lack of success.[4] The second group we attempted to exclude comprised former athletes currently involved in administration or coaching of their sport, who might have a vested interest in presenting their sport in the best possible light. Due to the number of retired successful athletes who continue some form of full-time or part-time involvement in their sport (coaching, refereeing/judging, administration), these subjects proved to be difficult to avoid. However, the ones who appeared in the sample seemed to be prepared to dwell on both positive and negative aspects of their own careers and to make constructive suggestions for change. Third, for several reasons we attempted to exclude those currently involved as athletes, which at first consideration might seem to be the most relevant group (children were, of course, excluded anyway for ethical reasons). We did not wish either to ask athletes to criticize their current coaches or administrators or to raise suspicions that may not have otherwise occurred to the athletes. Also, those who are currently involved in a sport frequently assume that they are involved voluntarily, and they tend to emphasize the positive attributes of their participation rather than considering the possible social, psychological and physical costs (cf., Cantelon, 1981). Several of the subjects were still participating, but they were adults, were at senior levels in their athletic careers, and were quite prepared to reflect on their childhood experiences. Details of the sample are presented in Table 4.1.

Table 4.1   Demographic and Career Details of the Sample

Sport	Males	Females
Gymnastics (including 1 rhythmic)	2	10
Figure skating	0	5
Synchronized swimming	0	4
Swimming	3	2
Skiing (downhill)	1	0
Ice hockey	1	1
Tennis	1	1
Track	1	5
Field	2	0
Football	1	0
Martial arts (1 kick boxing, 1 judo, 1 tae kwan do)	3	0
Rowing	0	1
Wrestling	1	0

$N = 45$; 16 male, 29 female.
Age: 19-35; $M = 24.5$ years.
Career length: $M = 8.5$ years.
Age first involved: 4-15; $M = 10$ years.
Age retired: $M = 19$ years.
Maximum hours/week: 15-56; $M = 25.6$.

Extremes:
    Skater who trained 56 hr/week between ages 15 and 17;
    swimmer who calculated that he spent 15,800 hr in the water, an astonishing 22 months
    (at 24 hr/day) of his life.

Data Collection Procedures

Subjects were contacted with a "snowball" sampling procedure, interview times were scheduled, and the interviews were taped. Interviews lasted from 45 to 90 min. As is frequently the case in this type of research, subjects presented further information during casual discussion after the tape recorder had been switched off, and this was recorded as field notes.

The interviews were divided into three parts: demographic and statistical details of the subject and his or her athletic career; positive and negative aspects of the subject's childhood athletic career; and a general set of discussion questions (e.g., Were your experiences typical? Can you describe the best and worst careers of people you knew? Would you do it again the same way? Would you involve your children in this sport? What would you do to change/improve the experiences of children in this sport?). Interviews were transcribed and analyzed for common themes with regard to the childhood athletic experiences of the subjects.

In an attempt to avoid the positive and voluntaristic type of statements that current elite athletes might make, we designed this study as a retrospective study of retired athletes who might be able to look back on their careers with more perspective than those currently involved. Although this type of research involves possible problems with recall and selective memory, the data are as valid as any type of oral history, and this research presents no more problems with subjectivity than any other type of survey research. Validity has also been confirmed in several classroom and conference presentations of these data, where a number of audience members have confirmed the accuracy of the experiences recounted here. In the final analysis, only athletes can determine if we have accurately captured their experiences.

Data Presentation

We have deliberately taken an extremely conservative approach to the presentation and interpretation of the data. Although some sensational data were communicated to us, particularly with regard to incidents of abuse, a number of examples were not used for the following reasons:

1. Some were second-hand or hearsay and could not be confirmed at this time.
2. There was a concern that confidentiality would have been breached in some instances because of the possibility that readers would recognize the subjects and their abusers.
3. The researchers occasionally had the impression that subjects were beginning to exaggerate their concerns—perhaps telling the interviewers what they thought we wanted to hear, or more likely embellishing the story in the retelling. Whenever this was suspected, the data were toned down.
4. Some of the material was clearly upsetting to our subjects, and we respected their wishes if they requested that material not be used.
5. A great deal of material was borderline. Was the motion that a coach used to encourage or psych up the athlete a gentle punch or was it a hit? Could we consider abusive the slap a coach used to get an athlete's attention or to demonstrate how ''fat'' a particular body part was? Was the slap to a particular out-of-position body part (by the spotter during the practice of a ''trick'') punitive rather than educational? How excessive were some particularly punitive drills? How many rubdowns, massages, or inappropriate touches (that apparently occurred ''accidentally'' during spotting) were sexually motivated? In all of these types of cases many athletes thought that many coaches and assistant coaches had gone too far, and this was often a topic of discussion among athletes. But many had built up a resistance to this issue and accepted it as part of the sport. Power differences made it extremely difficult to confront the coach with such behavior.

In future research, a means will have to be developed for dealing more appropriately with such borderline behavior; and athletes must be empowered to begin to "name" their negative experiences.

Athletes' Experiences in High-Performance Sport

As could be expected from a sample of successful athletes, all noted positive experiences resulting from their sport involvement. In terms of extrinsic benefits, travel was the single item most mentioned, and the opportunities to travel across Canada and abroad were both memorable and rewarding. Subjects also frequently mentioned prestige and the resulting attention from family, friends, and the media. Trophies, cups, medals and other awards were also appreciated, but our subjects did not attach the same importance to these as to travel and prestige.

The most significant intrinsic benefit was enjoyment of the sport, an attribute that was clearly related to competence. Friendships with fellow athletes were frequently mentioned, and travel played a significant part in expanding a network of friends. Feelings of good health and fitness were noted, as was the pleasure of skill improvement. Many subjects felt that as a result of their sport involvement they had developed self-discipline and confidence; had matured and "grown up quickly" in comparison to their nonathletic peers; could handle stress and deal with crises; were able to organize their time; and had developed mental sharpness.

Subjects were given every opportunity to expand on the positive aspects of their careers but did not spend much time on this section of the interview. Although they tended to enthuse about travel and friendships, some of the other positive aspects sounded like clichés. It is possible that the tangible benefits of high-performance sport are few and quite clear, but it seems more likely that the cultural value we place on the personal joy and pleasure of doing something really well is very limited, as is the vocabulary we have to describe these feelings. There are some excellent novelistic descriptions of such pleasure, and perhaps two athletes from the same sport could come close to addressing the "good times" while reminiscing about their careers, but no examples were evident during the interviews.

Subjects spent far more time on negative experiences, and these tended to fall into two categories: those that we expected from previous research, and those that were less expected. In the followng sections, relationships with family and friends, educational problems, physical and psychological problems, excessive behavior, doping, relationships with coaches, dietary problems, the internal politics of sports, and retirement problems are each considered separately.

Troubled Family Relationships

Some 65% of the athletes surveyed reported family problems of one type or another. These included regret that a large part of family life had been missed; both subtle and overt parental pressure; guilt about money, family time, and attention received in comparison to siblings; constant parental presence at practices and competitions at an age when independence was sought; and sibling rivalries and jealousies. We heard of some families splitting up so that the athlete and a parent (usually the mother) could live closer to a well-known coach.

Although some athletes reported excellent relationships with parents during their competitive careers, our general impression was of greater child/adolescent-parent problems than the norm. Even where athletes reported good relationships, they sometimes felt guilty about the time and money parents devoted to their sport involvement. And one gymnast was concerned about the extremely close relationship she had with her female coach ("it must have been hard on my mom").

At one extreme, some athletes were concerned about lack of support from their parents. The tae kwan do competitor reported that his parents refused to attend after he won the provincial championship because "it gets pretty brutal." Others reported disinterested and unsupportive parents, one noting his extreme anger at receiving no financial or emotional support from his parents. A gymnast told us about showing her father her bruised hips after practice—he just turned away and made it clear that he disapproved of her involvement. The mother of a gymnast who fell off the bars during a competition reportedly said, "I wish she would have broken her foot."

At the other extreme, parents take an unhealthy interest that results in severe pressure on the athlete. There are many cases of gymnasts' parents being banned from practices, and one figure skater's mother was not permitted to stay at the same hotel as her child at competitions. Another skater noted how her mother "freaked out" and did not speak to her for 3 weeks after she announced that she was quitting. The daughter eventually realized that her mother's identity and daily structure were completely aligned with her skating—"What was she going to do now?" Parental support and interest may also yield subtle pressure, creating a sense of obligation and making it difficult for the athlete to quit. As one gymnast said of her mother, "With a two-and-a-half-hour drive each day, who wants it more?" Some athletes pointed to the extreme financial sacrifices made by many parents.

However, many parents attempt to do the best for their children and try to help their children achieve their full potential. Unfortunately, they often find that they are powerless in the high performance sport system. Thompson (1992) found the following:

> None of these [mothers] felt they had any say in the nature of their child's experience within the sport. Many talked about needing to be at their child's tournaments to 'protect' them from the ugliness which they saw associated with that form of competition. They also spoke of the immense difficulty coping with the dilemmas which arose when their child was unjustly disappointed or punished by the sport's bureaucratic decisions. They felt silenced by the spectre of the 'ugly parent' mythology, believing that if they ever complained it would be their child and her or his [sport] career which would suffer. (p. 8)

Thus parents, who are frequently (and sometimes deservedly) blamed for problems in youth sport, also find themselves in ambivalent and constraining positions.

In addition, sibling problems were reported by 45% of the athletes. Siblings were often reportedly jealous over the time, money, and attention the athlete received from parents and over her or his athletic ability. One gymnast said, "We never ate supper together, so my parents made a big fuss when I was home for dinner," a practice that further alienated her from her siblings. Athletes' schedules also often created a loss of contact with siblings. As one skater said, "I couldn't tell you what [my sister] did from [ages] 14 to 18."

Problems in Social Relationships

For the majority of our sample, friendships were not a problem. Most subjects noted strong friendships with fellow athletes, and many reported networks of friends outside the sport, some subjects even suggesting that their sport involvement had helped them to feel socially competent. Others stated that they had no time for friends because of their heavy involvement in their sport or that their sport substituted for friends. Some even suggested that the competitive atmosphere at practices made it difficult to be friends with fellow athletes.

Some of our subjects noted specific problems with nonathletic peers. One gymnast would not tell her friends when she competed, because if her picture was in the local newspaper she would be ridiculed by her male peers. Another gymnast felt outcast because of her success in sport, and this was compounded in physical education classes where her abilities (often pointed out by the teacher) made her stand out and separated her further from her classmates. The rower noted, "I felt different from everyone else. . . . I was strong and big as compared to the other girls so I had a conflict in that respect. . . . I didn't fit in [but] in a way I wanted to be like the other girls." A male swimmer felt that people outside the sport saw him as conceited, and the kickboxer felt like an outcast in high school because he was accustomed to associating with older people.

Age differences sometimes caused problems; one-third of the athletes reported physical and mental abuse and peer pressure in this regard. Two of the martial arts participants experienced physical abuse as a result of winning contests against older competitors; a swimmer who trained with 14- to 17-year-olds when he was 7 said, "I used to cry . . . they put me in a locker for fun"; and many of the athletes reported pressure to be involved in adultlike behavior such as drinking, partying, and drug use (discussed subsequently).

Social problems also took other forms, one of which involved missed activities. As one subject said, "I missed out on birthday parties, family outings, Christmas holidays, and weekends away." Athletes reported that they had missed parties, dances, and just "hanging out" with friends. Some even missed formal occasions such as their own or their boyfriends' or girlfriends' high school graduation formals, and one swimmer who attended his own graduation formal rather than swim in a meet was victimized by his coach and club officials. Missed field trips, outdoor education weekends, and even particular television programs further limited athletes' interactions with friends at school.

All of these resulted in athletes feeling out of step with their nonparticipant peers, particularly so for those who retired from sport in their teens and found that they were far behind in such things as summer employment experience. Thus, for some the shock was the need to work for university tuition, whereas for others it was finding themselves low in the hierarchy of summer camp counselors. Almost a quarter of the sample reported that during their careers they had no interest in meeting peers outside their sport and now regretted not having been more open to new friendships. One gymnast described a friend whose whole life had been gymnastics and studying and who after retirement became a loner who did not know about friends or how to use free time.

Athlete-Coach Relationships

This study was spurred, in part, by a statement made in casual conversation by a retired figure skater, who noted that when she was a teenager, her relationship with her adult male coach had been "destructive." She went on to describe the emotional turmoil, the dependency and domination, the granting and withholding of affection, and the eventual romantic relationship, marriage, and inevitable divorce. Although we did not consider this a typical experience, it led us to consider what kind of problems young athletes experienced in the relatively closed world of practice for high-performance sport. Athletes spend a great deal of time with their coaches, often far more than with their families, and in some of the individual sports intense one-on-one relationships develop. But such relationships are not necessarily healthy, and coaches may become quite controlling and manipulative.

Well over half of the sample reported good to very good relationships with their coaches. But the majority of female athletes had had male coaches, which can lead to some extremely complex relationship problems, particularly in individual sports. Todd Crosset (1989) has collected numerous examples of physical, mental, and sexual abuse in male-coach/female-athlete relationships and is currently working through the difficulties of appropriately and sensitively interpreting and characterizing the data. Is the physical and mental abuse the same as that inflicted by authoritarian coaches on male athletes? Are the sexual encounters similar to those occasionally reported between schoolteachers and students? Crosset suspects that the male-coach/female-athlete cases are different and more intense, much more similar to cases of the domestic abuse of women and children.

The difficulties of interpretation are evident in the data collected for this study. Among the cases of "very good" relationships with coaches, phrases like "father figure" and "he was like a father to me" cropped up frequently for both female and male subjects. One female gymnast said, "He was everything to me, he took me everywhere." This coach had great difficulty dealing with an illness the athlete suffered because it was "something he could not control." Another described her coach's reaction on her return to the gym having put on some weight after a shoulder injury. "He was almost sick when it happened." Despite their genuine good feelings about their coaches, it appeared that some subjects were beginning to sense the dependency they had felt and the domination and control wielded by their coaches. In a number of the interviews with female subjects, it became apparent that they were beginning to ''name'' their experiences for the first time.

Although apparently unhealthy and overly dependent relationships may be relatively common, it is difficult to sensitively and accurately determine at what point coach-athlete relationships become abusive. Two female subjects reported sexual incidents that can be reported here. One athlete's male coach insisted on giving her rubdowns even after she had expressed her discomfort. Her father had died a short time before, and she now feels that the coach was taking advantage of her vulnerability to increase her dependency on him. The relationship became increasingly tense and was terminated soon thereafter.

Another athlete, although not directly involved, became implicated in an incident that she felt had had profound effects on her sport career and her life. When she was 15 years old, her best friend told her how confused and frightened she felt because the coach was making sexual advances. The situation quickly became more complex and rumors began to spread. Our subject felt obligated to tell the club administrators, and the coach was eventually fired. But she had been caught in the middle of the scandal, and while it was going on the coach spoke to her. He informed her that she could not possibly understand the ''love'' between him and her friend, that the subject's achievements were a result of his coaching, and that without him she would be nothing. Our subject was left hurt, angry, and confused by the incident, which highlighted the dependency of athletes. Despite everything, she felt as though she was betraying her ''father.'' As Crosset suggests, this type of abuse is similar to incest and other forms of family abuse, in which the victim feels at fault and tends to keep the abuse secret, ''within the family.''

Other problems in the coach-athlete relationship involved domination of the body. One coach regularly asked female athletes to squeeze their buttocks together; if any cellulite showed they were required to lose weight. A number of female subjects felt that they had been coerced into unnecessary dieting by weigh-ins and other such tests, and in some cases this got out of control (as discussed subsequently).

Female puberty was a particularly difficult time for male (and even some female) coaches. One athlete remembers puberty as the time when her coach constantly asked her, ''Are you gaining weight?'' It appears that coaches' attempts to control female athletes' body weight is a part of the domination that is the basis of some coach-athlete relationships.

Male athletes reported very few examples of relationship problems. One noted that his Korean coach ''didn't understand about school.'' Another discovered that his coach had been taking money from his ''carding'' fund (state financial support for high-performance athletes) to cover expenses not related to the athlete. That relationship was terminated. Finally, as noted previously, one swimmer chose to attend his graduation formal rather than swim in an important club meet (grant money depended on being the top-placing club). The coach has not spoken to him since that day, ''won't even say 'hi' to me.''

Educational Problems

Because of the particular characteristics of the athletes sampled, and the fact that the majority were studying for or held university degrees, there was little evidence of real educational problems. In fact, the majority of the sample did not feel that their grades would have improved if they had not been involved in sport. But the vast majority had had to cope with the conflict between sport and school, and they employed a variety of means to accomplish this.

Athletes completed homework whenever and wherever possible. Friends often helped by providing notes and tutoring to compensate for missed class time. Parents fought battles with school administrators over timetables, wrote notes to have tests and exams deferred, or allowed athletes to stay at home to study for tests or to complete required assignments that had been neglected because of travel commitments.

Some 40% of the subjects had attended school on a modified schedule. Skaters attended mornings or afternoons only, and one tennis player only attended half days, believing that he would receive an American scholarship regardless of his grades. Those who trained out of town had permission to leave school early to travel to their training sites. Some athletes encountered uncooperative school administrators, but two reported receiving "extra help" to pass courses (e.g., a football player had been given a watered-down exam in his final year of school to help him obtain an American college scholarship).

Academic difficulties that were reported were usually attributed to the time committed to sport. One gymnast had difficulties completing high school because of her repeated hospitalization with anorexia, and another graduated late because of his foreign travel for track meets. One hockey player had been advised by his coach and his father to deemphasize academics because he was talented enough to play in the National Hockey League. Although he played professional hockey, he now regrets not having pursued his academic interests.

Some subjects felt pressure from school physical education/coaching staff to participate on school teams in addition to club teams. One gymnast needed a note from home in order to "get them off my back," and another met with the disapproval of the school coach for competing for both school and club but only training with the club. A related problem resulted from overspecialization and nonparticipation in school physical education classes. Many of the athletes regretted not having developed skills in different sports. They were "useless in basketball" or "unable to throw a football," skills taken for granted in many forms of recreation for teenagers and young adults.

Physical and Psychological Problems

Injuries characteristic of overtraining among young athletes are widely reported in the literature (e.g., Rowley, 1986) and were reported by the majority of our sample. More serious injuries were reported by gymnasts (several of whom quit, conceding that it would have been too difficult to get back into shape after recovery) and by the contact-sport athletes. The kickboxer, who competed nationally at age 13, stated, "I've broken both my legs, both my wrists, I've fractured my cheek bones, I've damaged the right orbital of my eye, damaged the nerves of my face, fractured I don't know how many ribs. . . . When I used to compete in Europe (age 14 on) a lot of these injuries were at these meets and my father didn't go with me anymore; my parents don't know and I will never tell them." The football player noted that he was beaten up by older players in his first year as a junior (age 16), receiving dislocated shoulders and concussions. "I couldn't roll the window down of my little car because my shoulder was so bad."

Other athletes noted incidences of mononucleosis, lack of sleep, dietary problems (discussed subsequently), and psychological problems such as burnout.[5] A number of gymnasts and skaters were afraid of serious injury, because the tricks they were learning became difficult and dangerous. (A number of reports have suggested that current levels of performance among young athletes in sports such as women's gymnastics will result in long-term medical problems such as arthritis.) In retrospect, the most striking feature of subjects' responses on this topic was their rather bland acceptance of injury as part of the inbuilt risks of sport. Future research should focus on this aspect of risk taking.

Excessive Behavior

Although only about 40% of our sample admitted to the type of excessive and out-of-control behavior referred to by athletes as "bingeing," the majority were aware of it, knew of athletes involved, and could describe instances. Typical binge behavior occurred after important competitions, at the end of a season, or after retirement, and involved "eating, popping, drinking, injecting, and sniffing everything that wasn't nailed down." Vandalism in the form of throwing television sets out of hotel room windows and "wrecking everything" was also considered a part of bingeing, as was bar brawling.

We are aware that it is possible to overstate this issue because we are considering athletes. Because their lives are more ordered and disciplined than the lives of other children and adolescents, to find them engaged in or exceeding the type of experimentation and excess we acknowledge in other adolescents is somewhat surprising. And yet the extent to which some young athletes have gone may be precisely a reaction to that order and discipline. Such behavior among the male athletes at international meets may even have been encouraged in some countries where hosts sometimes provided "any type of entertainment desired" together with drugs, alcohol, and all-night parties.

Food and drink bingeing for some athletes on weight-control regimens may be a response to extended periods of privation and starvation (cf., Klein's 1986 study of bodybuilders). Athletes recently retired from their sports sometimes gained enormous amounts of weight (far more than would be expected from reduced calorie expenditure), engaged in extended truancy, abused alcohol, and used "drugs, lots of drugs." In fact, all bingeing might result from the temporary or permanent removal of the daily structure of training.[6]

Although bingeing may vary somewhat between sports, hockey players and swimmers having rather more serious reputations for partying than gymnasts and track athletes, none of the sports represented in our sample were free of the behavior. The subjects offered some quite detailed reflections on the reasons for its occurrence.

- "You had to make the most of it. Go for it. Do everything, to the max!"
- "You have to be so disciplined it's not a balance. . . . Maybe some personalities react badly."
- "A big load off. . . . 'OK, now it's time to party'. . . . A lot of it was in their heads."
- "She was 13, trying to be in with the 'big' kids; she's 'big' in terms of her competing level [but] she's so young she doesn't fit in . . . [so] she's smoking, drinking . . ."
- "When you partied, you just partied your face off. . . . You knew that you have to get into the grind tomorrow or the next day."

Another interpretation proposed by a subject suggested that bingeing might result from an athlete's constantly being under adult (parent, teacher, coach) supervision and having little control over his or her life. This lack of autonomy was largely attributed to parental overprotection. Generally, parents who insist on driving their children to and from practices and attend all practices and meets/ games do not grant their children any privacy or independence in their interactions with peers. Intentionally or not, parents supervise their children very closely, and once this surveillance is gone the reaction may be extreme.

As one skater remarked, "Parents are so naive when they think you're going to a skating party. . . . They think it's all so innocent because all these people are really into skating and they wouldn't dare do anything—but it's a hell of a lot worse . . . the drugs and rowdiness. . . . You go to school [parties] and it's so mellow." Athletes with more autonomy and independence were less involved in bingeing, although one gymnast attributed it more to extreme naiveté. She noted that her first exposure to the party scene at age 16 was a "culture shock . . . to actually find that your friends drank alcohol. . . . You thought that wasn't until you got married and had kids." The problem of talented young athletes spending time with older teammates is again apparent here. One hockey player remembered the older players taking her to bars and teaching her about drinking and partying.

Use of Performance-Enhancing Drugs

Most of the interviews took place before the Dubin Commission revelations (Dubin, 1990), and athletes were understandably reluctant to talk about any aspect of doping. A number admitted to having heard about drug use in their sport or even to knowing other athletes who took or were suspected of taking drugs. Two of the track-and-field athletes felt that steroids were a major issue in their sport, and one was quite bitter about it, feeling that his chances of success had been compromised by remaining drug free. He admitted to seriously considering taking steroids in order to reenter his sport.

The football player noted that his coach had pressured him to take steroids and had referred him to the team doctor (university level), who supplied the drugs. The rower also reported that the senior team was bicarbonate loading and that she suspected that coaching pressure was involved. Some of the female athletes noted incidences of laxative abuse as a weight-control strategy. But, in general, doping was not a serious issue with these subjects.

Dietary Problems

All of the female subjects in our sample except the hockey player either had experienced dietary and body-image problems or were very conscious of the existence of such problems in their sports. Although the problem has existed in women's sports since the 1970s, it has only recently become an issue of discussion and perhaps concern. Celebrities such as Cathy Rigby, the retired American gymnast, have recently been outspoken about their own problems with anorexia nervosa and bulimia, and Canada's three leading figure skaters in the mid-1980s, Elizabeth Manley, Tracy Wainman, and Charlene Wong, all experienced dietary problems.

Three women in the sample admitted to having suffered from anorexia. One gymnast retired before she entered high school because of her illness. Another noted that her intense drive to become a world-class gymnast included, in her mind, control of her body size. She confirmed this daily at the gym, frequently hearing the coaches telling older girls to lose weight and observing that those with the smallest and most "girlish" bodies were the best athletes. Her problem with anorexia led to her hospitalization, and she spent the remainder of her adolescence in and out of institutions. One synchronized swimmer started dieting before she reached puberty, after hearing a coach tell older girls to lose weight. She lost weight, and her eating disorder continued for a number of years even after her retirement. This athlete also noted continuing medical problems resulting from malnourishment while she was still growing.

Subjects reported that concerns about weight, appearance, and changing body shapes were evident in almost every setting involving young female athletes— gyms, pools, tracks, and rinks. A synchronized swimmer addressed the concern with appearance: "When you walked into the pool, the way you looked, you had to create an awe." A gymnast recalled being pressured to lose the weight gained as a result of an injury with the comment from a coach that, after all, "it is a very visual sport."

Female subjects considered puberty to be the most difficult time, with coaches' concerns about changing body size and shape being expressed to the athletes both directly and indirectly. Weighing in at every practice (and being sent home as punishment if "overweight"), being teased about weight ("aren't you getting a little fleshy?"), being placed on restricted-calorie diets (as little as 500 kcal/ day for a growing child!), and overhearing coaches talking about athletes ("she needs to lose a little weight around her behind'') all combined to make the athletes feel that they should be "doing something" about normal body changes. One runner recalled training without a bra in the hope that it would stop the development of her breasts, and another athlete recalled a friend sleeping with weights on her chest for the same reason.

Despite the fact that some supposedly ideal body shape was extremely difficult for some athletes to achieve and impossible for others, female athletes made the sacrifices, believing they were justified by examples of fellow athletes with anorexia who were still performing well.

This problem was almost nonexistent for male athletes. Only the kickboxer recalled counting calories, and only the wrestler was involved in making weight.[7] However, some commentators have recently drawn a parallel between girls' eating disorders and boys' steroid abuse, both of which involve similar concerns with appearance and perfection.

Politics in Sport

Many of the subjects noted the internal politics of their sport as a problem. Of particular concern were such things as team selection, subjective judging, and poorly trained coaches. Subjects felt that these and other issues such as racism, doping (in the contact sports and field events), and athlete funding were the responsibilities of club administrators and the executives of national sport organizations. These issues have been widely considered in Canada as a matter of athletes' rights (Beamish & Borowy, 1988; Kidd & Eberts, 1982), that is, athletes have the right to be consulted and/or involved, and to receive fair treatment. Macintosh and Whitson (1990) have considered the problems that result when sports are administered by both volunteers and professional bureaucrats. The result is often a lack of due process, and athletes are left unsure of specific criteria for team selection and are disciplined arbitrarily. Subjects felt that the fact that internal politics negatively affected their lives "far too often" was an issue in need of attention.

Retirement From Competition

Athletes in the sample retired from competition for a variety of reasons, including injury, burnout, turning professional (skaters), and getting married. Their retirements tended to follow the patterns widely reported in the literature. Some athletes experienced adjustment difficulties or engaged in excessive behavior, some felt isolated and lost, others felt bored or bitter, and some missed the physical routine. Many avoided contact with their sport for a time.

Most adjusted well, and those who turned to coaching their sport felt that their new careers eased the transition to nonathlete. In a few cases the transition was easy. These athletes tended to have lower expectations for their athletic careers, made the decision to retire themselves, and had positive athletic experiences. Retirement was most difficult for those who regretted not having accomplished all that they felt they could have. Often their retirements were involuntary (due to injury); one gymnast felt that she should have persisted through a burnout stage.

In Canada, and most other Western societies, retirement from high-performance sport is essentially a process athletes have to work through on their own. There are no support systems, and the sport governing bodies are not responsible for athletes who have ceased to be productive team members (unlike the system that existed until the recent 1989-1990 political changes in Eastern Europe, where postretirement programs were the norm). Only the Sport Canada career-counseling program, started at the demand of athletes in 1985, comes close to providing some support. But there is no counseling to see athletes through such a traumatic change of lifestyle, and the career counseling service is of little use to those who retire young.

Interpreting the Research Results

The following sections discuss these results in two parts: the first in terms of factors affecting the problems that subjects experienced, and the second in terms of how these results might be interpreted.

Factors Contributing to Negative Experiences in Sport

Three related factors appear to have affected the problems experienced by our subjects: the way in which a sport was organized, a combination of age and time spent practicing, and gender.

Organizational Structure of the Sport. The organizational structure of the sport was a major determinant of the number of problems athletes experienced. Organizational concerns involved elements such as whether the sport had Olympic or adult professional levels, how well developed the youth levels of competition were, to a certain extent whether the sport was a team or individual sport. This latter issue concerns the amount of one-on-one time that athletes spent with a coach. However, some individual sports, such as downhill skiing, have instituted teams of coaches, which appears to result in fewer problems. Thus, the female hockey player regretted that there had been no real national team when she was competing and little in the way of high-level competition, but she experienced less problems than many of the other athletes. Similarly, the judo competitor could think of no detrimental aspects of his involvement, but the limited youth competition in his sport meant that he started at a later age and practiced less (at a young age) than many of our subjects.

Major Time Commitments at an Early Age. Our data show a very considerable relationship between time committed to the sport and the number of negative experiences reported. This is particularly true of time commitment at younger ages. The example of the judo competitor is typical, as is the case of the 100-m runner who did not begin to make major time commitments until his late teens leading to international competition in his early twenties. In these and other sports for which later maturation is the norm, athletes tended to report the most positive and the least negative experiences (e.g., the subject involved in judo described sport as "the most significant positive growth experience I ever had"). Those who had major time commitments in their preteen and early teenage years tended to report the most negative experiences.

Age also points to another difference between female and male athletes. In the sports we have considered, females tend to peak much earlier and go through the most intensive parts of their careers at much younger ages than males (which, in part, accounts for the lower number of male subjects meeting our selection criteria). The extreme youth of the female participants in particular has also been criticized because of some of the robotlike performances that are being produced in the expressive/artistic sports. Technical excellence at a very young age, followed by retirement before age 20, precludes the development of any emotional and mature artistic dance content as demonstrated by gymnasts such as Ludmilla Turischeva. Figure skating has been criticized even more strongly, and critics such as Toller Cranston believe that teenagers cannot be expected to capture the sport's expressive potential. The ages and the slow progress to skating maturity of the Duschenes and of Torvill and Dean clearly adds to the emotive content of their skating.

Gender. In almost all cases the problems for female athletes are more serious than for male athletes (and dietary problems are almost exclusively female). The following are areas of difference:

1. There still appears to be a tendency (although this varies somewhat by sport) for people to consider a boy's athletic career more important than a girl's and to make more allowances for boys in the areas of family, social relationships, and education.

2. Excessive behavior (bingeing, or "blowing off steam") may be generally more tolerated among boys and may be more severely sanctioned for girls (it is considered "unladylike").

3. The data clearly indicate that the male-coach/female-athlete relationship poses difficulties of greater number and of a different order than those likely to be experienced by male athletes. Homosexual relationships with coaches, though reportedly far less frequent than heterosexual relationships, can present similar difficulties and possibly new problems.

4. There is almost no male counterpart to female dietary problems (see Note 7), although some steroid use has some similarities. Anorexia nervosa, bulimia, and other less serious dietary and dieting problems are apparently widespread among gymnasts, figure skaters, and synchronized swimmers but are also evident in diving, swimming, skiing, track, and even basketball. Although there are some earlier examples, most observers trace the new gymnastic standard of slim and girlish figures, extreme youth, and risky tricks to the successes of Olga Korbut and Nadia Comaneci at successive Olympics during the 1970s. The two gymnasts became media darlings (rather than, for example, the older and more mature

Ludmilla Turischeva, who won the overall gold medal in 1972) at a time when the male-dominated medium of television—and, perhaps even more so, film and advertising—were beginning to embrace girlishness and that particular form of "Twiggy"-like feminity in an apparent reaction to the growing social and political strength of women. The new standard was also adopted by female figure skaters, even to the extent that they greatly increased the difficulty and risk of the moves. Coaches began to expect all of their charges to conform to such standards, and the ideal began to spread even to sports in which appearance could not be considered an issue. As with many such fashions, the standard began to be justified in pseudoscientific terms.[8] Slight and girlish builds were promoted as necessary for the strength/weight ratio athletes needed to perform difficult moves, and postpubertal curves were presumed to slow the performance speed of twists and turns. The success of 1984 Olympic gymnast Mary Lou Retton and 1990 world champion Stretlana Boginskaya, who did not have the prerequisite body types, should have laid to rest such thinking. But athletes are still weighing in, being teased about their weight, and having severe calorie and body-fat limitations imposed on them by their coaches, and athletes' attempts to conform have resulted in widespread dietary problems. The tyrannical standards are frequently imposed on athletes whose bodies are still growing, a time when food limitations can have severe consequences. Several of our subjects noted that it took them some years after retirement to reestablish appropriate eating habits and weights. What is most interesting, though, is that these standards have persisted despite a further shift in male-defined standards of female beauty (from Twiggy of the 1970s to "hardbodies"—the fit female body—of the 1980s) and despite successes by several gymnasts and figure skaters who cannot be considered to have "girlish" figures. This lends support to Crosset's (1989) belief that control of an athlete's body shape is associated with the abusive domination of an athlete.

These aspects of female sport experience must be seen in contrast to the experiences of young male athletes, even those in the same sport. Whereas girls fight natural growth, and sometimes retire when those postpubertal curves inevitably appear, boys embrace their natural growth. Whereas girls deny themselves food in order to conform to some artificial standard, boys eat in order to grow bigger and stronger. And whereas girls appear to cram their careers into a few years, retiring at 16, 17, or 18 years of age (at universities, varsity gymnastics is now considered to be a "second" career), boys mature at a slower and more relaxed pace in order to peak at a later age. Such contrasts may be taken even further by looking at a common stereotype. For example, female athletes may be subject to questions about their sexual preference, whereas male athletes may be seen as desirably heterosexual. And extended careers as professional athletes or coaches are far more available to males.

These contrasts contain many symbolic messages, one of which must surely be a message to girls to get this foolish flirtation with high-performance sport out of their systems during childhood and adolescence. It is apparent that appropriate physical activity for females and the form and meaning of that activity are still primarily defined by males—coaches, administrators, fathers, and media representatives.

Interpretation of Past Experiences

When asked if they would repeat their careers, slightly fewer than 10% of the subjects said "no," about 65% said "yes" if they had their present knowledge of the problems or could make some changes, and approximately 30% answered with an unequivocal "yes." Given that only one subject in the entire sample did not recommend changes for his sport, it is possible that the view of the latter group was colored by current knowledge. When asked if they would want their children to participate in their sport, slightly more than 60% of subjects said they would and almost 40% said they would not, or at least not at an elite level.

From one perspective, these results confirm the athletes' positive experiences: More than 90% of subjects would repeat their sport careers, and more than 60% would involve their children in similar careers. From another perspective, more than 70% of these retired athletes who had enjoyed positive and successful careers would not repeat that experience, at least not in the same way. And although 40% indicated that they would not want their children to experience high-performance sport, some of those 60% favoring the experience suggested that their backgrounds and knowledge would permit them to protect their children from some of the problems they had experienced and to provide their children a more positive experience.

Given that the subjects were selected for their generally positive and successful experiences, their careers involved a surprising number of negative experiences. Evidence collected from various informal sources indicates that the situation may be even more negative for the current generation of child athletes than for our sample. And, of course, if we had concentrated on somewhat less successful high-performance athletes, or on more athletes who had retired prematurely because of injury, abuse, or other problems, we would have expected even more negative results.

So the question that we must ask is this: How and why have we as a society done this, and permitted this to be done to, our children? Two related factors appear to be involved: the rationalization of sport and the disappearance of childhood.

Rationalization of Sport. High-performance sport has been rationalized to the extent that performance has become more important than the fact that human beings are producing that performance. Thus, the body has become an instrument, an object to be worked on, trained, tuned, and otherwise manipulated, in order to achieve performance. Those close to athletes (coaches, trainers, commentators) and even athletes themselves refer to the athlete's body as if it or the performance it produces exists distinct from the person (in some cases even substituting for the person). Detachment of the body and its performance from the person legitimizes the use of drugs and other techniques, even violation and abuse, in the name of improved performance. The body's education, social and familial relationships, safety, and future well-being do not have to be considered; if "it" is having problems, call in the physician or the sport psychologist to fix it.

Of course the person continually intrudes in this rational relationship, particularly if the person is a child who has not yet learned to objectify his or her own body. In the past, coaches and sport administrators justified their involvement of children in the rationalized training techniques of modern sport with reference to East Europeans (those under the former regimes in Eastern Europe).

Such justifications went as follows: Because the (then) Soviets, East Germans, and others identified athletically talented children, took children from their parents to train full-time at specialist residential sport schools, and practiced a wide range of nefarious techniques in order to win international sport competitions, the least we could do to remain competitive was to involve talented children in intensive specialist training and competition. Such arguments are easy to dismiss. Eastern European sport had a variety of problems (cf. Riordan, 1991), but in a number of sports (e.g., hockey and wrestling) high-performance training started at a later age than in North America. In Eastern Europe, having one's child selected to a sport school probably carried even more prestige than winning an athletic scholarship or sending one's child to places such as Nick Bollettieri's Tennis Academy. And postcareer care and opportunities in Eastern Europe were far more available than in North America. In addition, whereas in North America the athlete's parents, educators, coaches, and physicians often appeared to have conflicting interests and to pull on the athlete in opposite directions, such Eastern European agents frequently worked more in harmony. However, the myth has been a powerful justification for some time now for involving our children in a highly specialized and rationalized system of training.

The Disappearance of Childhood. These actions have been carried out in an era of what Postman (1982) called "the disappearance of childhood" or Suransky (1982) referred to as "the erosion of childhood." Postman and Suransky's perspectives portray childhood as a social and historical construct first appearing during the 17th and 18th centuries (Aries, 1962). Those elements of human experience that are a creation of human agency are, of course, subject to change, and Postman has provided numerous examples to indicate that we are witnessing an end of the innocence of childhood. Yuppie parents are beginning to place their infants on educational and career paths (e.g., Glenn Doman's "hothousing" techniques), and such parental achievement pressures clearly extend to the highly worklike careers of young athletes.

One of the original subjects in this study, a figure skater, felt that her later life problems resulted from having lost her childhood/adolescence, and another figure skater noted, "I didn't have any childhood." This initially suggested to us that the individual experiences of athletes were influenced by a lost-childhood syndrome. Other tendencies appeared to support the thesis, particularly in light of the number of regrets the athletes had about missed events and experiences, inappropriate behavior, and occasional evidence of social incompetence. But our general impression was that despite the fact that the adults involved (particularly coaches) did not treat the athletes like children or allow for the fact that they were children, the athletes had discovered ways in which to play and to "make space" for themselves. They did this the way children always do when faced with a highly authoritarian setting—they turned some activities into fun, they enjoyed their social interaction with other same-age athletes, and they behaved very irresponsibly when unsupervised, frequently breaking training demands. The lost childhood thesis did not receive any substantial support.

Thus, the childhood experiences of our subjects are of a very different order than the "stolen childhoods" of modern child slaves and laborers (Lee-Wright, 1990; Vittachi, 1989) or the lost childhoods of concentration camp and ghetto children in World War II (although, as Eisen, 1990, pointed out so sensitively, even these children found some room to play). But our subjects clearly experienced modified childhoods. If a medical analogy can be drawn, it might be that cancer is to a lost childhood what influenza is to a modified childhood. That is to say, although influenza isn't as dangerous as cancer, it should still be taken seriously.   The fact that very, very few children are dying as a consequence of their childhood experiences with high-performance sport does not mean that we should not be concerned. Despite the fact that a lost-childhood syndrome was not widely apparent among our subjects, the fact that they were involved in such worklike sport careers is more symptomatic of the disappearance of childhood as a social construct.

Cantelon's (1981) seminal work in this area and Beamish and Borowy's (1988) more recent work point to the very distinct parallels between children's involvement in high-performance sport and child labor. However, Cantelon (1981) pointed to four reasons why "for most people, child labour in sport is a non-issue" (p. 274); although these are still largely valid, a number of changes occurred in the 1980s and early 1990s that may make such labor more of an issue. Cantelon's reasons, together with these new developments, are as follows:

1. In historical terms, the issue of children's rights is a relatively recent phenomenon: Only approximately 100 years have passed since education became a requirement and child labor became illegal in many of the more developed nations. Conflicts between parents' rights to raise children as they choose and state-legislated children's rights have continued to the present day, and the right of parents to determine their children's sport involvement has clearly been exempt from legal constraint.

However, recent years have produced a rapidly growing interest in the rights of children (e.g., Gross & Gross, 1977; Vittachi, 1989; Winn, 1983); greatly increased concern about child abuse in Canada, the United Kingdom, and the United States; and a renewed concern about child labor, for example, the U.S. Labor Department's "Operation Child Watch" (Bingham, 1990) and work by Lee-Wright (1990). Governments are clearly becoming less reluctant to legislate in favor of children's rights, often against the more traditional parents' rights (e.g., the antispanking law passed in Sweden in 1980). This trend culminated in November 1989 with the adoption of the United Nations Convention of the

Rights of the Child. As governments begin to ratify the Convention, it may provide a platform from which to consider the rights of children in high-performance sport.

2. In philosophical terms, there is a powerful assumption that sport is the opposite of work and cannot possibly be considered as a labor issue. This assumption has been greatly reinforced by the notion of amateurism.

However, there is a growing recognition that preparation for a career in professional or high-performance amateur sport is a full-time occupation, an understanding that has been reinforced by revelations about how much money leading "amateur" athletes earn from appearances, sponsorships, and prizes and about the American scholarship and Canadian carding systems. So far, though, this understanding does not seem to include the fact that children are involved in such full-time preparation.

3. Also in philosophical terms, there is a powerful voluntaristic assumption at work. The assumption is that children are not forced to participate but decide to become involved and to remain committed to a sport training regimen.

However, the more recent sociological understanding of choice that guides my work shows that personal decisions are never independent of the social structures in which they occur, structures that limit and constrain the types of choices that people make. Some of the evidence presented previously indicates that a number of athletes experienced both subtle and overt pressures to remain involved in their sports.

4. A final assumption concerns the idea that participation in high-performance sport is good for children. In addition to providing physical benefits, such participation is supposed to cultivate moral and ethical character by requiring self-discipline, organization, hard work, and goal orientation. Many parents believe such participation keeps children off the streets and off drugs.

Again, there is a growing awareness that such characteristics do not necessarily carry over from sport to other areas of an athlete's life, an awareness usually deriving from journalistic revelations about illiteracy, drug abuse, gambling, and various other crimes and misdemeanors perpetrated by young athletes.

Thus, Cantelon's reasons for believing child labor in sport to be a nonissue in 1981 may be more vulnerable today. Child labor is becoming an issue and can exist only when we do not think of childhood as a distinct stage in development during which "unrestrained play activity" (Cantelon, 1981) is both necessary and important. Children's work in high-performance sport is one characteristic of the disappearance of childhood.

Recommendations for Resolving Problems

During the interviews, subjects were asked for their recommendations to remedy some of the problems they identified in high-performance sport for children. A summary of these is presented, followed by some suggestions for structural change in the system of high-performance youth sport.

Athletes' Recommendations

As noted previously, only one athlete had no suggestions for improving his sport. Athletes' recommendations focused primarily on coaching but also touched on the administration of the sport, support systems, and conflicts with education.

If there is one underlying concern that appears throughout these athlete recommendations it is that young athletes should be treated as children first and athletes second, and that training programs should be adjusted to meet the social, physiological, and psychological capabilities of children. Subjects felt that research, information, and qualified personnel were crucial to achieving these ends.

Guidelines for Coaching Qualifications. Subjects expressed great concern that coaches did not have requisite knowledge in a wide range of areas considered important by the athletes, and they felt that many coaches who had been athletes themselves simply coached the way they had been coached. Thus, subjects considered advanced coach education in technique, training, and sports medicine to be very important, as well as knowledge of counseling and child psychology. With advanced education, coaches might be less likely to follow nonscientific fads and fashions in areas such as body-fat content, might be able to lower the incidence of overuse injuries, might be less controlling and manipulative, and might gear training methods and techniques to the developmental levels of children. Subjects considered the emphasis on performance, achievement, and success to be a problem, and some athletes pointed to coaches who had resorted to dishonest methods to achieve success (from illegal recruitment to drugs and "fixing" judged scoring). But subjects made no practical suggestions regarding the reduction of this emphasis other than to note that participation should be more educational.

A number of female athletes pointed to the potential for exploitation and abuse in male-coach/female-athlete relationships, and suggestions included greater involvement of parents, more supervision and control of coaches by club administrators, and the training of more female coaches. Subjects also considered team coaching to be an asset, not only to avoid the one-on-one abuse potential but also to assist in conflict situations and to pool knowledge. A number of subjects were also aware that coaches, unlike teachers and others who care for children, are not subject to a high degree of accountability.

In fact, there was evidence that a double standard may exist for the behavior of coaches. One athlete reported being hit by her coach; when she informed her parents, they replied that it was good for her. When asked how her parents would respond if she was hit by a teacher she replied, "They would have the teacher fired and sue the school board." The limited accountability, when joined with few professional standards and yet massive social support for the coaching role, creates a dangerous combination. Coaches are not entirely to blame for this situation and should not be the scapegoats for the problems in high-performance children's sport. There are many excellent and informed coaches who exhibit the highest moral and ethical standards; however, coaches also work in a system of structures and constraints in which their future employment may depend on children's performances.

Reassess Administrative Objectives in Sport. Subjects considered both coaches and administrators to be responsible for the large amounts of training time that very young athletes endure and for overspecialization at young ages. These issues were considered to be especially problematic in sports such as track and the contact sports, in which athletes are presumed to peak at later and more physically mature ages. Several athletes suggested that they could have accomplished a great deal more if intensive training had not started until they reached full growth and maturity, if they hadn't "wasted all that intensity" before they were ready. In other words, the athletes considered the youth movement in these sports to be both unnecessary and detrimental.

The extreme youth of participants (particularly females) in the more artistic sports has also been criticized, as noted previously, because of the immature performances that result. A number of athletes proposed minimum age limits in international competitions in order to reduce the emphasis on early specialization and intensive training; women's gymnastics organizations have recently taken some steps in this direction.

Athletes sampled also held sport administrators responsible for underfunding, for the problems associated with subjective judging, and for not easing athletes' transitions out of their sports. Athletes made recommendations for resolving each of these problem areas, and some changes are under way. For example, the establishment of employment counseling by Sport Canada is aimed at relieving the latter problem. However, most recommendations were either unrealistic or not well thought out (e.g., "There should be more money"; "There should be more objective ways to judge performance").

Create Support Systems for Athletes. Subjects felt that a variety of support systems were necessary to assist child athletes in coping with stress. Such systems included greater parental involvement and family support (although several athletes felt that there should be less parental involvement), counseling or regular sessions with psychologists, tutors for those having educational difficulties, and simply "someone to talk to."

Maintain Sound Education for Athletes. Some of the recommendations highlighted unstated criticisms. For example, when asked if school and sport should be integrated in order to ease the difficulties of acquiring an education, several subjects were adamant that the two should remain separate. Their reasons are revealing. They felt that while school and sport were separate athletes could, with some difficulty, maintain a quality level of education. So cynical were their views of their particular sport governing bodies that they felt integration would subvert education; education would be slanted toward peaking an athlete's training at a time convenient for the sport but not necessarily for the athlete's education. Some high schools in Ontario have now begun to modify their schedules in order to accommodate the needs of young high-performance athletes.

Structural Changes in High-Performance Sport

Participation in high-performance sport was clearly an enormously positive experience for the vast majority of these athletes, as one would expect given the successes they achieved. But athletes did not achieve these successes without costs that, in a number of cases, appear to be disproportionate; the findings of this study support a number of less formal data sources that point to clear systemic problems in high-performance sport for children. Changes to improve the system may derive from two sources: those instituted by the present structures and those imposed externally.

Internal Changes. The athletes' recommendations generally involved a fine-tuning of the present system rather than a complete restructuring of high-performance sport for children. Such proposals are to be expected given that our subjects were successful products of the system. There was also an underlying feeling that "if I got through it, others can and should get through it"; but despite this, numerous changes were recommended.

If we were to put these recommendations together into an "ideal," they could produce a child-centered system in which parents, coaches, physicians, administrators, and teachers worked together in the best interests of the child under the auspices of the sport-governing body. Involvement would still have some costs (e.g., reduced social life, longer time required to complete education), but these would not be disproportionate. Sport-governing bodies would implement changes in their policies, procedures, and rules to account for the rights and interests of children, and children's growth, development, and empowerment would be ensured in a less controlling sport environment.

This is an ideal time in the development of Canadian high-performance sport to implement such changes. With the release of the report of *The Commission of Inquiry Into the Use of Drugs and Banned Practices Intended to Increase Athletic Performance* (Dubin, 1990), the sport community has the opportunity to positively restructure the entire system, a system that not only has resulted in use of performance-enhancing drugs but has also sacrificed children on the altar of international and professional sport success. Such changes are unlikely, however, because too many vested interests and ingrained ways of thinking are embodied in sport institutions, and because funding and sponsorship of sport-governing bodies will likely continue to be based on the achievement of international success. Given this situation, even minor changes will likely be reinterpreted to maintain as nearly as possible the status quo. Structural changes in the system of sport appear far more likely in Eastern Europe, where the restructuring of society has permitted serious questioning of the high-performance sport system and increased interest in mass recreational sport and sport for all (Riordan, 1991).

Externally Imposed Changes. When the Child Labor Laws (e.g., the Ontario Factories Act of 1884) were introduced in Canada in the late 19th century, among their only supporters were the moral reformers who forced the laws through Parliament. The Freed Commission on Canadian Labor (1889) asked children if they would rather work in the mines and factories or go to school. The majority preferred work, and "even those who related examples of employer abuse, preventable accidents, or beatings, were reluctant to leave their employers" (Cantelon, 1981, p. 278). The parents, of course, preferred that their children continue working, and both parents and children made the type of voluntarist assumptions that we hear today from child athletes and parents (although family income frequently depended on children's contributions). And employers claimed that the economy would collapse if the cheap labor provided by children was withdrawn. The laws were eventually enforced,[9] compulsory secondary education became the norm, and the economy did not collapse; profits were still made despite the absence of a cheap labor pool.

The parallel with the current situation in high-performance sport is apparent. When asked if legislation should be instituted to limit the number of hours children train and to ensure other rights and protections, half of the sample opposed the idea. Comments included, "you can't really put a law on it," "if [athletes are] committed to a national team, the team has the right to set the hours," "kids need pushing," and "give the choice to the parents, they are the ones to decide." And coaches and sport administrators have assured us that the entire system of high-performance sport would collapse if legal limitations were imposed on training time and other issues.

Beamish and Borowy (1988) have applied the various legal tests for an employer/employee relationship to the contract between Canadian high-performance athletes and their sport-governing bodies through Sport Canada, and these authors have found that the circumstances meet the criteria of employment in every case, even to the athletes' receipt of (limited) remuneration. Because there is no minimum age limit for the receipt of carding money, it is entirely possible for children with international rankings in sports such as swimming to be in the apparent employ of the Canadian government. Thus, a highly ranked 14-year-old can earn over $7,000 (Canadian) per year, an income that is beyond the dreams of most elementary and junior high school students but which may not even cover the expenses of, for example, a figure skater.

Sponsorships may bring additional income. Jennifer Capriati, the American tennis player, signed a deal for $3 to $5 million with a sportswear manufacturer at age 13 and began to receive even more endorsement deals at age 14 (e.g., $1 million from Prince rackets). And there have been reports of a 7-year-old British girl who is being coached in track by her father (but is not yet competing). He has obtained sponsorship for the child of over $3,000 (Canadian) per year from a vitamin manufacturer and additional support from a sporting goods manufacturer. These amounts will presumably increase once she starts to compete. Children may also turn professional, as has been particularly evident in tennis (e.g., Tracy Austin and Andrea Jaeger in the late 1970s, Jennifer Capriati and Mary Pierce in the 1990s).

Although it is possible for children to be employees or professionals in sport, to receive income from governments, from endorsements, or from prizes, they appear to fall into a legal loophole. Such children are supposedly protected by the same laws that apply to all children, such as compulsory education and child labor laws, but the legal system has been slow to adapt to the rapid changes that have occurred in sport. This is an area that, for children at least, is still pervaded as far as the law is concerned with the ideology of amateurism.

The fundamental problem now stems from the fact that adult careers and incomes may be contingent on the performances of children.[10] In few other areas of life (and particularly not in education) is this the case, the major exception being the entertainment and advertising industries for which special laws have been introduced to protect children. As a consequence of the scandalous behavior of some parents of child stars as well as some Hollywood executives during the 1940s and 1950s, laws were introduced to determine the number of hours and days that children may work or rehearse, the maximum amount of time that they work each day, and the amount of time that must elapse between performances. Income is protected from parents and agents in trust funds, and government health and safety regulations are in force in the places of employment.

The only apparent legal protection specifically for child athletes involves income in the Olympic sports. Sponsorship, prize, and appearance money received by an athlete is placed in a trust fund until the athlete retires, not to protect that income from parents and agents but to maintain the last vestiges of the hypocrisy of amateurism for the International Olympic Committee and the sport-governing bodies. There are no limits on training time or number of competitions, no real enforcement of the amount of time that athletes should devote to compulsory education, and certainly no protection under government health and safety regulations. In no other occupation would the high rate of burnout, the high rate of overuse injuries, the serious potential for traumatic injury, the serious possibility of long-term disability (from such things as arthritis and growth-plate damage), and the possible abuse and harassment of employees be allowed to pass without question. When these risks exist for children, it is time to be seriously concerned about children's rights and to consider extending child labor laws to protect young athletes.

Summary

Available evidence indicates that specialized intensive training and high-level competition at an early age are neither advantageous or necessary and may be detrimental to future athletic potential and performance. The somatic changes resulting from puberty are so unpredictable that much of the level of performance an athlete achieves prior to puberty may be lost. Elements that contraindicate early intensive involvement include the risks associated with developing high levels of prepubertal skill (e.g., burnout, damage to growth plates, and serious overuse injuries), the costs (for girls) of attempting to maintain prepubertal body types, the social and educational costs, the immature levels of performance achieved in the artistic sports, and the possibility that early effort is "wasted" in sports in which athletes peak at a later age, such as middle- and long-distance running.

Despite the growing weight of research evidence contraindicating early intensive involvement, we have no reason to be optimistic that sport will put its own house in order, although that would clearly be the best solution. There are too many vested interests and in situ structures to allow voluntary changes. Nor is it reasonable to expect a major restructuring of North American society in the near future in which sport is deemphasized, or a return to the values of an earlier age before adults began to organize sport for children. Sport, as in other areas of life, is still imbued with the 1980s philosophy of ''excellence.'' Thus, rather than striving for personal best, young athletes are presented with the continually shifting and invariably unattainable goal of excellence as something to strive for (cf. Kidd, 1988).

It is appropriate, of course, that parents want their children to achieve their full potential in whatever field of endeavor, but parents' aspirations will be met in a responsible manner only when more data are available. Athletes must continue to be able to ''name'' their experiences, and parents, coaches, and administrators must become aware of their fiduciary responsibilities for children in the high-performance sport system. Informed consent must become the guiding principle, and risk management must be taken seriously. Parents need to know if normal growth and development are at risk when children participate in high-performance sport, and parents also need to know if adequate supervision with appropriate professional standards is available.

Serious advocacy of the protection of young athletes under child labor laws may lead to more focused research and may encourage a change in the policies and structures of high-performance sport, creating less emphasis on early performance.[11] The current system of high-performance sport for children has a great many good points, but it also has far too many bad points and even some ugly and shameful aspects. It is time to consider a change.

Notes

[1]This paper defines *child* according to Article I of the United Nations Convention on the Rights of the Child (1989): ''every human being below the age of 18 years unless, under the law applicable to the child, majority is attained earlier'' (DCI/UNICEF, 1989). This extends the youth sport conference definition somewhat, but the research reported here was in progress before the guidelines for the workshop were established. Also the terms *elite* (American), *high-performance* (Canadian), and *top* (European) are used interchangeably to refer to athletes at the highest levels of their sports.

[2]Sutton-Smith (1981) and Gruneau (1981) have pointed out that children's unstructured play should not be romanticized because it can contain its own forms of oppression and constraint.

[3]This chapter is derived from an ongoing study of young high-performance athletes. Earlier parts of this research were presented at the 7th Annual Conference of the North American Society for the Sociology of Sport, Las Vegas, NV,

November 1986, and at the Jyvaskyla Congress on Movement and Sport in Women's Life, Jyvaskyla, Finland, August 1987. The author would like to acknowledge the support of the Arts Research Board at McMaster University in providing partial funding for this research.

[4]Clearly this is an important group that needs to be considered at some future time. While the interview instrument was being refined, we felt that it was more important to determine if problems existed among those who had less reason to complain.

[5]Psychological problems are considered in far more detail in chapters 1, 2, and 3; however, our subjects frequently reported examples of guilt, stress, and extreme behavior (from overcontrolled to out-of-control).

[6]We should not make too much of the daily structure of training because the young athletes (like all individuals in authoritarian settings) frequently resisted demands that they considered unreasonable. They went on dates, stayed up late, broke curfews when traveling, and even drank alcohol and used drugs.

[7]There are, of course, some serious potential problems associated with "making weight" in wrestling (cf. Tipton, 1987), although weight problems are less serious in boxing. Such problems also exist for male and female jockeys and bodybuilders.

[8]This, and some of the material that follows, is adapted from Burstyn (1986).

[9]Hurl (1987) has suggested that this was as much a consequence of union intervention and changing economic conditions as it was of more general humanitarian concerns.

[10]Bruce Kidd (1988) has referred to athletes as "sweat-suited philanthropists, ensuring the careers of hundreds of well-paid coaches, sports scientists and sport administrators" (p. 23). An example involves the disappointing 1991-92 season for the Canadian Alpine Ski Team. With no first-place finishes and a number of disappointing performances, the coaches and sport bureaucrats were under a great deal of pressure. When Kerrin Lee Gartner won the gold medal in the Women's Downhill at the Albertville Olympics, the relief among coaches and officials was so evident that it was reported on the CBC television Olympic coverage.

[11]Stricter laws can also lead, of course, to forgery of birth certificates and other forms of cheating.

References

Aries, P. (1962). *Centuries of childhood*. New York: Vintage.

Beamish, R., & Borowy, J. (1988). *Q. What do you do for a living? A. I'm an athlete*. Kingston: The Sport Research Group, Queen's University.

Bingham, C. (1990, March 26). The child-labor sting. *Newsweek*, p. 36.

Burstyn, V. (1986, October 9). *Play, performance and power* (Hour 2). Toronto: CBC Radio, Ideas.

Cantelon, H. (1981). High performance sport and the child athlete: Learning to labor. In A.G. Ingham & E.F. Broom (Eds.), *Career patterns and career contingencies in sport* (pp. 258-286). Vancouver: University of British Columbia.

Crosset, T. (1989). *The abusive coach: A preliminary description and analysis of abusive male coach-female athlete relationships.* Unpublished manuscript, Department of Physical Education, Brandeis University.

DCI/UNICEF Briefing Kit (1989). *The future United Nations convention on the rights of the Child, 3rd edition*, May, p. 2.

Devereux, E.C. (1976). Backyard versus Little League Baseball: Some observations on the impoverishment of children's games in contemporary America. In D. Landers (Ed.), *Social problems in athletics* (pp. 37-56). Urbana: University of Illinois Press.

Dubin, C.L. (1990). *Commission of inquiry into the use of drugs and banned practices intended to increase athletic performance.* Ottawa: Minister of Supply and Services.

Eisen, G. (1990). *Children and play in the Holocaust: Games among the shadows.* Amherst: University of Massachusetts Press.

Geldbach, E. (1977). Protestantism, capitalism, sports. *Journal of Sport History*, **4**(3), 285-294.

Gross, B., & Gross, R. (Eds.) (1977). *The children's rights movement: Overcoming the oppression of young people.* New York: Anchor/Doubleday.

Gruneau, R. (1981). Considerations on the politics of play and youth sport. In A.G. Ingham & E.F. Broom (Eds.), *Career patterns and career contingencies in sport* (pp. 48-79). Vancouver: University of British Columbia.

Grupe, O. (1985). Top level sport for children from an educational viewpoint. *International Journal of Physical Education*, **22**(1), 9-16.

Hurl, L. (1987). *Questioning historical myths: A study of child labor in late-19th century Ontario.* Unpublished manuscript, School of Social Work, McMaster University.

Kidd, B. (1988). The philosophy of excellence: Olympic performances, class power, and the Canadian state. In P.J. Galasso (Ed.), *Philosophy of sport and physical activity: Issues and concepts* (pp. 11-31). Toronto: Canadian Scholars' Press.

Kidd, B., & Eberts, M. (1982). *Athletes' rights in Canada.* Toronto: Ministry of Tourism and Recreation.

Klein, A. (1986). Pumping irony: Crisis and contradiction in bodybuilding. *Sociology of Sport Journal*, **3**(2), 112-133.

Lee-Wright, P. (1990). *Child slaves.* London: Earthscan.

Macintosh, D., & Whitson, D. (1990). *The game planners: Transforming Canada's sport system.* Kingston, ON: McGill-Queen's University Press.

McPherson, B.D. (1982). The child in competitive sport: Influence of the social milieu. In R.A. Magill, M.J. Ash, & F.L. Smoll (Eds.), *Children in sport* (pp. 247-278). Champaign, IL: Human Kinetics.

Postman, N. (1982). *The disappearance of childhood.* New York: Delacorte.

Riordan, J. (1991). The changing relationship between sport and the state in Eastern Europe. In F. Landry, M. Landry, & M. Yerles (Eds.), Sport: the third millennium (pp. 287-293). Sainte-Foy, PQ: Les Presses de L'Universite Loval.

Rowley, S. (1986). *The effect of intensive training on young athletes: A review of the research literature.* London: The Sports Council.

Suransky, V.P. (1982). *The erosion of childhood.* Chicago: University of Chicago Press.

Sutton-Smith, B. (1981). *Play theory and 19th century play history.* Paper presented at the Anthropological Association for the Study of Play annual meeting, Fort Worth, TX.

Thompson, S. (1992). *Sport for others, work for women, quality of life for whom?* Paper presented at Olympic Scientific Congress, Malaga, Spain, July.

Ulrich, H.E. (1976). The social structure of high-level sport. *International Review of Sport Sociology,* **11**(2), 139-152.

Tipton, C.M. (1987). Commentary: Physicians should advise wrestlers about weight loss. *The Physician and Sportsmedicine,* **15**(1), 160-165.

Vittachi, A. (1989). *Stolen childhood: In search of the rights of the child.* London: Polity Press.

Winn, M. (1983). *Children without childhood.* New York: Pantheon.

Physiological Perspectives

Oded Bar-Or

Physical training induces physiological changes in several body tissues and organs, the extent of which has been termed *trainability*. Although training effects can be induced by mild and moderate training programs, such effects are particularly evident when training is intensive. With the increase in popularity of high-level competitive sports among children, increasing numbers of prepubescent and early pubescent girls and boys are participating in highly intensive training programs. The two chapters in Part III focus on physiological and some medical changes that such participation induces in the child. Specifically, these chapters address differences in trainability between children and more mature groups, the benefits of high-intensity training to a child's fitness and sport performance, and some medical risks that such a regimen may induce.

It would be highly desirable to learn about the carryover of training-induced physiological and medical changes from childhood to adulthood. For example, does intensive weight training during childhood give the mature athlete an advantage over another athlete who started weight training at age 20? Does distance running in early life affect the risk for coronary heart disease? Does the delay in menarche (appearance of the first menstrual period), often seen in young female athletes, affect fertility? Although such questions are important to coaches, parents, health professionals, and scientists, information on the carryover effects of intensive training is scarce. Part III therefore summarizes the evidence regarding short-term effects of intensive training in children, with some speculations regarding its long-term effects.

Because of the relative paucity of specific data on the effects of intensive training on the child athlete, one must sometimes extrapolate from available information on more mature groups or on milder training regimens. Indeed, some of the statements made here are based on data obtained from adolescent and adult athletes or from nonathletic children.

Constraints in Research on Children

Due to methodological and ethical constraints in performing research with children, knowledge regarding the effects of training on children has lagged behind that generated for adults. A major methodological hurdle is that numerous physiological functions and aptitudes for sports are affected not only by training but also by growth and maturation (physical, mental, and emotional). It is therefore hard to tease out the net effect of training. Nor is it clear how to equate, for the purpose of research, the training dose (intensity, in particular) among groups that differ in body size and maturation.

The main ethical constraints are related to research on the deleterious effects of training. Whereas adults can volunteer to participate in studies that are intended to assess exercise-induced damage (e.g., hyperthermia, dehydration, overuse injuries, or suppression of immunoresponse), it would be unethical to subject children to any study whose end point is damage to health. Another ethical limitation is that invasive (e.g., muscle biopsy, catherization) and pain-inducing procedures, or those that require irradiation, may not be performed with children unless clinically indicated.

The following is a brief overview of the physiological benefits (proven or assumed) and the medical risks that an intensive training program may entail. The two chapters in Part III provide in-depth analyses of this topic.

Physiological Benefits of Intensive Training

Trainability and Performance in Sports

Early studies have suggested that prepubescents, although improving their endurance performances (e.g., in running or swimming) with training, may not increase their maximal aerobic power to the same extent as do adults. However, more recent works have shown that when the training dose is sufficient, training does increase children's maximal oxygen uptake. There is also evidence that sprint and high-power training programs of 4- to 12-weeks' duration can increase a child's muscle endurance and peak power by 5 to 12%. The extent of this increase is similar to that reported for adults. Likewise, resistance training of several months' duration can induce similar gains in muscle strength (calculated as a percentage of the pretraining strength) of prepubescents, adolescents, and young adults. A phenomenon typical for prepubescents is that their strength can be increased without a concomitant increase in muscle bulk.

In spite of the adequate trainability of prepubescents there is little scientific evidence to support a relationship between improvement in athletic performance and the extent of physiological improvement. Some evidence suggests that enhanced muscle strength is accompanied by improved motor performance (e.g., as in the vertical jump). In adults, cessation of training leads to a rapid decrease in those physiological functions that increased with training, but there is no information on the rate at which such functions decline in children once training has stopped. It is apparent, however, that motor skills acquired during childhood are retained longer than functions such as aerobic power, anaerobic power, muscle strength, or muscle endurance.

Bone Density

Bone density and mineral bone mass increase during childhood and adolescence, peak during early adulthood, and decline thereafter. It has been suggested, but not yet proven, that enhanced motor activity during the growth years may increase this peak, thereby reducing the risk for osteoporosis in later years. Scientists do not know which activities, and at what dosage, might induce such a benefit. (See also "Health Risks of Intensive Participation.")

Injury Prevention

It has often been stated that training (mostly resistance training) helps prevent athletic injuries. This has not been documented for children.

Health Risks of Intensive Participation

Heat Intolerance and Heat-Related Illness

Because of their geometric and physiological characteristics, prepubescents are potentially more affected by hot and cold climates than are adolescents and adults. For example, children have a shorter tolerance time to heat or cold, particularly if extreme. In addition, prepubescents take longer (2 weeks, compared with 1 week in adults) to acclimate to a sudden increase in climatic heat stress. Even in the absence of epidemiological data that compare the risk of heat- or cold-induced illness among athletes of different ages, one should assume that children are at greater risk for heat- and cold-induced illnesses. The more extreme the climate the greater the risk. This is potentially the most severe risk to health that a young athlete may incur.

As do adults, children underestimate the amount of fluid that they should ingest during prolonged exercise, especially when their sweating losses are high. For the same degree of dehydration (percent initial body weight), a child's core temperature rises faster than an adult's, which, during conditions that induce much sweating, may increase the risk for heat-related illness.

Injuries from Resistance Training and Weight Lifting

Several retrospective studies have documented accidents and musculoskeletal injuries in prepubescents who participate in resistance training. However, in recent prospective studies (several weeks to several months long) in which children used proper equipment and were supervised by experienced staff, researchers found no damage to bone or soft tissues or decreases in joint flexibility. However, the safety of competitive weight lifting (and power lifting) has not been demonstrated in children.

Aberrations in Eating Habits

To maintain low body fat (e.g., gymnasts, figure skaters, and dancers) or low body mass (e.g., wrestlers), young athletes sometimes resort to abnormal eating and drinking practices as well as artificial means of losing body mass or fluids. With some athletes, such aberrant eating patterns become habits. The relatively high prevalence of anorexia nervosa in female athletes may be an extreme stage of such an aberrant eating pattern.

Iron Deficiency

Adolescent endurance athletes, females in particular, have a high incidence of iron deficiency, usually without overt anemia. The risk of iron deficiency in prepubertal athletes has not been reported. Whether such nonanemic iron deficiency impairs health is unknown, but it does seem to impair performance in endurance events.

Delayed Menarche

Cross-sectional observations show an association between participation in some sports and a delay in menarche. Although some authors contend that this association reflects a preselection of late-maturing individuals to certain sports, others suggest a cause-and-effect relationship. Prolonged exertion sometimes induces acute changes in the pattern of release of gonadotropins, in females and males alike. This may hint at a mechanism by which intensive training might induce a delay in menarche.

Osteopenia

Although an active lifestyle may increase peak bone density (see "Benefits of Intensive Training in Children"), the low estrogenic activity that is associated with prolonged intensive training in females sometimes reduces bone density.

Myocardial Changes

Inadequate measuring methods limit the investigation of myocardial function and possible damage in young athletes. These youngsters demonstrate some, but not all, of the characteristics of "athlete's heart" observed in endurance-trained adults. No adverse effects of these alterations have been observed.

Recommendations

The following recommendations are based on findings reviewed in chapters 5 and 6. Recommendations are divided into physiology-related aspects and those that address prevention or amelioration of risk to the child's health. It is beyond the scope of this book to recommend specific intensive training regimens that are suitable for children.

Optimizing Performance

Is there a developmental stage at which training will yield the highest (or lowest) physiological benefits? No scientific data address this question, but experience in various countries that cultivate young athletes for future excellence suggests no physiological benefits in starting specialized training prematurely. For example, it may not be advantageous for a prepubescent boy who plans a career in sprinting to focus his training exclusively on strength and speed. Nor is it an advantage for a young would-be distance champion to limit her training to distance running. Experience suggests that before puberty the child's training regimen should include a broad spectrum of activities. An exception are sports such as gymnastics or figure skating in which skill is the dominant component. This important area requires much research. More research is also needed to determine the importance of fitness training to a child's performance in sports, taking into account the relative contribution of motivation, tactics, and other behavioral aspects.

Before puberty, girls and boys have similar body heights, weights, and muscle strength. Based on physiological considerations, there is no reason why prepubescent girls and boys cannot compete against each other, even in contact and collision sports. In boys, particularly around the time of their growth spurt, the increase in muscle strength may lag behind increases in height or weight. This may contribute to a certain decline in athletic performance (sometimes referred to as "adolescent clumsiness,") of which coaches and athletes should be aware.

Preventing Detrimental Effects of Intensive Participation

Some of the following health-related recommendations are based on scientific evidence. Others, in the absence of evidence, are based on common sense and clinical judgment. For safety and ethical reasons, coaches and other professionals should adopt restraint, cautioning children and especially parents against practices that might be detrimental to health.

For example, even though there are no epidemiological data about damage that weight lifting and power lifting may induce in children, it would be prudent not to recommend these sports before the child has reached puberty. Resistance training (e.g., using dumbbells, resistance machines, pulleys, springs, the child's own weight, and that of a partner), on the other hand, seems safe. But it is highly recommended that the child perform resistance training only when supervised by an experienced adult, using equipment modified for the child's body size and low muscle strength. More research is needed to determine whether resistance training helps to prevent sports-related injuries in children.

Another issue, often queried by parents, educators, and coaches is whether they should impose limits on the distances children run in competition. Current knowledge suggests that if indeed there are any adverse effects of distance running, they are related to the cumulative training mileage rather than to the distance run on the day of competition. Therefore, one cannot recommend specific distances for competition that are compatible with a child's health.

More substantive information is available regarding precautions that trainers should take when a child trains or competes in a hot or cold climate. As stated in chapter 6, a child's thermoregulatory capacity is compromised in extreme climates. Even in the absence of epidemiological data regarding the exact risk that children incur under such conditions, the following recommendations are warranted:

1. When exposed to a hot (or warm and humid) climate, the unacclimatized child athlete should assume a training regimen lighter than she or he has been accustomed to in thermoneutral climates. Specifically, training sessions should become shorter, include frequent rest periods in the shade, and be less intense than normal. Length and intensity of practice sessions can be increased gradually during the 10 to 14 days of acclimatization.
2. Because children underestimate their fluid needs, they should be encouraged to drink above and beyond their thirst. The coach or trainer should encourage the child to drink often (every 15 to 20 min) during practice and competition until not thirsty and then add another 100 ml (half a cup).
3. Because of their large surface-area-to-mass ratio, children lose heat rapidly when they are in cool water (e.g., less than 25°C). The smaller the child the faster the heat loss. To prevent excessive cooling, children should come out of the water when they are not swimming. If water temperature is less than 22°C, the swimming child should not stay in the water more than 15 min.

Children who compete in sports such as wrestling or judo should be strongly advised not to dehydrate excessively as a means of making weight before competition; and legislation should be enforced to discourage such a practice. For example, sports bodies should increase the number of weight categories in children's competition or forbid children from competing at weight categories below their preseason body weights.

To avoid aberrant eating patterns and excessive loss of body fat in young athletes, coaches should temper their demands that their athletes slim down at all costs. When a young endurance athlete, female in particular, shows excessive fatigue and loss of performance, coaches should suspect (and, if needed, seek treatment for) iron deficiency; serum ferritin levels are diagnostic.

Chapter 5

Benefits and Risks
of Resistance Training
in Children

Cameron J.R. Blimkie

The issue of resistance training during childhood has received increased interest from both the lay public and the scientific community since the 1980s. The effectiveness, benefits, and risks of resistance training for adults have been extensively studied, documented, and promulgated in both the scientific and lay literature. These same issues as they relate to children, however, have received far less, and the dearth of information on these topics has resulted in a number of concerns relating to resistance training during childhood.

The issues of the effectiveness of resistance training, the relative trainability of strength, the persistence of resistance training-induced strength changes, and the mechanisms underlying strength gains brought about by resistance training during late childhood have been reviewed recently (Blimkie, in press). In brief, it appears that resistance training, under conditions of high intensity and volume loading, significantly increases strength in both prepubertal and early pubertal boys and girls. The mechanisms underlying strength gains with resistance training in this population have not been unequivocally established. Resistance training appears to have little if any effect on muscle size but has resulted in neurological (percent motor unit activation) changes and intrinsic muscle function changes (twitch torque) that could account for part of the training-induced increases in voluntary strength. Changes in motor skill coordination (e.g., activation level and pattern of prime mover, agonist, and antagonist muscles) probably also contribute substantially to resistance training-induced strength increases during late childhood. Most but not all studies indicate that prepubertal and early pubertal boys and girls make similar relative (percent improvement) strength gains compared to later stages of development and young adulthood but usually demonstrate smaller absolute strength increases following training. Training-induced strength gains appear not to be wholly sustained during detraining, and maintenance training consisting of only one training session per week does not appear to preserve prior strength gains.

Besides increasing strength, resistance training can impart numerous other benefits to the child trainee; however, it might also be risky in terms of injury, growth, and health outcomes, particularly during childhood. This review will address the benefits versus risks of resistance training during childhood.

For the purposes of this review, prepuberty and early puberty encompass ages 6 to 11 years for girls and 6 to 13 years for boys. These age ranges correspond to pubic hair Stages 1 and 2 (Tanner, 1962), the period of development that will be referred to as late childhood. Resistance training is defined as the use of progressive resistance methods to increase one's ability to exert or resist force (Cahill, 1988). Resistance training methods vary in terms of the physiological demands placed upon muscle, bone, and connective tissue (e.g., isometric, isotonic, isokinetic, concentric, and eccentric contractions) and in the degree of sophistication and precision of progressive resistive loading (e.g., body weight, stretch tubing, free weights, pneumatics, hydraulics, and depth jumping). Not surprisingly, then, resistance training methods may also vary in terms of their potential for imparting benefits and imposing risks. Resistance training is distinguished from the sports of weight lifting and power lifting, which consist of specific maximal or near-maximal lifts performed during competition (e.g., the clean and jerk).

Resistance Training and Injuries

Perhaps the most serious concern regarding resistance training during childhood is the potential for acute and chronic soft-tissue and musculoskeletal injury (Table 5.1). In this context, *injury* is defined as any acute or chronic physical trauma evident at the clinical or subclinical level that is caused by the physiological or biomechanical stresses of training and that impairs body function. A 1979 U.S. Consumer Product Safety Commission report indicated that over half of the 35,512 weight-lifting injuries requiring emergency room treatment during 1979 involved 10- to 19-year-olds. A 1987 report indicated that 68% of the 44,962 weight-lifting injuries that occurred in 1987 involved people between 0 and 24 years of age; there were 8,590 weight-lifting-associated injuries in the age range 0 to 14 years, with a twofold to threefold higher occurrence in boys than girls (Table 5.2). These reports do not distinguish between injuries resulting from resistance training and those resulting from weight-lifting or power-lifting competitions. Nevertheless, it is clear that specialized activity programs that involve heavy resistive loads either in training or in competition may cause injuries in children.

Epiphyseal Injuries

Of particular concern is the potential for damage to the immature epiphysis, or growth plate of bone, with the consequent potential detrimental effects on growth

Table 5.1   Injury Concerns Relating to Weight Lifting During Childhood

- Injury to the epiphyseal plate
  - Osteoarthritis
- Juvenile osteochondritis dissecans
  - Overuse injuries
- Low back spondylolysis
  - Spondylolisthesis
  - Soft-tissue injury
  - Fracture
  - Crush injury

Table 5.2   Acute Weight-Lifting Injuries During Childhood

- 44,962 weight-lifting injuries (requiring emergency-room treatment) total in 1987
- 68% of these injuries in individuals between 0 and 24 years
- 19% of injuries (8,590 actual) in children between 0 and 14 years
- Twofold to threefold higher occurrence in boys than girls between 0 and 14 years
- 39% of injuries occurred in the home
- Most common types of injury by prevalence
  - strains/sprains
  - contusions/abrasions
  - lacerations
  - fractures
- Most common site of injury by prevalence
  - lower trunk
  - finger
  - toe
  - foot

Note. Data from the 1987 National Electronic Injury Surveillance System (NEISS) (U.S. Consumer Product Safety Commission, 1987).

and development. There are numerous case reports of epiphyseal fractures resulting from weight lifting during childhood (Benton, 1983; Brady, Cahill, & Bodnar, 1982; Gumbs, Segal, Halligan, & Lower, 1982; Rowe, 1979; Ryan & Salciccioli, 1976). The majority of these injuries occurred in pubescents and adolescents with only one reported case (Gumbs et al., 1982) of an epiphyseal fracture in a 12-year-old boy. The low prevalence of epiphyseal fractures during late childhood probably reflects lower participation rates of younger children in weight-lifting activities, either training or competition, and perhaps even a less aggressive and intensive nature of training by the younger children. The possibility exists, however, that prepubescent children might be less prone to fractures than older children because growth plates may be stronger and more resistant to sheer stress during prepubescence than during later stages of development (Micheli, 1988). Furthermore, the majority of the injuries reported appear to have been preventable, in that they have been attributed to improper lifting technique, excessive loading, or the performance of ballistic movements that apparently result in high sheer forces and a greater potential for fracture (Gumbs et al., 1982; Jesse, 1979; Micheli, 1988; Ryan & Salciccioli, 1976; Sale, 1989).

In closely supervised prospective resistance-training studies, there have been no reported incidences of epiphyseal fracture in prepubertal children (Blimkie et al., 1989; Servedio et al., 1985; Sewall & Micheli, 1986; Weltman et al., 1986). Furthermore, epiphyseal fractures are apparently relatively rare in prepubescent and early pubescent children even in sport-related injuries (Caine, 1990; Larson & McMahon, 1966; McManama & Micheli, 1977; Micheli, 1988) and appear in most cases to have no detrimental effect on growth when diagnosed and properly treated (Caine, 1990). The concern over epiphyseal fractures caused by resistance training during prepuberty and early puberty may be overstated. Close adult supervision, instruction in proper lifting technique, gradual progression in training loads, and avoidance of excessive loads may minimize the risk for such injuries in this population (Kraemer, Fry, Frykman, Conroy, & Hoffman, 1989).

Musculoskeletal Injuries

The majority of injuries caused by resistance training during childhood are neither epiphyseal nor acute in nature but appear due to repetitive microtrauma to musculoskeletal structures with gradual onset of pain, dysfunction, and disability (Brady et al., 1982; Brown & Kimball, 1983). Brady et al. (1982) reported the incidence of weight-training-associated injuries over a 4-year period in 43 young athletes between 13 and 19 years of age. Lumbosacral injury was most frequent, followed by avulsion at the anterior superior iliac spine and equal incidences of injury to the knee and cervical spine. The severity of disability varied both within (at a certain location) and across different injury types, and treatment varied from hospitalization and surgical intervention to rest and discontinuance of training. Jackson, Wiltse, Dingeman, and Hayes (1981) studied 37 young athletes presenting with persistent lumbar pain; using the technetium pyrophosphate bone-scan technique, these authors reported three cases (males 17 to 19 years of age) of stress reactions involving the pars interarticularis of the lumbosacral region associated with weight training. Brown and Kimball (1983) reported 98 injuries associated with power lifting in 71 males between 14 and 19 years of age who were contestants in the 1981 Michigan Teenage Powerlifting Championship. Fifty percent of the injuries occurred to the lower back, and the more benign soft-tissue injuries (e.g., muscle pulls, tendinitis, cramps) accounted for over 83% of all injury types. The incidence of more severe injuries such as fracture and nerve damage was low, 2% and 3.1%, respectively. (Figure 5.1).

These retrospective and case studies indicate that resistance training is associated with a certain risk of injury during puberty and adolsecence. Soft-tissue

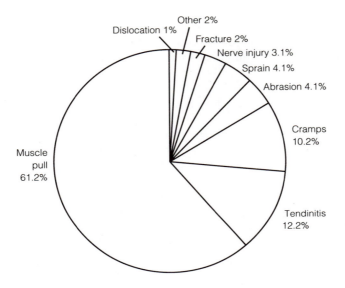

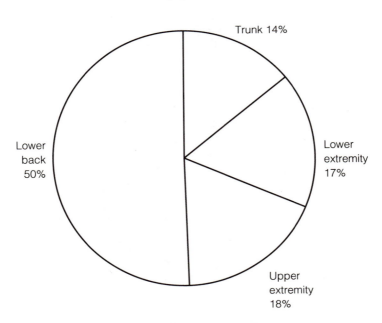

Figure 5.1 Injury type and location associated with adolescent power lifting. *Note.* Based on data by Brown and Kimball (1983).

injury appears to be most prevalent, and the lower back seems the most susceptible site for weight-lifting injuries. Although these findings point to the potential for injury, they are specific to pubescents and adolescents and therefore may not be generalizable to the prepubescent and early pubescent child. Nevertheless, the prevalence and types of injuries associated with less structured weight-lifting activities (as summarized in the U.S. Consumer Product Safety Commission reports) are similar to those found in more structured weight-lifting programs and indicate that there is indeed a real risk of injury associated with weight lifting during childhood.

There have been only a few prospective studies on the safety of resistance training during late childhood. Servedio et al. (1985) found that 8 weeks of weight training in which subjects used Olympic-style lifts (snatch, clean and jerk) failed to cause any injuries in six prepubescent boys. Likewise, Sewall and Micheli (1986) reported no injuries in a group of prepubertal boys and girls following 9 weeks of isotonic and accommodating resistance training. Rians et al. (1987) found that 14 weeks of predominantly isokinetic concentric resistance training resulted in only one overt clinical injury, diagnosed as shoulder strain, in a group of prepubertal male ice hockey players. By comparison, six injuries occurred that were associated with participation in other sports and activities of daily living, and these injuries resulted in a 16-fold higher training discontinuance rate compared to absenteeism caused by the single resistance-training injury. Furthermore, there was no evidence of subclinical musculoskeletal injury as judged by biphasic scintigraphy, or of muscle damage indicated by serum creatine phosphokinase (CPK) levels, associated with this training program.

Blimkie et al. (1989) reported that 20 weeks of high-intensity resistance training incorporating isotonic exercises involving both concentric and eccentric muscle contractions failed to cause any overt clinical musculoskeletal injuries in prepubertal boys. Single bouts of weight training during either the early (2nd week) or late (19th week) stages of the training program did not cause any significant increases in serum CPK, an enzyme marker for muscle damage, or urinary hydroxyproline, a nonspecific marker for collagen and connective tissue damage. There was, however, a significant increase in resting CPK (Figure 5.2), but not hydroxyproline, over the 20-week training period. There was no evidence of chronic cartilaginous damage as reflected by the serum marker keratin sulfate. These results suggest that individual bouts of resistance training, whether in the early or later stages of training, probably do not cause extensive muscle or connective tissue damage but that the cumulative effect of repetitive bouts of heavy exercise may leave the muscle in a continuous, but not debilitated, state of breakdown. Collectively, these results suggest that closely supervised, properly instructed, and appropriately prescribed resistance training is not a particularly stressful or risky activity in terms of the integrity of the musculoskeletal tissues of prepubertal children (Table 5.3).

With resistance training, as with most forms of exercise, the potential for musculoskeletal injury is present at all stages of development during childhood and even during adulthood. There is no evidence that prepubertal children are

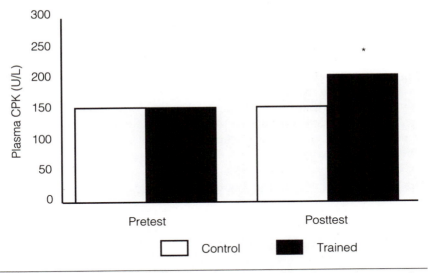

Figure 5.2   Creatine phosphokinase (CPK) levels in prepubertal boys before and after 20 weeks of heavy resistance training. *Note.* Based on data by Blimkie et al. (1989). *Indicates a significant difference between pre- and posttest values for the trained group.

Table 5.3   Injuries Associated With Resistance Training in Prospective Studies Involving Prepubescent and Early-Pubescent Children

Study	Age (years)	Gender	Duration (weeks)	Injury occurrence	Type
Servedio et al. (1985)	11.9	M	8	No	—
Sewall & Micheli (1986)	10-11	M,F	9	No	—
Rians et al. (1987)	6-11	M	14	Yes	Shoulder strain
Blimkie et al. (1989)	9-11	M	20	No	—

more prone to resistance training-related injuries than pubescents, adolescents, or adults. Studies using adequate controls for the length, type, and intensity of resistance training, and for levels of supervision and technical instruction, have yet to be conducted to ascertain the relative risk of injury at different stages of development. Additionally, there is no evidence that resistance training during childhood is more risky in terms of the incidence and severity of musculoskeletal injury than participation in many popular youth sports or recreational activities. Studies comparing resistance training with other youth sports would need to control for participation rates and activity-specific exposure time, and this clearly has yet to be done. Nevertheless, experts recommend a prudent approach to resistance training (Blimkie, 1989; Freedson, Ward, & Rippe, 1990; Kraemer et al., 1989; Sale, 1989) that adheres to the basic principles of training and is tempered with an appreciation of the physical and psychological limitations imposed by immaturity.

The 1 Repetition Maximum Load Myth

A number of reports have expressed concern and reservation over the use of maximal load lifting (1 RM) during childhood (American Academy of Pediatrics, 1983; Cahill, 1988; National Strength and Conditioning Association, 1985; Sewall & Micheli, 1986). Underlying this concern is the fear that high-intensity loading that requires maximal or near-maximal effort may cause structural damage and acute cardiac complications. There is no evidence that maximal load lifting (1 RM performance lifts) or near-maximal or maximal efforts (e.g., maximal isometric testing and isokinetic strength testing) performed following adequate progression of loading and warm-up in laboratory testing procedures cause injury to children. Greater concern is probably warranted, however, for maximal load lifting during weight-lifting training and competition, where the mechanics of lifting are more complex, usually involving multijoint action, and where proper warm-up, progression, technique, and supervision may be somewhat wanting.

Resistance-Training Fatalities

Whereas most resistance-training injuries that occur during childhood and adolescence are benign and treatable, the possibility always exists for more catastrophic injury. George, Stakiw, and Wright (1989) reported a fatality in a 9-year-old boy when a barbell fell on his chest from a bench press support stand. Death was attributed to rupture of the right atrium at the junction of the inferior vena cava resulting from blunt compression of the heart against the vertebral column. Because this fatality did not occur in the context of a formalized resistance-training or competitive weight-lifting program, it appears more an indictment of safety standards for weight-lifting equipment than of the practice of resistance training itself. Furthermore, because the accident occurred under unsupervised conditions, it underscores the need for close and experienced adult supervision, especially for younger children.

Preventing and Rehabilitating Injuries

Compared to the injury potential associated with resistance training, far less attention has been paid to the possibility that resistance training can prevent and rehabilitate injury during childhood. The physiological basis underlying the possible protective effects of resistance training against injury has been described elsewhere (Fleck & Falkel, 1986). There is some albeit limited evidence that strength training significantly decreases the number and severity of knee injuries in male adolescent high school football players (Cahill & Griffith, 1978) and substantially reduces the injury rates and recovery times of adolescent males and females (Hejna, Rosenberg, Buturusis, & Krieger, 1982) (Figure 5.3). Whether prepubertal and early pubertal children can achieve the same benefits with resistance training remains to be demonstrated. Differences in volume and intensity of sports training and competition, in degrees of aggressiveness and competitiveness, and in participation rates in contact and noncontact sports across developmental stages might limit the generalizability of these seemingly positive effects to younger age groups.

Resistance Training and Flexibility

Parents and coaches are often concerned that resistance training will result in muscle-boundness with a consequent decrease in flexibility and a subsequent increase in risk of injury to the child. There is no retrospective evidence of reduced flexibility in children who have participated in weight training or in weight-lifting competitions. A number of prospective studies have investigated the effects of resistance training on flexibility during prepuberty and early puberty (Table 5.4). Resistance training has resulted in either no change (Servedio et al., 1985), slight (< 5%) but insignificant improvements (Sewall & Micheli, 1986), or moderate and significant (8 to 12%) improvements (Rians et al., 1987; Siegel, Camaione, & Manfredi, 1989) in flexibility in prepubertal boys and girls. Stretching exercises were incorporated in the studies that demonstrated improvements in flexibility (Rians et al., 1987; Siegel et al., 1989), and based on only one study (Sewall & Micheli, 1986) the improvement in flexibility was greater for the joints that were preferentially stretched during the training program. Based on these few studies, it appears that strength-training programs either will have no detrimental effect on flexibility or may, if they also include specific stretching exercises, result in slight to moderate improvements in flexibility in prepubertal and early pubertal children.

Effects of Resistance Training on Sport Performance

Sport performance is influenced by a number of factors including those that are primarily genetically determined (e.g., stature) and those that may be modified by training (e.g., motor skill, strength). Many of the sports in which children participate have a substantial strength or power component, and theoretically performance in these sports can be improved with resistance training. There are numerous ways in which resistance training may either directly or indirectly affect sport performance (Table 5.5). To date, only a few studies have attempted

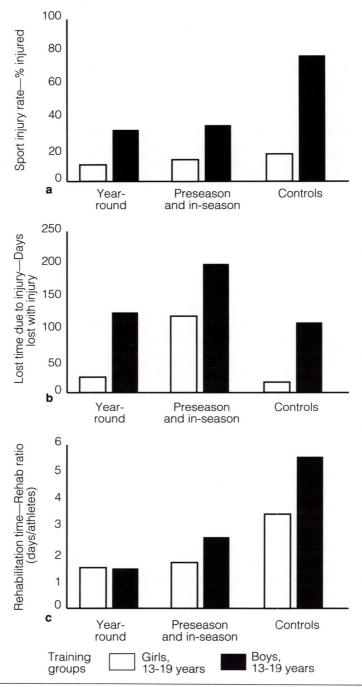

Figure 5.3 Effects of resistance training on injury rate (a), lost time due to injury (b), and rehabilitation time (c) following injury. *Note.* Based on data by Hejna et al. (1982).

Table 5.4   Changes in Flexibility Associated With Resistance Training During Prepuberty and Early Puberty

Study	Age (years)	Gender	Flexibility measure	% Δ Trained group	% Δ Control group
Servedio et al. (1985)	11.9	M	Unknown	None	None
Sewall & Micheli (1986)	10-11	M & F	Shoulder flexibility	− 0.5	+2.7
			Hip flexibility	+10.3	−0.8
			Knee flexibility	+ 3.5	+8.7
Rians et al. (1987)	6-11	M	Sit and reach	+ 8.4	−1.2[a]
Siegel et al. (1989)	8.4-8.6	M	Sit and reach	+11.8	−2.9[a]
		F	Sit and reach	+ 9.1	+2.8[a]

[a]Significant difference between trained and control groups.

to determine directly the importance of resistance-training-induced strength changes to improved sport performance during childhood. Ainsworth (1970) found that 6 weeks of supplemental resistance training failed to significantly improve strength or swimming speeds in male and female swimmers between 7 and 17 years of age. However, a more intensive and longer duration supplemental resistance-training program (Blanksby & Gregor, 1981) resulted in significant improvements in both strength and 100-yd swim performance in male and female age-group swimmers. Based on these studies, it appears that the positive effect of resistance training on swimming performance may depend on intensity and duration. Besides these two swimming-related studies, there have been no other attempts to directly determine the effects of resistance training-induced strength increases, or to determine the relative importance of changes in strength and in these other possible outcomes of resistance training, to improved sport performance during prepuberty and early puberty.

The effect of resistance training on sport performance in children has been indirectly implied, however, from changes in motor fitness test scores following training (Table 5.6). Nielsen, Nielsen, Behrendt-Hansen, and Asmussen (1980) reported a significant 12% improvement in vertical jump performance in a group of mostly prepubertal girls following 5 weeks of isometric knee extension training. Weltman et al. (1986) reported a significant increase (10.4%) in vertical jump performance, but not in standing long jump (3%) performance, in prepubertal boys following 14 weeks of hydraulic resistance training. These authors also indicated that parents anecdotally reported improved sport performances by the boys who took part in the training program.

Whereas resistance training appears to improve performance on selected motor fitness tests, and although there is probably a positive correlation between motor

Table 5.5   Possible Ways in Which Resistance Training Can Influence Sport Performance During Childhood

- Physiological changes at muscle level
- Psychological changes
- Somatic growth changes
- Body composition changes
- Injury and rehabilitation rate changes
- Others

Table 5.6   Changes in Motor Fitness Performance Associated With Resistance Training During Prepuberty and Early Puberty

Study	Age (years)	Gender	Performance test	% Δ Trained group	% Δ Control group
Nielsen et al. (1980)	<13.5	F	Vertical jump	+12.0	+2.0[a]
Weltman et al. (1986)	6-11	M	Vertical jump	+10.4	−3.0[a]
			Standing long jump	+ 3.0	+1.7

[a]Significant difference between trained and control groups.

fitness and sport performance, these few studies do not provide compelling evidence that resistance training has any effect whatsoever on sport performance during prepuberty and early childhood. The presence or absence of such an effect would seem fairly easy to prove in quantifiable sports such as jumping and throwing events, weight-lifting and power-lifting competitions, and timed events in track and swimming. The task may be more difficult for judgment sports or for team sports in which individual contribution and performance outcome are more subjective and less quantifiable. However, independent and trained observers, who would not know whether athletes were involved in formal resistance training, could assess performance changes even in these less quantifiable sports. Whether resistance training during prepuberty and early puberty can be justified on the basis of improving sport performance remains to be established.

Resistance Training, Body Size, and Composition

Stature

The repetitive nature of resistance training, coupled with the inherent high compressive and sheer forces associated with this form of exercise, poses the possibility of damage to growth tissue and of growth arrest. A report by Kato and Ishiko

(1964) provided weak support for this hypothesis and seems to have fueled this myth of the growth-arresting potential of lifting heavy loads during childhood. Kato and Ishiko (1964) noted decreases in stature in some Japanese children who performed heavy lifting or loading activities during manual labor. But this study failed to control for other factors (e.g., nutrition) that could also account for the apparent growth arrest, and thus the data should not be taken as evidence in support of this hypothesis.

Several of the more recent prospective resistance-training studies have, however, provided additional insight into this issue (Table 5.7). In the six studies reporting changes in stature, three studies reported slightly larger gains in the trained groups compared to the control groups over the course of training. There was no difference between trained and control groups in the other two studies. The differences between control and trained groups in all of these studies were extremely small (< 1%) and never statistically significant. These studies indicate that short-term (< 21 weeks), closely supervised, and highly controlled resistance-training programs have no detrimental effect on stature during late childhood. Whether high-intensity programs begun at earlier ages and conducted over longer time periods have any effect on stature during the prepubertal and early pubertal years remains to be determined.

Body Mass

Resistance training is often recommended as a means of increasing body mass for the possible enhancement of sport performance. With the exception of the study by Sewall and Micheli (1986), which reported a slight reduction in body mass, all other prospective studies of resistance training during prepuberty and early puberty have reported small increases (1 to 5.5%) in body mass in the trained groups (Table 5.7). In none of these studies, however, were the increases statistically different between control and trained groups, and the average increase in mass was small, only on the order of 2.7%. These studies suggest that short-term resistance-training programs have no major influence on development of body mass during prepuberty and early puberty.

Body Composition

For adults, resistance training is often recommended as a means of increasing lean body mass and reducing body fat. Only one study has assessed changes in lean body mass during late childhood resulting from resistance training (Table 5.8). Weltman et al. (1986) reported a slight reduction (0.4%) in body density as determined by hydrostatic weighing, and by inference a slight decrease in lean body mass, in prepubertal boys following 14 weeks of resistance training. This change was not significantly different from the slight (0.4%) increase in density in the control group. Body fatness as indicated by the sum of 11 skin folds increased slightly (3.3%) in the trained group and decreased (5.1%) in the control group. Based on these changes, it appears that the ratio of fat to lean

Table 5.7   Changes in Somatic Growth Associated With Resistance Training During Prepuberty and Early Puberty

Study	Age (years)	Gender	% Δ Height Trained	% Δ Height Controls	% Δ Weight Trained	% Δ Weight Controls
Vrijens (1978)	10.5	M	+0.9	None	+1.9	None
Servedio et al. (1985)	11.9	M	—	—	Equal but unspecified increase in both groups	
Sewall & Micheli (1986)	10-11	M & F	—	—	−0.5	+6.7
Weltman et al. (1986)	6-11	M	+1.5	+0.7	+5.5	+2.2
Sailors & Berg (1987)	12.6	M	+1.0	+1.2	+1.0	+4.2
Siegel et al. (1989)	8.4-8.6	M	+1.1	+0.3	+1.0	+2.8
		F	+1.1	+0.7	+2.5	+0.7
Ramsay et al. (1990)	10.5-10.8	M	+0.5	+0.6	+4.5	+3.9

tissue and the percentage body fat increased slightly in the trained group and decreased slightly in the control group. In the other prospective studies (Table 5.8), the combined changes in body mass and skin folds all indirectly imply small and insignificant increases in lean body mass, and either no change or only small and insignificant changes in percent body fat resulting from training. It appears from these studies that short-term resistance training does not have a dramatic effect on either somatic growth or body composition in prepubertal and early pubertal children.

Cardiorespiratory Fitness

Resistance and endurance training are often practiced together both for sport and for general fitness and conditioning. The adaptive responses to these forms of training are different and sometimes may even be antagonistic (Dudley & Fleck, 1987; Sale, MacDougall, Jacobs, & Garner, 1990). Because cardiorespiratory fitness appears protective against atherogenic disease, and given the possible antagonism between resistance- and endurance-trained adaptive responses, concern has been raised about the possible detrimental effects of resistance training on cardiorespiratory fitness and atherogenic risk during childhood.

...anges in Body Composition Associated With Resistance Training During Prepuberty and Early Puberty

Study	Age (years)	Gender	% Δ Body density		% Δ Σ Skinfolds		% Δ % Body fat	
			Trained	Control	Trained	Control	Trained	Control
Vrijens (1978)	10.5	M	—	—	-2.4 (Σ 10 skinfolds)	None	—	—
McGovern (1984)	Fourth, fifth, and sixth graders	M, F	—	—	None	None	—	—
Servedio et al. (1985)	11.9	M	—	—	—	—	None	None
Weltman et al. (1986)	6-11	M	-0.4	+0.4	+3.3 (Σ 11 skinfolds)	-5.1	Not reported	
Siegel et al. (1989)	8.4-8.6	M F	— —	— —	-10.8 -11.9 (Σ 7 skinfolds)	+4.1 +3.2	-0.8 -4.2	+ 7.7 +12.6
Ramsay et al. (1990)	10.5-10.8	M	—	—	-2.2 (Σ 2 skinfolds)	-1.9	-4.4	-3.9

Table 5.9 Changes in Cardiorespiratory Fitness Associated With Resistance Training During Prepuberty and Early Puberty

Study	Age (years)	Gender	% Δ Absolute V̇O₂max		% Δ Relative V̇O₂max	
			Trained	Control	Trained	Control
McGovern (1984)	Fourth grade	M & F	No change		No change	
	Fifth grade	M & F	Not reported		Not reported	
	Sixth grade	M & F	Not reported		Not reported	
Weltman et al. (1986)	6-11	M	+19.4	−2.7[a]	+13.8	−5.4[a]
Docherty et al. (1987)	12.6	M	+21.5	+4.7[a]	+18.4	+4.2[a]
			+17.9	+4.7[a]	+17.2	+4.2[a]
Blimkie et al. (unpublished data)	10.5-10.8	M	− 1.3	+5.9	− 6.0	+1.6

[a]Significant difference between trained and control groups.

Antagonism caused by concurrent resistance and endurance training has not been studied in children; however, several studies have investigated the effects of resistance training on development of cardiovascular fitness during childhood (Table 5.9). McGovern (1984) reported that 12 weeks of circuit training had no significant effect on maximal oxygen uptake of fourth-grade boys and girls. Details of this study are scarce, and there was no mention of changes in maximal oxygen uptake in either the fifth- or sixth-grade children who were also involved in the study. Weltman et al. (1986) reported substantial increases in both absolute (19.4%) and relative (13.8%) maximal oxygen uptake in prepubertal boys after 14 weeks of predominantly concentric, hydraulic resistance training. Likewise, Docherty, Wenger, and Collis (1987) also reported significant increases in both absolute (17.9 to 21.5%) and relative (17.2 to 18.4%) maximal oxygen uptake in 12.6-year-old boys following 4 weeks of predominantly concentric, hydraulic resistance training. Bouts of short-duration, high-intensity cycle ergometry exercise were incorporated into the training programs in both of these studies (Docherty et al., 1987; Weltman et al., 1986), and this additional training mode may account for part of the improvement in maximal oxygen uptake in these studies, independent of the effects of resistance training. The similarity in magnitude of increases in maximal oxygen uptake between the studies by Weltman et al. (1986) and Docherty et al. (1987) is perplexing, given the lower training volume and much shorter training duration in the latter study. Recently, we have observed only small and insignificant reductions in absolute (1.3%) and relative (6%) maximal oxygen uptake in prepubertal boys following 20 weeks of traditional high-intensity isotonic resistance training (Blimkie et al., unpublished data). These results were probably due more to poor motivation during posttesting than to reduced conditioning, based on observed lower posttest maximal heart rate and respiratory quotient responses in the trained group (Figure 5.4).

Although the data are limited, it appears that traditional high-intensity isotonic-type resistance training has little or no effect on development of cardiorespiratory fitness as reflected by maximal oxygen uptake during prepuberty and early puberty, provided there is no curtailment of other activities of daily living, including sport participation. In contrast, it appears that cardiorespiratory fitness may be more sensitive and responsive to high-repetition concentric resistance loading than to high-intensity isotonic loading during childhood. This may be due to the higher volume of work and greater caloric expenditure associated with reciprocal concentric exercises during hydraulic resistance training compared to isotonic or free-weight training modes. The changes in maximum oxygen uptake reported in the studies that used hydraulic resistance training are comparable to reported improvements in cardiorespiratory fitness in children following high-intensity endurance-training programs (Rowland, 1985). If these observations are accurate, reciprocal concentric resistance training may be the best training mode for optimal improvement of both strength and cardiorespiratory fitness during childhood. Although it is tempting to espouse the virtues of this type of training for children, the issue is at best equivocal and needs further study.

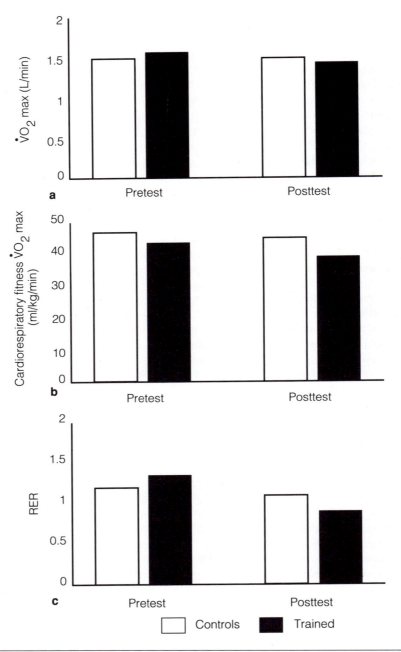

Figure 5.4   Effects of 20 weeks of resistance training on absolute (a) and relative (b) $\dot{V}O_2$max and respiratory exchange ratio (RER) (c) during maximal treadmill running in prepubertal boys. *Note.* Based on unpublished data by Blimkie et al.

Cardiovascular Adaptations

Blood Pressure

The cardiovascular adaptations to resistance exercise vary considerably from those occurring in response to endurance exercise, at least in adults (Fleck & Kraemer, 1988; Petrofsky & Phillips, 1986). Much less is known, however, about children's acute and chronic cardiovascular adaptations to resistance exercise or training. Dynamic resistive exercise results in significant transient increases in systolic and diastolic blood pressures, and subsequent increases in cardiac afterload, in adults (Fleck & Dean, 1987; MacDougall, Tuxen, Sale, Moroz, & Sutton, 1985). Only one study has investigated acute blood pressure responses during weight lifting in children. Nau, Katch, Beckman, and Dick (1990) investigated acute intra-arterial blood pressure responses during bench press exercise in eight males and three females ages 8 to 16 years. Subjects performed the bench press to fatigue at intensities of 60, 75, 90, and 100% of their 1-RM lift. Peak systolic and diastolic pressures increased by 35 to 48% and 55 to 72%, respectively, and peak heart rate increased above baseline by 62 to 72% under the various lifting conditions. The highest peak systolic and diastolic pressures occurred at the 75% 1-RM load; however, there were no significant differences in either peak pressures across conditions. Furthermore, pressures increased continuously with increasing number of repetitions, and peak pressures always occurred during the last repetition, representing the point of voluntary fatigue. Although the absolute baseline and peak pressures were lower in children than those reported for adults under similar conditions, the relative changes (percent increase above baseline) in peak pressures during lifting were apparently similar to those in adults performing similar lifts. Results from this study suggest that resistance exercise evokes a substantial transient pressor response and cardiac afterload in children and that the blood pressure adaptations during resistance exercise appear similar for children and adults.

Concern has been raised over the possibility of blackout (syncope) secondary to the transient increases in blood pressure during resistance exercise. Isolated cases of blackout during weight lifting have been reported in adults (Karpovich, 1951; Reilly, 1978) and appear to be related to breath holding (Valsalva maneuver) during the execution of heavy lifts. There have been no reported cases of children fainting either during weight-lifting competition or during prospective resistance-training studies involving children. Although the possibility of weight-lifting blackout exists, it is probably a rare occurrence in children and can most likely be prevented by proper instruction in breathing and lifting techniques.

Whereas the transient effects of resistance exercise on the pressor response are well established, the chronic adaptations in resting blood pressure to resistance training are somewhat more equivocal. Borderline hypertension has been reported in adult bodybuilders and power lifters (Spitler, Diaz, Horvath, & Wright, 1980; Staron, Hagerman, & Hikada, 1981); however, these studies did not consider the possible effects of anabolic steroid use on the pressor response. When steroid use is discounted, other cross-sectional studies have reported normal resting blood pressures in resistance-trained adult athletes (Colliander and Tesch, 1988; Longhurst, Kelly, Gonyen, & Mitchell, 1980), and short-term training studies have shown either no change in pressures (Allen, Byrd, & Smith, 1976) or significant decreases in systolic (Fahey, Akka, & Rolph, 1975; Stone, Wilson, Blessing, & Rozeneck, 1983) and both systolic and diastolic pressures (Goldberg, Elliot, Schutz, & Kloster, 1984).

There are no published retrospective or cross-sectional reports of abnormal blood pressures in children who have trained for or competed in competitive weight lifting. Only a few prospective studies have investigated changes in children's blood pressures in response to resistance training. Servedio et al. (1985) reported a reduction in resting diastolic, but not systolic, blood pressure in a group of largely prepubescent boys following 8 weeks of Olympic-style weight lifting. Weltman et al. (1986) reported that 14 weeks of hydraulic resistance training did not significantly affect resting blood pressure in a group of prepubertal boys. However, neither of these studies presented actual blood pressure data. Last, Blimkie et al. (unpublished data) found that 20 weeks of heavy isotonic resistance training had no significant differential effect on resting systolic or diastolic blood pressures in a group of prepubertal boys (Figure 5.5). In the only other related study, Hagberg et al. (1984) reported slight reductions in systolic (3%) and diastolic (5%) pressures in previously (before 5 months of endurance training) hypertensive adolescents following 5 months of resistance training. Collectively, these results suggest that acute pressor adaptations to resistance training are similar between children and adults, and that at least short-term resistance training (as was involved in the majority of studies with adults) does not cause sustained hypertension in children.

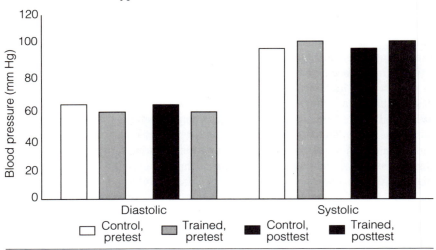

Figure 5.5   Effects of 20 weeks of resistance training on resting diastolic and systolic blood pressures in prepubertal boys. *Note*. Based on unpublished data by Blimkie et al.

Cardiac Dimensions and Function

As for adults, the possibility of cardiac hypertrophy also exists for the child as a chronic adaptation to resistance training-induced increases in blood pressure and afterload. Only two studies have investigated the effects of resistance training on cardiac dimensions and function in prepubertal and early pubertal children. Servedio et al. (1985) reported significantly larger left ventricular end diastolic dimensions (but did not specify whether these were internal diameter or posterior wall dimensions) and also reported significantly larger calculated stroke volume and cardiac output in prepubescent boys following 8 weeks of Olympic-style weight lifting. The abstract does not specify whether there were any differences in cardiac dimensions and function between trained and control groups prior to training, and actual echocardiographic data were not presented in this report. More recently, Blimkie et al. (unpublished data) used M-mode echocardiography to assess changes in resting cardiac dimensions and functions in prepubertal boys following 20 weeks of heavy resistance training. There were no significant differential effects of training on resting septal or left ventricular posterior wall thicknesses, on left ventricular internal diameters during systole or diastole (Figure 5.6), or on left ventricular shortening and ejection fractions. Too few studies have been conducted to state unequivocally the effects of resistance training on cardiac dimensions and function during prepuberty and early puberty. It appears, however, from our study that relatively short-term high-intensity isotonic resistance training may not alter resting cardiac dimensions or function during late childhood. The effects of longer term training, and of different resistance training modes on cardiac adaptations, remain to be determined.

Blood Lipids and Lipoproteins

Epidemiological studies have demonstrated a clear association between certain lipoprotein-lipid profiles and risk of coronary artery disease in adults (Castelli, Doyle, Gordon, Hames, & Hjortland, 1977; Stamler, Wentworth, & Neaton, 1986). Additionally, there is fairly extensive information about the effects of both endurance (Dufaux, Assman, & Hollman, 1982; Superko & Haskell, 1987) and resistance (Kokkinos & Hurley, 1990) training on lipoprotein-lipid profiles in adults. By contrast, there is only limited information about lipoprotein-lipid risk factors during childhood (Despres, Bouchard, & Malina, 1990; Gilliam, Katch, Thorland, & Weltman, 1977; Lauer, Connor, Leaverton, Reiter, & Clarke, 1975; Wilmore & McNamara, 1974) and about the association between these childhood profiles and adult risk of coronary artery disease. There is also little information on the effects of exercise in general (Despres, Bouchard, & Malina, 1990; Gilliam & Burke, 1978; Linder, Du Rant, & Mahoney, 1983; Nizankowska & Abramowicz, 1983; Savage, Petratis, Thomson, Berg, Smith, & Sady, 1986; Thorland & Gilliam, 1981; Widhalm, Niaxa, & Zyman, 1978) and resistance training in particular (Fripp & Hodgson, 1987; Weltman et al., 1986) on lipoprotein-lipid profiles during childhood.

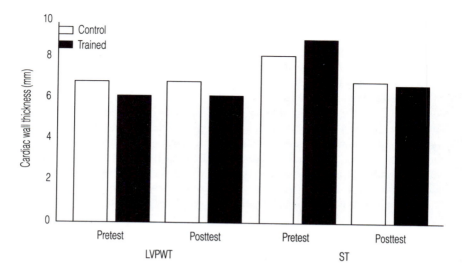

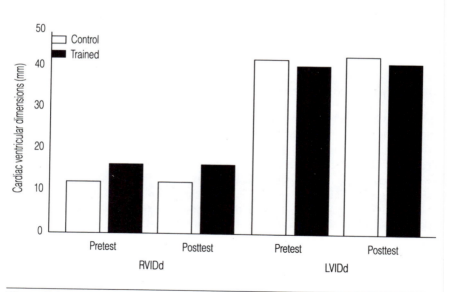

Figure 5.6 Effects of 20 weeks of heavy resistance training on resting cardiac wall thicknesses (a) and cavity dimensions (b) in prepubertal boys. LVPWT = left ventricular posterior wall thickness; ST = septal thickness; RVIDd = right ventricular internal diameter during diastole; LVIDd = left ventricular internal diameter during diastole. *Note.* Based on unpublished data by Blimkie et al.

Weltman et al. (1986) reported a significant reduction in serum cholesterol and a significant increase in the ratio of high density lipoprotein-c (HDL-C)/total cholesterol in prepubertal boys following 14 weeks of hydraulic resistance training (Figure 5.7). There were no significant changes, however, in serum triglyceride or in the fraction of HDL-C. Prestudy levels of total cholesterol were elevated in the trained group, and as suggested by the authors this probably partly accounted for the reduction in total cholesterol observed in the trained group following training. Although this study suggests that resistance training may have a positive effect on lipoprotein-lipid profiles, the authors pointed out that the reductions in total cholesterol could not be ascribed entirely to resistance training, because other physiological changes known to influence these profiles (e.g., improved cardiorespiratory fitness) also occurred in this study. The results from this study are also confounded by lack of dietary controls and by failure to separate residual effects of the last training bout from the chronic effects of training on lipoprotein-lipid profiles.

In the only other related study, Fripp and Hodgson (1987) reported significant improvements in the lipoprotein-lipid profiles (e.g., decreased low density lipoprotein cholesterol, or LDL-C, increased HDL-C, increased HDL-C/total cholesterol ratio) of adolescent males following 9 weeks of high-intensity isotonic weight training (Figure 5.8). These changes persisted even when the researchers adjusted for changes in body weight (body mass index), and the changes occurred without any change in cardiorespiratory fitness.

These studies suggest but do not prove unequivocally that resistance training may induce favorable lipoprotein-lipid changes during childhood. Research has

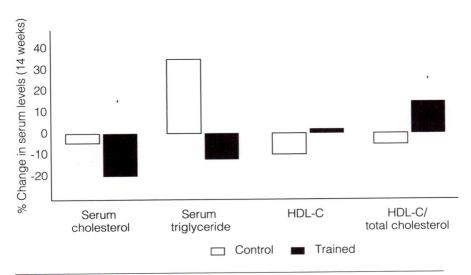

Figure 5.7   Changes in serum lipids and lipoproteins in prepubertal boys following 14 weeks of resistance training. HDL-C = high-density lipoprotein cholesterol. *Significant difference. Based on data by Weltman et al. (1987).

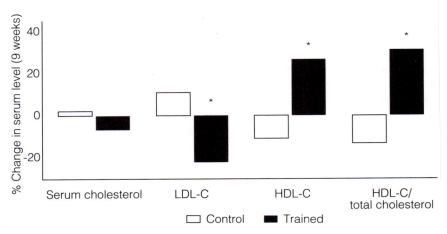

Figure 5.8 Changes in serum lipids and lipoproteins in adolescent males following 9 weeks of resistance training. HDL-C = high-density lipoprotein cholesterol; LDL-C = low-density lipoprotein cholesterol. *Significant difference. Based on data by Fripp and Hodgson (1987).

yet to determine whether these changes are due to the physiological effects of resistance training per se or rather to the secondary effects of this type of training on other factors such as body weight, body composition, or improved cardiorespiratory fitness. From a therapeutic or clinical perspective, however, the mechanism underlying these changes may be less important than the fact that resistance training appears associated with improvements in lipoprotein-lipid profiles of children. Future studies should control for initial lipoprotein-lipid levels, for diet, and for changes in body composition and cardiorespiratory fitness; should distinguish between acute and chronic training effects; should include children from both high- and low-risk groups in terms of lipoprotein-lipid profiles; and should compare the effects of different resistance training modes.

Anabolic-Androgenic Steroid Abuse

A number of recent studies have indicated that children and adolescents are abusing anabolic-androgenic steroids (American Academy of Pediatrics, Committee on Sports Medicine, 1989; Buckley et al., 1988; Johnson, Jay, Shoup, & Rickert, 1988; Krowchuk et al., 1989; Salva & Bacon, 1989; Strauss, 1989; Terney & McLain, 1990). Estimates of the prevalence of anabolic steroid use among the general adolescent population including both junior and senior high school students (Grades 8 to 12) range from less than 1% (Corder et al., 1975) to 6.6% (Buckley et al., 1988) (Figure 5.9). Given that steroids are presumed to enhance athletic performance, it is not surprising that an even higher prevalence rate of steroid use—between 1.4% (Krawchuk et al., 1989) and 12.5% (Johnson et al., 1988)—has been reported for adolescent athletes (Figure 5.10). Among

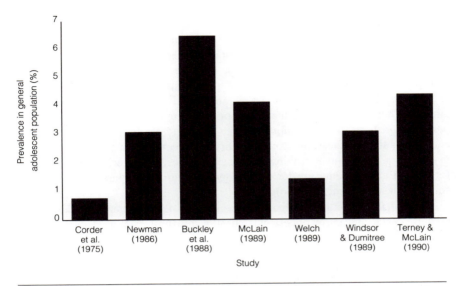

Figure 5.9 Prevalence of anabolic steroid use among the general adolescent population. Prevalence was determined as the percent of respondents in questionnaire studies who indicated steroid use.

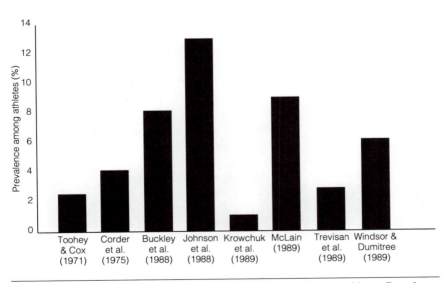

Figure 5.10 Prevalence of anabolic steroid use among adolescent athletes. Prevalence was determined as the percent of respondents identified as athletes in questionnaire studies who indicated steroid use.

sports there is also some evidence of greater abuse in the so-called strength sports such as football, wrestling, basketball, and track and field, each of which has a formidable enrollment of children in North America (Buckley et al., 1988; Terney & McLain, 1990) (Figure 5.11). Because resistance training is often incorporated into the training programs for these sports, resistance training per se becomes implicated, by association, in steroid abuse by these adolescent athletes. There is no evidence that resistance training itself, independent of sport participation (e.g., for recreational or fitness purposes), is associated with or encourages steroid abuse among children or adolescents. When resistance training is used as a means of improving sport performance, however, the inducement for steroid abuse seems greater and presents a real and apparently increasing concern for adolescent sport programs.

Although there is little information about the prevalence of steroid abuse during prepubescence and early pubescence, health care professionals, coaches, and parents must be ever vigilant against the spread of this abuse among younger athletes. In addition, anabolic steroid abuse appears to be an ethical dilemma that is not reserved solely for the young athlete. According to a report by Salva and Bacon (1989), a fairly high percentage (20%) of requests for steroids for adolescents are made by parents, especially by parents whose sons play football. Clearly, educational programs that deal with the medical and ethical issues surrounding ergogenic abuses must be targeted not only to the young athlete but to others of significant influence, including parents, coaches, trainers, and sport organizers.

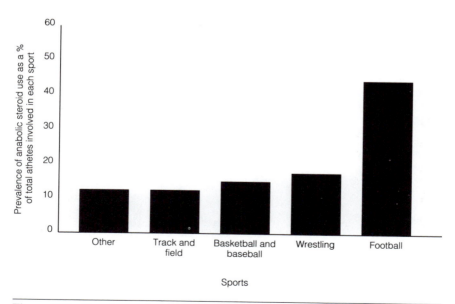

Figure 5.11   Prevalence of anabolic steroid use during adolescence, classified by sport. *Note.* Based on data by Buckley et al. (1988).

Contraindications for Resistance Training

Resistance training may be a potentially beneficial and relatively low-risk form of exercise for most healthy children. With the exception of the studies by Fripp and Hodgson (1987) and Vignos and Watkins (1966), there are no reports of the benefits and risks of this type of highly specialized training for prepubertal and early pubertal children with chronic diseases or medical conditions. It seems prudent, however, that resistance training should be recommended cautiously, and should be conducted only under close medical supervision and with strict monitoring, for children with the following conditions: arthritic conditions, cardiovascular and respiratory diseases, neurological and muscular disorders, endocrine and metabolic conditions, and psychological and mental disorders. Resistance training may prove to provide both direct and indirect therapeutic effects in some of these conditions; however, this remains to be established and should be the focus of future research.

Summary

There are numerous rationales for the recommendation of resistance training during childhood. Results from a national fitness survey (Ross & Gilbert, 1985) indicate declining and poor levels of strength among North American youth, a trend that resistance training may reverse. Reduced strength may also be associated with poor posture during childhood (Mersch & Stoboy, 1989), and a program of resistance training may reduce the prevalence of this condition in children. Additionally, resistance training may contribute to enhanced sport performance, improved body composition, and a reduction in injury rate and rehabilitation time. These rationales are based largely on anticipated potential, and not yet proven, outcomes of resistance training during childhood. The absence of proof, however, does not prove absence, and there is sufficient evidence to anticipate numerous beneficial effects (besides improvements in strength) of resistance training during childhood. On the other hand, there are numerous potential yet mostly unproven risks associated with resistance training during childhood. Coaches and others must follow a prudent yet practical approach that balances these potential benefits and risks when prescribing resistance training for children. Guidelines for such an approach to resistance training during childhood have been published recently (Blimkie, in press; Freedson et al., 1990; Kraemer et al., 1989; Sale, 1989; Weltman, 1989). Resistance training is a highly specialized and advanced form of training and must be placed in proper perspective during childhood. Resistance training should be recommended as only one of a variety of physical activity and sport pursuits, should be closely supervised, and should be a voluntary and pleasurable experience for the child.

Acknowledgments

The author thanks Mary Cleland for assisting with typing the manuscript. Thanks also to the Ontario Ministry of Tourism and Recreation for its financial support of my work in this area.

References

Ainsworth, J.L. (1970) *The effect of isometric-resistive exercises with the Exer-Genie on strength and speed in swimming.* Unpublished doctoral dissertation, University of Arkansas.

American Academy of Pediatrics. (1983). Weight training and weight lifting: Information for the pediatrician. *The Physician and Sportsmedicine,* **11,** 157-161.

American Academy of Pediatrics, Committee on Sports Medicine. (1989). Anabolic steroids and the adolescent athlete. *Pediatrics,* **83,** 127-128.

Benton, J.W. (1983). Epiphyseal fractures in sports. *The Physician and Sportsmedicine,* **10,** 63-71.

Blanksby, B., & Gregor, J. (1981). Anthropometric, strength and physiological changes in male and female swimmers with progressive resistance training. *Australian Journal of Sport Sciences,* **1,** 3-6.

Blimkie, C.J.R. (1989, October). Strength training for the child athlete: The Institute Report. *Scholastic Coach,* p. 9.

Blimkie, C.J.R. (in press). Resistance training during pre- and early puberty: Efficacy, trainability, persistence, and mechanisms. *Canadian Journal of Sport Sciences.*

Blimkie, C.J.R., MacDougall, D., Sale, D., Thonar, E., Smith, K., & Garner, S. (1989). Soft-tissue trauma and resistance training in boys. *Medicine and Science in Sports and Exercise,* **21**(Suppl. 533), S89.

Brady, T.A., Cahill, B., & Bodnar, L. (1982). Weight training-related injuries in the high school athlete. *American Journal of Sports Medicine,* **10,** 1-5.

Brown, E.W., & Kimball, R.G. (1983). Medical history associated with adolescent power-lifting. *Pediatrics,* **72,** 636-644.

Buckley, W.E., Yesalis, C.E., Friedl, K.E., Anderson, W.A., Streit, A.L., & Wright, J.E. (1988). Estimated prevalence of anabolic steroid use among male high school seniors. *Journal of the American Medical Association,* **260,** 3441-3445.

Cahill, B.R. (Ed.) (1988). *Proceedings of the Conference on Strength Training and the Prepubescent.* Chicago: American Orthopaedic Society for Sports Medicine.

Cahill, B.R., & Griffith, E.H. (1978). Effect of pre-season conditioning on the incidence and severity of high school football knee injuries. *American Journal of Sports Medicine,* **6,** 180-184.

Caine, D.J. (1990). Growth plate injury and bone growth: An update. *Pediatric Exercise Science,* **2,** 209-229.

Castelli, W.P., Doyle, J.T., Gordon, T., Hames, C.G., & Hjortland, M.C. (1977). HDL cholesterol and other lipids in coronary heart disease: The Cooperative Lipoprotein Phenotyping Study. *Circulation,* **55,** 767-772.

Colliander, E.B., & Tesch, P.A. (1988). Blood pressure in resistance-trained athletes. *Canadian Journal of Sport Sciences*, **13**, 31-34.

Corder, B.W., Dezelsky, T.L., Toohey, J.V., et al. (1975). An analysis of trends in drug use behavior at ten central Arizona high schools. *Arizona Journal of Health, Physical Education, Recreation and Dance*, **18**, 10-11.

Despres, J-P., Bouchard, C., & Malina, R.M. (1990). Physical activity and coronary heart disease risk factors during childhood. *Exercise and Sport Sciences Reviews*, **18**, 243-261.

Docherty, D., Wenger, H.A., & Collis, M.L. (1987). The effects of resistance training on aerobic and anaerobic power of young boys. *Medicine and Science in Sports and Exercise*, **19**, 389-392.

Dudley, G.A., & Fleck, S.J. (1987). Strength and endurance training. Are they mutually exclusive? *Sports Medicine*, **4**, 79-85.

Dufaux, B.G., Assman, G., & Hollman, W. (1982). Plasma lipoproteins and physical activity: A review. *International Journal of Sports Medicine*, **3**, 123-136.

Fahey, T.D., Akka, L., & Rolph, R. (1975). Body composition and VO_2max of exceptional weight-trained athletes. *Journal of Applied Physiology*, **39**, 559-561.

Fleck, S.J., & Dean, L.S. (1987). Resistance training experience and the pressor response during resistance training. *Journal of Applied Physiology*, **63**, 116-120.

Fleck, S.J., & Falkel, J.E. (1986). Value of resistance training for the reduction of sports injuries. *Sports Medicine*, **3**, 61-68.

Fleck, S.J., & Kraemer, W.J. (1988). Resistance training: Physiological responses and adaptations (part 3 of 4). *The Physician and Sportsmedicine*, **16**, 63-66, 69, 72-74.

Freedson, P.S., Ward, A., & Rippe, J.M. (1990). Resistance training for youth. *Advances in Sport Medicine and Fitness*, **3**, 57-65.

Fripp, R.R., & Hodgson, J.L. (1987). Effects of resistive training in plasma lipid and lipoprotein levels in male adolescents. *Journal of Pediatrics*, **111**, 926-931.

George, D.H., Stakiw, K., & Wright, C.J. (1989). Fatal accident with weight-lifting equipment: Implications for safety standards. *Canadian Medical Association Journal*, **140**, 925-926.32.

Gilliam, T.B., & Burke, M.B. (1978). Effects of exercise on serum lipids and lipoproteins in girls ages 8-10 years. *Artery*, **4**, 203-213.

Gilliam, T.B., Katch, V.L., Thorland, W.G., & Weltman, A.W. (1977). Prevalence of coronary heart disease risk factors in active children 7 to 12 years of age. *Medicine and Science in Sports and Exercise*, **9**, 21-25.

Goldberg, L., Elliot, D.L., Schutz, R.W., & Kloster, F.E. (1984). Changes in lipid and lipoprotein levels after weight training. *Journal of the American Medical Association*, **252**, 504-506.

Gumbs, V.L., Segal, D., Halligan, J.B., & Lower, G. (1982). Bilateral distal radius and ulnar fracture in weight-lifters. *American Journal of Sports Medicine*, **10**, 375-379.

Hagberg, J.M., Ehsani, A.A., Goldring, D., Hernandez, A., Sinacore, D.R., & Holloszy, J.D. (1984). Effect of weight training on blood pressure and hemodynamics in hypertensive adolescents. *The Journal of Pediatrics*, **104**, 147-151.

Hejna, W.F., Rosenberg, A., Buturusis, D.J., & Krieger, A. (1982). The prevention of sports injuries in high school students through strength training. *National Strength and Conditioning Association Journal*, **4**, 28-31.

Jackson, D.W., Wiltse, L.L., Dingeman, R.D., & Hayes, M. (1981). Stress reactions involving the pars interarticularis in young athletes. *American Journal of Sports Medicine*, **9**, 304-312.

Jesse, J.P. (1979). Misuse of strength development programs in athletic training. *The Physician and Sportsmedicine*, **7**, 46-52.

Johnson, M.D., Jay, M.S., Shoup, B., & Rickert, V.I. (1988). Anabolic steroid use in adolescent males. *Journal of Adolescent Health Care*, **9**, 263.

Karpovich, D.V. (1951). Incidence of injuries in weight lifting. *Journal of Physical Education*, **48**, 71-72.

Kato, S., & Ishiko, T. (1964). Obstructed growth of children's bones due to excessive labor in remote corners. In S. Kato (Ed.), *Proceedings of the International Congress of Sport Sciences* (pp. 476). Tokyo: Japanese Union of Sport Sciences.

Kokkinos, P.F., & Hurley, B.F. (1990). Strength training and lipoprotein-lipid profiles: A critical analysis and recommendations for further study. *Sports Medicine*, **9**, 266-272.43.

Kraemer, W.J., Fry, A.C., Frykman, P.N., Conroy, B., & Hoffman, J. (1989). Resistance training and youth. *Pediatric Exercise Science*, **1**, 366-350.

Krowchuk, D.P., Anglin, T.M., Goodfellow, D.B., Stancin, T., Williams, P., & Zimet, G.D. (1989). High school athletes and the use of ergogenic aids. *American Journal of Diseases of Children*, **143**, 486-489.

Larson, R.L., & McMahon, R.O. (1966). The epiphysis and the child athlete. *Journal of the American Medical Association*, **196**, 607-612.

Lauer, R.M., Connor, W.E., Leaverton, P.E., Reiter, M.A., & Clarke, W.R. (1975). Coronary heart disease risk factors in school children: The Muscatine study. *Journal of Pediatrics*, **86**, 697-703.

Linder, C.W., DuRant, R.H., & Mahoney, O.M. (1983). The effect of physical conditioning on serum lipids and lipoproteins in white male adolescents. *Medicine and Science in Sports and Exercise*, **15**, 232-236.

Longhurst, J.C., Kelly, A.R., Gonyea, W.J., & Mitchell, J.H. (1980). Echocardiographic left ventricular masses in distance runners and weight-lifters. *Journal of Applied Physiology*, **48**, 154-162.

MacDougall, J.D., Tuxen, D., Sale, D., Moroz, J., & Sutton, J. (1985). Arterial blood pressure response to heavy resistance exercise. *Journal of Applied Physiology*, **58**, 785-790.

McGovern, M.B. (1984). Effects of circuit weight training on the physical fitness of prepubescent children. *Dissertation Abstracts International*, **45**(2), 452A-453A.

McLain, L.G. (1989). Anabolic steroids and high school students. *Medicine and Science in Sports and Exercise*, **21**(2)(Suppl. 150), S25.

McManama, G.B., & Micheli, L.J. (1977). The incidence of sport related epiphyseal injuries in adolescents. *Medicine and Science in Sports and Exercise*, **9**, 57.

Mersch, F., & Stoboy, H. (1989). Strength training and muscle hypertrophy in children. In S. Oseid & K-H. Carlsen (Eds.), *Children and exercise XIII* (pp. 165-182). Champaign, IL: Human Kinetics.

Micheli, L.J. (1988a). The incidence of injuries in children's sports: A medical perspective. In E.W. Brown & C.E. Branta (Eds.), *Competitive sports for children and youth* (pp. 279-284). Champaign, IL: Human Kinetics.

Micheli, L.J. (1988b). Strength training in the young athlete. In E.W. Brown & C.E. Branta (Eds.), *Competitive sports for children and youth* (pp. 99-105). Champaign, IL: Human Kinetics.

National Strength and Conditioning Association. (1985). Position paper on prepubescent strength training. *National Strength and Conditioning Association Journal, 7,* 87-90.

Nau, K.L., Katch, V.L., Beckman, R.H., & Dick, M., III . (1990). Acute intraarterial blood pressure response to bench press weight lifting in children. *Pediatric Exercise Science,* **2**(1), 37-45.

Newman, M. (1986). *Michigan consortium of schools student survey.* Minneapolis: Hazelden Research Services.

Nielsen, B., Nielsen, K., Behrendt-Hansen, M., & Asmussen, E. (1980). Training of "functional muscular strength" in girls 7-19 years old. In K. Berg & B.D. Eriksson (Eds.), *Children and exercise IX* (pp. 69-78). Champaign, IL: Human Kinetics.

Nizankowska, T., & Abramowicz, T. (1983). Effects of intensive physical training on serum lipids and lipoproteins. *Acta Paediatrica Scandinavica,* **72**, 357-359.

Petrofsky, J.S., & Phillips, C.A. (1986). The physiology of static exercise. *Exercise and Sport Sciences Reviews,* **14**, 1-44.

Ramsay, J.A., Blimkie, C.J.R., Smith, K., Garner, S., MacDougall, J.D., & Sale, D.G. (1990). Strength training effects in prepubescent boys. *Medicine and Science in Sports and Exercise,* **22**(5), 605-614.

Reilly, T. (1978). Some observations on weight-training. *British Journal of Sports Medicine,* **12**, 45-47.

Rians, C.B., Weltman, A., Cahill, B.R., Janney, C.A., Tippett, S.R., & Katch, F.I. (1987). Strength training for prepubescent males: Is it safe? *American Journal of Sports Medicine,* **15**, 483-489.

Ross, J.G., & Gilbert, G.G. (1985). National children and youth fitness study: A summary of findings. *Journal of Physical Education, Recreation and Dance,* **56**, 45-50.

Rowe, R.A. (1979). Cartilage fracture due to weight lifting. *British Journal of Sports Medicine,* **13**, 130-131.

Rowland, T.W. (1985). Aerobic response to endurance training in prepubescent children: A critical analysis. *Medicine and Science in Sports and Exercise,* **17**, 493-497.

Ryan, J.R., & Salcicciolo, G.C. (1976). Fracture of the distal radial epiphysis in adolescent weight-lifters. *American Journal of Sports Medicine,* **4**, 26-27.

Sailors, M., & Berg, K. (1987). Comparison of responses to weight training in pubescent boys and men. *Journal of Sports Medicine,* **27**, 30-36.

Sale, D.G. (1989). Strength training in children. In C.V. Girolfi & D.R. Lamb (Eds.), *Perspectives in exercise science and sports medicine: Vol. 2. Youth, exercise and sport* (pp. 165-222). Indianapolis: Benchmark Press.

Sale, D.G., MacDougall, J.D., Jacobs, I., & Garner, S. (1990). Interaction between concurrent strength and endurance training. *Journal of Applied Physiology,* **68**, 260-270.

Salva, P.D., & Bacon, G.E. (1989). Anabolic steroids and growth hormone in the Texas Panhandle. *Texas Medicine*, **85**, 43-44.

Savage, M.P., Petratis, M.M., Thomson, W.H., Berg, C., Smith, J.L., & Sady, S.P. (1986). Exercise training effects on serum lipids of prepubescent boys and adult men. *Medicine and Science in Sports and Exercise*, **18**, 197-240.

Servedio, F.J., Bartels, R.L., Hamlin, R.L., Teske, D., Shaffer, T., & Servedio, A. (1985). The effects of weight training using Olympic style lifts on various physiological variables in pre-pubescent boys. *Medicine and Science in Sports and Exercise*, **17**, 288.

Sewall, L., & Micheli, L.J. (1986). Strength training for children. *Journal of Pediatric Orthopedics*, **6**, 143-146.

Siegel, J.A., Camaione, D.N., & Manfredi, T.G. (1989). The effects of upper body resistance training on prepubescent children. *Pediatric Exercise Science*, **1**, 145-154.

Spitler, D.L., Diaz, F.J., Horvath, S.M., & Wright, J.E. (1980). Body composition and maximal aerobic capacity of body builders. *Journal of Sports Medicine*, **10**, 181-188.

Stamler, J., Wentworth, D., & Neaton, J.D. (1986). Is the relationship between serum cholesterol and risk of premature death from coronary heart disease continuous and graded? Findings in 356,222 primary screenees of the Multiple Risk Factor Intervention Trial (MRFIT). *Journal of the American Medical Association*, **256**, 2823-2828.

Staron, R.S., Hagerman, F.C., & Hikada, R.S. (1981). The effects of detraining an elite power lifter: A case study. *Journal of Neurological Sciences,* **51**, 247-257.

Strauss, R.H. (1989). High school kids: Looking better, living worse? *The Physician and Sportsmedicine*, **17**, 35.

Superko, H.R., & Haskell, W.H. (1987). The role of exercise training in the therapy of hyperlipoproteinemia. *Cardiology Clinics*, **5**, 285-310.

Tanner, J.M. (Ed.) (1962). *Growth at adolescence*. Oxford, England: Blackwell Scientific.

Terney, R., & McLain, L.G. (1990). The use of anabolic steroids in high school students. *American Journal of Diseases of Children*, **144**, 99-103.

Thorland, W.G., & Gilliam, T.B. (1981). Comparison of serum lipids between habitually high and low active pre-adolescent males. *Medicine and Science in Sports and Exercise*, **13**, 316-321.

Toohey, J.V., & Cox, B.A. (1971). Steroids and the athlete. *Arizona Journal of Health, Physical Education and Recreation*, **14**, 15-17.

Trevisan, L., Bents, R., Bosworth, E., Elliot, D., & Goldberg, L. (1989). A sequential study of anabolic steroid use and availability among high school football athletes. *Medicine and Science in Sports and Exercise*, **21**(2)(Suppl. 149), S25.

U.S. Consumer Product Safety Commission (1979; 1987). *National electronic injury surveillance system*. Washington, DC: Directorate for Epidemiology, National Injury Information Clearinghouse.

Vrijens, J. (1978). Muscle strength development in the pre- and post-pubescent age. *Medicine and Sport*, **11**, 152-158.

Welch, M.J., & Priest, R.F. (1989). Anabolic steroid use among high school athletes. *Medicine and Science in Sports and Exercise,* **21** (Suppl. 148), S25.

Weltman, A. (1989). Weight training in prepubertal children: Physiologic benefit and potential damage. In O. Bar-Or (Ed.), *Advances in pediatric sport sciences* (Vol. 3, pp. 101-129). Champaign, IL: Human Kinetics.

Weltman, A., Janney, C., Rians, C.B., Strand, K., Berg, B., Tippitt, S., Wise, J., Cahill, B.S., & Katch, F.I. (1986). The effects of hydraulic resistance strength training in pre-pubertal males. *Medicine and Science in Sports and Exercise,* **18**, 629-638.

Weltman, A., Janney, C., Rians, C.B., Strand, K., & Katch, F.I. (1987). The effects of hydraulic-resistance strength training on serum lipid levels in prepubertal boys. *American Journal of Diseases of Children,* **141**, 777-780.

Widhalm, K., Niaxa, E., & Zyman, H. (1978). Effect of diet and exercise upon the cholesterol and triglyceride content of plasma lipoproteins in overweight children. *European Journal of Pediatrics,* **127**, 121-126.

Wilmore, J.H., & McNamara, J.J. (1974). Prevalence of coronary heart disease risk factors in boys, 8 to 12 years of age. *Journal of Pediatrics,* **84**, 527-533.

Windsor, R., & Dumitree, D. (1989). Prevalence of anabolic steroid use by male and female adolescents. *Medicine and Science in Sports and Exercise,* **21**, 494-497.

Chapter 6

The Physiological Impact of Intensive Training on the Prepubertal Athlete

Thomas W. Rowland

The emergence of the child athlete in the world's sports arenas has been viewed with a measure of both awe and concern (Maffulli & Helms, 1988; Zauner, Maksud, & Melichna, 1989). Children are achieving world-class performances as early as their midteen years in an increasingly broad range of sports, particularly swimming, gymnastics, figure skating, and tennis. Though it is not clearly documented, there is little question that the number of these highly trained young athletes is on the rise, a trend that is likely to continue as media coverage creates role models for following generations.

Do intense training and competition pose risks for growing elite athletes? It would not be unusual to find that a 15-year-old cross-country champion has been training over 50 mi a week regularly since the prepubertal years—a time normally devoted to physical, emotional, educational, and social growth. Such an athlete's legs, heart, and lungs will have been placed under training stresses once considered rigorous even for elite adult athletes. Can adverse effects be expected from this intensive participation during the growing years, effects that predispose the athlete to long-term consequences? If so, should the young athlete's amount of training and competition be limited?

The scientific basis for addressing these questions has clearly lagged far behind the growing number of young athletes, and the limited research information currently at hand has not yet provided conclusive answers. Training is designed to create stresses on body systems, and the potential for injury to growing tissues—with possible long-term implications—is troublesome. On the other hand, it is tentatively reassuring that young athletes appear to be healthy, as do adult athletes who began training during childhood. Moreover, athletes may gain certain benefits, both physiological (e.g., reduction of coronary artery risk factors, reduction of body fat) and psychological (e.g., gains in self-confidence, discipline), from early sport involvement.

Assessing the impact of intensive training on child athletes is not easy. Noting that "what effect these [training] programs have on the dynamics of growth of young children are questions that warrant considerable study" (p. 33), Bailey and Mirwald (1988) outlined the difficulties involved:

1. Young athletes are involved in a wide variety of sports, each with its own unique training stresses. The physiological impact of lacrosse, for instance, might be very different from that of gymnastics.
2. The age at which training begins, the developmental status of the child, and the intensity of training all influence the stresses of sports participation.
3. The prepubertal athlete is a relatively new phenomenon. Numbers of elite child athletes are not large, and sufficient time has not passed in which researchers can gauge the long-term effects of early training.
4. Physiological responses to training mimic those created by biological growth and development, making it difficult to distinguish the "fitness effect" of training from the effect of normal maturation alone.
5. In examining the physiological characteristics of child athletes compared to nonathletes, researchers find it difficult to separate out the effects of sport participation from those of genetic preselection.

These hindrances notwithstanding, this chapter will assess the potential physiological risks and benefits incurred by intensive training during the prepubertal years. Physiological differences that separate child athletes from nonathletes will be reviewed, and current data addressing stresses to specific organ systems in young competitors will be examined. Following a discussion of potential physiological benefits from early athletic training, a proposed set of guidelines for training and competition by prepubertal children will be presented.

Physiological Characteristics of Child Athletes

Comparing the physiological profiles of young competitors to those of nonathletic children would seem to be the simplest means of assessing the physiological impact of sport participation during childhood. That is, we would expect the characteristics of elite child athletes to provide information regarding the physiological alterations that result from early sports training and competition. Unfortunately, several confounding factors limit the usefulness of such comparisons.

Foremost among these, it is impossible in cross-sectional studies to determine if characteristics of child athletes represent the result of training or are simply expressions of inherited physiological traits that permit elite athletic performance. If the latter is true, these characteristics are not indicative of the effects of early training and competition. There is no question that genetically acquired talents contribute greatly to physiological fitness. Estimates of this inherited influence vary, but most studies suggest that at least 30 to 50% of maximal aerobic power can be related to genetic effects (Bouchard, 1986).

It is not altogether clear whether prepubertal children respond physiologically to exercise training to the same degree as do adults (Rowland, 1985). If they don't, the physiological profiles of child athletes will not reflect the influence of training and competition. If physiological responses to training in children are the same as those of adults, they closely mimic the same changes that occur normally with growth and development. Physiological differences between child athletes and nonathletes could then simply reflect differing levels of biological maturation.

With these considerations in mind, what do we know about the physiological characteristics of well-trained child athletes? Participants in several sports have been investigated, but there has been little in-depth evaluation of any particular athletic activity. This chapter concentrates on reports dealing with highly trained prepubertal athletes, ignoring studies of older adolescent athletes who may have trained in the childhood years.

Runners

Most information pertains to runners. Mayers and Gutin (1979) compared physiological characteristics of eight elite cross-country runners ages 8 to 11 years with characteristics of nontrained control subjects, both during treadmill testing. Average values for $\dot{V}O_2$max for the runners and controls were 56.6 and 46.0 ml/kg/min, respectively ($p < .05$). The runners demonstrated significantly lower heart rates and $\dot{V}O_2$ at a given submaximal speed, but economy differences disappeared when researchers considered the subjects' heights. Mean maximal heart rate was 203 bpm for the runners and 205 bpm for the controls ($p > .05$).

Sundberg and Elovainio (1982) reported findings in 12 boys age 12 years who had 2 to 5 years of intensive running training. The runners exhibited significantly higher $\dot{V}O_2$max during cycle testing than untrained controls (59.3 vs. 51.1 ml/kg/min), whereas respective average maximal heart rates were 192 and 197 bpm ($p > .05$). No significant differences in resting pulmonary function (vital capacity, FEV_1), heart rate, heart volume (by X ray), or blood pressure were observed between the two groups.

Vaccaro and Poffenbarger (1982) described resting pulmonary function studies in eight female runners ages 10 to 14 years who had been training 25 to 35 mi per week for 1 year. Mean values for forced vital capacity, maximal voluntary ventilation, FEV_1, and diffusion capacity (resting and exercise) were higher in the athletes than control subjects, but the differences did not reach statistical significance.

Van Huss et al. (1988), studying young elite female runners, found that 22 girls ages 9 to 15 years showed an average $\dot{V}O_2$max of 59.9 ml/kg/min compared to 47.2 ml/kg/min in age-matched nonathletic subjects. For male runners and controls the values were 65.9 and 56.7 ml/kg/min, respectively ($p < .01$). Pooled average values for all athletes indicated lower submaximal blood pressure, lactate level, and heart rate, but there were no significant differences from controls at maximal exercise.

Thoren and Asano (1984) compared physiological findings between the top and bottom five finishers among 481 youth competitors in a 1,700-m run. The highest finishers had been in training for an average of 4 years for males and 2-1/2 years for females, 2 to 10 km for two to three sessions weekly. The lowest finishers had not been in running training. $\dot{V}O_2$max was greater in the trained children (51.4 vs. 39.2 ml/kg/min for the boys and 54.5 vs. 41.2 ml/kg/min for the girls). Resting heart rates were lower and stroke volumes higher in both male and female trained subjects, but no differences in heart rates and stroke volumes were noted between trained and untrained subjects during submaximal cycle exercise. Resting and exercise blood pressure levels were similar in the runners and controls, as were resting pulmonary function tests (vital capacity, maximal voluntary ventilation).

Nudel et al. (1989) evaluated aerobic power in 10 boys and 6 girls ages 8 to 17 years who had been training for 3 to 5 years an average of 30 to 105 mi per week; seven subjects had completed marathons. Average $\dot{V}O_2$max was 61.0 ml/kg/min in the runners compared to 43.2 in the nontraining controls.

Other Athletes

Andrew, Becklake, Guleria, and Bates (1972) showed that trained prepubertal swimmers exhibited greater vital capacity, FEV_1, and diffusion capacity (related to height) than nontrained controls. Yost, Zauner, and Jaeger (1981) could not find any differences in forced vital capacity in 9- to 17-year-old competitive swimmers compared to controls, although diffusion capacity was greater at rest and during exercise in the swimmers. Bloomfield, Blanksby, Beard, Ackland, and Elliott (1984) reported no significant differences in resting lung function tests in 112 swimmers and 65 tennis players ages 7 to 12 years and control subjects. Schmucker and Hollman (1974) reported no significant difference in maximal aerobic power during cycle exercise testing of 10 male trained swimmers ages 6 to 11 years compared to untrained controls (48.3 and 47.5 ml/kg/min, respectively).

Maximal aerobic power during treadmill testing of small groups of elite prepubertal tennis players was reported in two studies that did not include nonathletic subjects for comparison. Carlson and Cera (1984) described $\dot{V}O_2$max values of 60.3 and 52.3 ml/kg/min in males and females, respectively, comparable to levels of 56.3 and 52.6 ml/kg/min reported by Buti, Elliott, and Morton (1984).

Gratas, Dassonville, Beillot, and Rochcongar (1988) compared ventilatory responses to exercise in 14 prepubertal trained boys (who participated in football, cycling, swimming, and ice skating) to responses of untrained subjects. Mean $\dot{V}O_2$max during cycle testing was 49.4 ml/kg/min in the athletes and 41.3 ml/kg/min in the controls. Average values for ventilation, ventilatory equivalent for oxygen, and breathing frequency were significantly lower for the trained boys at all absolute work levels, whereas tidal volumes were greater. Anaerobic threshold (by ventilatory parameters) was 70% of $\dot{V}O_2$max for both groups.

Hamilton and Andrew (1976) measured oxygen uptake, heart rate, and cardiac output (by CO_2 rebreathing) during submaximal cycle exercise in 12 trained 12-year-old hockey players. At identical work loads, the athletes and nonathlete control subjects demonstrated no differences in heart rate or stroke volume. Likewise, no differences in lung volumes, flow rates, or diffusion capacity were detected. Cunningham, Telford, and Swart (1976) reported a mean $\dot{V}O_2$max value of 56.6 ml/kg/min in 15 boys ages 9 to 10 years who had been involved in competitive hockey for an average of 4.4 years.

Hakkinen, Mero, and Kauhanen (1989) compared physiological profiles of prepubertal (ages 11 to 13 years) runners, sprinters, weight lifters, and controls; in this study there were only four subjects in each group. The runners exhibited significantly greater $\dot{V}O_2$max during treadmill testing than the other subjects (66.5 ml/kg/min), and the weight lifters were able to generate greater maximal isometric force with testing of leg extensor muscles. No significant differences were observed in explosive performance (vertical jump) among the three groups of athletes.

In summary, although far from comprehensive, these data appear to indicate that the physiological profile of competitive prepubertal athletes is similar to that of adult athletes when compared to nonathletic subjects. Most specifically, maximal aerobic power is significantly greater in child endurance athletes than in their nontraining peers, reflecting superior cardiovascular functional capacity.

Some information suggests, however, that these athlete-nonathlete differences may be quantitatively less in the pediatric population. For instance, elite male prepubertal distance runners show $\dot{V}O_2$max levels of 60 to 65 ml/kg/min, compared to mean normal values of about 50 ml/kg/min for this age. In young adults, on the other hand, world-class marathon runners and cross-country skiers can exhibit $\dot{V}O_2$max levels of 70 to 80 ml/kg/min, whereas the norm for a sedentary male is approximately 45 ml/kg/min. Possibly, failure of the child athlete to reach the level of physiological adaptation observed in the adult elite athlete can be explained by a longer period of training for the adult athlete, impaired ability of the prepubertal athlete to improve aerobic function, or a "weeding out" over time of young athletes with lower fitness capacities.

Likewise, several explanations can be offered for the "improved" physiological profile of prepubertal athletes compared to their nontraining peers: Prepubertal athletes are developmentally advanced compared to nonathletes, prepubertal athletes have benefited from a true fitness effect through training, or child athletes possess the genetic capacity for superior aerobic fitness. Current research information allows little insight into the relative contribution of these factors.

Physiological Risks of Early Intensive Training

What evidence is available to indicate that excessive physical training creates unacceptable physiological insult to the growing child? In this context, *unacceptable* implies impairment of normal biological maturation that may have long-range consequences. The list of potential problems is long, yet the body of research examining the reality of these concerns is small. At the same time, the need to provide safe training guidelines for young competitors is increasing. The following sections outline the current understanding of the physiological risks incurred by intensive training regimens in the growing child.

Cardiac Stress

Concern that extremes of physical activity might adversely tax the cardiovascular system probably began with Pheidippides, who keeled over dead in 490 B.C. after running 175 mi to carry the news of the Greeks' victory over the Persians on the plain of Marathon. (His final words, "Rejoice, we conquer," provide little clue, however, as to the mechanism of his demise.)

Animal research does provide credence to the concept of exercise-induced cardiac damage. When rats are exercised to exhaustion, histological examination of ventricular muscle indicates extensive mitochondrial injury, with swelling and disruption of cristae (King & Gollnick, 1970; Sugimoto, Allison, & Guyton, 1973). These changes appear to be rapidly reversible, however, and usually disappear altogether within 24 hr. Maher et al. (1972) investigated the functional implications of these morphological alterations, reporting that isolated cardiac muscle of rats exhausted by exercise, compared to hearts of control animals, demonstrated reduced peak isometric tension, diminished velocity of shortening, and depressed development of isometric tension in response to exogenous norepinephrine.

The nature and temporal aspects of these findings bear an interesting parallel to certain echocardiographic features observed in human adult endurance athletes after extended competition (Raven & Stevens, 1988). Niemela, Palatsi, Ikaheimo, Takkunen, and Vuori (1984) studied 13 experienced ultramarathoners before and after an uninterrupted competitive 24-hr run. Resting left ventricular end diastolic dimension (LVED) decreased by 7%, with a fall in shortening fraction from 38 to 32%. Mean velocity of circumferential fiber shortening declined by 9%. No electrocardiographic abnormalities were observed, and echocardiographic changes resolved by 2 to 3 days after the race. Similar echocardiographic features suggesting a rapidly reversible impairment of resting left ventricular function from extreme exercise have been reported by others (Seals et al., 1988). These alterations may at least be partially explained by changes in hydration status (preload); they are not accompanied by electrocardiographic changes, acidosis, or abnormalities in concentrations of serum electrolytes. As Douglas, O'Toole, Hiller, Hackney, and Reichek (1987) pointed out, the results of these studies "suggest that irreversible cardiac injury is insignificant, if indeed it is present at all" (p. 1210). Such echocardiographic studies have not yet been performed with prepubertal athletes.

Several reports have indicated a rise in both total serum creatine kinase (CK) and proportion of CK–MB isoenzyme, a traditional marker of myocardial ischemia, following distance events by adult competitive runners. Early concerns that these observations indicate cardiac stress with exercise have been dispelled by the findings of normal myocardial scintigrams and electrocardiograms in these athletes (Siegel, Silverman, & Holman, 1981). It appears that trained skeletal muscle is the source of elevated postexercise serum CK-MB activity.

Kabara and Morris (1988) could find no significant differences in resting total CK between elite runners, wrestlers, and nonathletes ages 9-18 years. In a few cases CK-MB was present. In a study of active but untrained prepubertal boys, total CK rose in response to a 30-min downhill treadmill run, but no CK-MB was detected (Webber, Byrnes, Rowland, & Foster, 1989).

Highly trained adult athletes exhibit a constellation of clinical cardiac findings collectively termed the "athlete's heart" (Douglas, 1989; Rost & Hollman, 1983). These characteristics, which include resting bradycardia, cardiomegaly, soft systolic murmur, electrocardiographic signs of ventricular enlargement, and echocardiographic changes, presumably reflect the physiological consequences of long-term training. It is therefore pertinent to determine if these features are evident in prepubertal athletes and to examine the implications of these findings for long-term health.

Echocardiographic features of the "athlete's heart" in the adult have been extensively studied, and several excellent reviews are available (Maron, 1986; Rost & Hollman, 1983). Dimensions of cardiac chambers are usually significantly greater than those of nonathletes. It is important to note, however, that the differences between cardiac dimensions for athletes and nonathletes are usually small, and values for athletic subjects rarely exceed the normal range. For instance, the mean LVED value in endurance athletes (swimmers, runners) is typically 54 to 56 mm, compared to an expected value in the nonathlete of about 46 mm. Even the largest dimensions reported in athletes (about 60 mm) are much less than dimensions of patients with significant left ventricular disease. The thickness of the ventricular septum (VS) and left ventricular posterior wall (LVPW) is also often greater in athletes (particularly those involved in weight training), but again these values are usually within normal range and are typically only 14% to 19% greater than those of sedentary subjects.

There is no clear evidence that physiological cardiac findings reflected as the "athlete's heart" are detrimental to long-term health (Crawford & O'Rourke, 1979). Sudden cardiac death occurs in athletes of all ages but can almost always be traced to underlying congenital or acquired heart disease. Features of the "athlete's heart" regress if training is discontinued but persist if training is continued through the middle adult years. Longevity studies of athletes have shown neither a consistent increase nor decrease in life span.

Several studies have addressed the "athlete's heart" in prepubertal athletes. Clinically, Rowland, Delaney, and Siconolfi (1987) could find no auscultatory or electrocardiographic differences between trained prepubertal swimmers and nonathletic control subjects, although the mean resting heart rate was significantly lower in the swimmers. The electrocardiograms of the child distance runners described by Nudel et al. (1989) were all normal as well.

Table 6.1 outlines the studies that have examined resting echocardiographic data in trained prepubertal athletes compared to nontrained control subjects matched for height, weight, body surface area, or fat-free mass. Of the seven studies, five describe a greater mean LVED in athletic subjects (although two studies presented insufficient information to allow statistical comparisons). Among the four studies with data regarding left ventricular end systolic dimension (LVES), only one showed greater values for the athletes. Approximately one-half of the studies indicated greater VS and LVPW thicknesses in the athletic subjects.

Two reports have compared echocardiographic findings in young athletes with literature-based control data. The 17 10- to 11-year-old distance and sprint runners described by Tharp, Thorland, Johnson, and Peter (1986) had a mean LVED of 41 mm (compared to an expected value of 39 mm reported by Henry et al., 1978), whereas measurements of VS and LVPW were actually slightly less than published norms. Allen, Goldberg, Sahn, Schy, and Wojcik (1977) found no difference in mean LVED in 77 trained swimmers (ages 5 to 17) from the norms of Henry et al. (1987), although the athletes' heart walls were thicker. Echocardiographic data displayed an unusually wide scatter in this study (39% of subjects had an LVED less than the 5th percentile and 38% were over the 95th percentile).

In the only echocardiographic study of nonendurance prepubertal athletes, Bassett, Ruttenburg, Johnson, and Sands (1990) found no difference in LVED or LVPW between 15 highly trained female gymnasts (ages 7 to 12) and active controls, but VS was significantly greater in the gymnasts.

Rost, Gerhardus, and Schmidt (1985) reported longitudinal data on prepubertal athletes. They studied 36 children age 10 years at the beginning of an intensive swim training program. After 2 years of training, differences in LVED and LVPW became significant between the trained children and controls, and these differences increased during a 3rd year of training. No abnormalities of cardiac function were observed during the course of this study, except for one swimmer who demonstrated a progressive decrease in LVED, significant increase in LVPW, and electrocardiographic findings of Wenckebach phenomenon.

In summary, these studies appear to indicate that echocardiographic findings indicating "athlete's heart" are not unexpected in the endurance prepubertal athlete. This conclusion is in accord with echocardiographic studies of untrained children that demonstrate a close association between $\dot{V}O_2$max and LVED, LVPW, resting stroke volume, and calculated left ventricular mass (Blimkie, Cunningham, & Nichol, 1980; deKnecht, Saris, Daniels, Elvers, & deBoo, 1984). Whether the presence of the "athlete's heart" in the child reflects a training effect or hereditary predisposition (or both) has not been clarified. Limited evaluation has failed to reveal evidence of electrocardiographic changes in prepubertal athletes other than resting bradycardia. Except for possibly

Table 6.1 Echocardiographic Findings in Child Athletes

Study	Subjects (N)	Sport	Age (yrs)	LVED (cm) Athletes	LVED (cm) Non-athletes		LVES (cm) Athletes	LVES (cm) Non-athletes		VS (cm) Athletes	VS (cm) Non-athletes		LVPW (cm) Athletes	LVPW (cm) Non-athletes	
Telford et al. (1988)	48	Running	11-12	4.66	4.59	NS	2.98	2.98	NS	—	—		.76	.74	NS
	37	Other	11-12	4.57	4.55	NS	2.88	2.95	NS	—	—		.74	.72	NS
Nudel et al. (1989)	5	Running	8-12	4.44	4.01	?	—	—		—	—		—	—	?
Shepherd et al. (1988)	13	Running	5-12	4.10	4.10	NS	2.6	2.7	NS				.62	.55	*
Medved et al. (1986)	72	Swimming	8-14	4.08	3.65	*	—	—		.73	.69	NS	.68	.63	NS
				4.34	3.99	*	—	—		.79	.75	NS	.71	.62	*
				4.52	4.25	*	—	—		.82	.85	NS	.77	.81	NS
				5.28	4.48	*	—	—		.99	.82	*	.89	.74	*
Rowland et al. (1987)	14	Swimming	8-13	3.95	3.62	*	2.39	2.32	NS	.71	.65	*	.68	.62	*
Gutin et al. (1988)	11	Running	6-14	4.32	4.10	*	2.77	2.56	*	.66	.69	NS	.63	.67	NS
Rost et al. (1985)	36	Swimming	6-10	4.1	3.9	?	—	—		—	—		.7	.6	?

Note. All measurements are related to body size (body surface, weight, or fat-free mass). LVED = left ventricular end diastolic dimension; LVES = left ventricular end systolic dimension; VS = ventricular septum; LVPW = left ventricular posterior wall; NS = nonsignificant difference (p > .05), athletes vs. nonathletes.

*p < .05.

the case reported by Rost et al. (1985), there is no published evidence of adverse cardiac effects of exercise training in childhood in the absence of underlying heart disease.

Stresses on Other Systems

Measurements of pulmonary function in adult athletes following prolonged distance running have suggested that these types of events increase airway closure at high lung volumes (Rasmussen, Elkjaer, & Juhl, 1988). Reduced vital capacity, increased residual lung volume, decreased diffusing capacity, and diminished expiratory flow rates are frequently observed in adult runners following marathon races, with resolution to normal within 24 hr (Maron, Hamilton, & Maksud, 1979). Dempsey, Aaron, and Martin (1988) suggested that peribronchiolar edema, contraction of bronchiolar smooth muscle, or both, might be responsible for these changes. Whether prepubertal athletes exhibit similar alterations in pulmonary function with competition has not been evaluated.

Mahlamaki, Pekkarinen, Partanen, and Michelsson (1989) could find no differences in neurological findings on physical examination of the lower extremities between 233 young cross-country skiers ages 10 to 14 years and 208 controls.

No data are available regarding changes in child athletes' nonexercising organ systems, which generally experience diminished blood flow during exercise. Gastrointestinal disturbances are common in adult athletes, particularly distance runners, who often suffer from abdominal cramping, diarrhea, blood in the stools, and heartburn. Intestinal ischemia from splanchnic vasoconstriction, increases in gastrointestinal peptides, or both may be responsible. Adult athletes also not uncommonly demonstrate transient proteinuria and hematuria, perhaps related to renal vasoconstriction (Eichner, 1988).

The absence of published reports of renal or gastrointestinal complications in child athletes is reassuring; however, the risk of damage from chronic recurrent reduction in vascular supply to these organs during growth is unknown.

Skeletal Damage

Musculoskeletal stress imposed by exercise stimulates bone growth; conversely, a period of immobility depresses bone development (Loucks, 1988). Yet there are limits to such "positive" stress, beyond which growth processes may be impaired. Consequently, any adverse effects of intensive training during childhood that interfere with normal biological maturation might be most readily recognized by evidence of skeletal damage and retardation of linear growth. In fact, several lines of evidence suggest that early vigorous sport training and competition have the potential to adversely affect the growth of child athletes.

Growth Plate Vulnerability. The growth centers of long bones, or epiphyseal plates, are soft areas that are particularly susceptible to traumatic injury. It has been estimated that the growth plate of the child athlete may be two to five times weaker than surrounding supporting tissues (Maffulli & Helms, 1988); acute trauma to these areas that might cause ligamentous injury in an adult may produce more serious epiphyseal plate fractures in the child. These fractures resulting from *macrotrauma* (such as a blow to the knee) have the potential for retarding limb growth and may lead to bone deformity and chronic joint disease.

Most athletic training regimens do not involve high risk for macrotraumatic injury but are more often characterized by *microtrauma*, smaller but repetitive compressive forces to growth plates. The key question is whether repetitive microtrauma—the 7,500 footstrikes in a typical 10-mi run, repeated several times a week—can translate into the same kinds of damage to leg bone growth centers as a single blow that causes an epiphyseal fracture.

Recognized effects of exercise stress on skeletal development in animals have fueled concerns regarding training in children (Apple, 1985; Borms, 1986). It has been observed since the mid-1800s that epiphyseal plates do not tolerate extreme levels of compression well (Arkin & Katz, 1956; Strobino, French, & Colonna, 1952). Complete arrest of growth is achieved with epiphyseal stapling in both animals and humans, and lesser degrees of compression also compromise bone development in dogs and rats (Blount & Clarke, 1949). This presumably explains the finding that prolonged exercise training in animals shortens their long bones.

Given this premise for concern, is there actual clinical evidence for disturbances of epiphyseal plates in prepubertal athletes? Caine (1990) comprehensively reviewed reports of growth plate injuries from physical activity in children. The most frequently cited reference involved child laborers rather than athletes. In 1966 Kato and Ishiko described premature closure of the proximal tibial and distal femoral epiphyses in 116 young Japanese children (out of 4,000) who carried heavy loads on their shoulders. Whether these changes resulted entirely from excessive forces applied to growth centers is unclear, however, because the children lived in an economically and nutritionally deprived area of Japan.

In two sports, baseball pitching and gymnastics, chronic stress-related damage has been well documented in young athletes. Although in neither case is stature affected, such bone damage may interrupt or even terminate athletic competition.

Degenerative and inflammatory changes in the elbows of pitchers have been termed "Little League elbow" (Micheli & Smith, 1982). These alterations include medial epicondylitis with partial or complete avulsion, osteochondral injuries to the capitellum and subchondral bone of the capitellum, and premature arrest of the proximal radial epiphysis. Such injuries result from the repetitive valgus strain of overhand throwing, which can presumably be prevented by training limitations. Most athletes recover after a short period of rest and rehabilitative exercises, although in some cases disability may continue for extended periods of time.

Caine (1990) described 11 reports in the literature that indicate the potential for epiphyseal damage, caused by intensive training, in the wrists of young competitive gymnasts ages 11 to 21 years. Included are examples of widening, "beaking," and stress fractures of the distal radial epiphysis; shortening of the radius compared to the ulna; and rarefaction of wrist bones. The true frequency of these changes is unknown. Epidemiological studies have indicated a very low prevalence of abnormalities of the distal radius in young gymnasts. Caine (1990) pointed out that the athletes involved in these epidemiological studies were training at lower levels of intensity than those in the articles cited.

Intensively training gymnasts may also be at increased risk for vertebral compression fractures, pars interarticularis defects, and degenerative disk disease, although a recent report that used magnetic resonance imaging to assess disk status in 35 competitive gymnasts ages 8 to 19 years is reassuring. Only three had evidence of disk degeneration, and in two of these cases the abnormal findings were related to congenital bony anomalies in the lumbosacral region (Tertti et al., 1990).

Epiphyseal overuse injuries in child athletes involved in other sports have not been reported. Particularly interesting is the absence of published descriptions of such injuries in prepubertal distance runners. Godshall, Hansen, and Rising (1981) reported that running caused stress fractures through the distal femoral epiphysis in two teenagers, one a 220-lb football player trying to reduce weight in preseason training and the other a 14-year-old basketball player. Cahill (1977) described a 15-year-old cross-country runner who developed a stress fracture of the proximal tibial epiphysis after running 40 to 50 mi per week for 2 months.

The incidence of overuse running injuries in children and adolescents appears to be at least as high as that of adults, but large sports medicine clinics report that these injuries have not involved epiphyseal growth plates. As Apple (1985) noted,

> If one theorizes about the compressive loading forces that occur with running, one would expect there to be an increased incidence of pressure injuries to the epiphysis as a consequence of extensive long distance running prior to epiphyseal closure. Such has not been the case. At the present time, until further evidence is forthcoming, there does not seem to be any adverse effect to pressure on epiphyses induced by running. (p. 645)

Training and Growth Hormone. Given that normal growth of children is related to plasma levels of both growth hormone and somatomedin, it is important to examine the effects of exercise training on these growth-stimulating factors. Acute bouts of exercise stimulate the secretion of growth hormone at all ages (Amirov et al., 1990). In adults, this response is greater in unfit compared to fit athletes at a given exercise load, but the two groups have equal growth hormone responses at the same relative exercise intensity (percent $\dot{V}O_2max$) (Sutton & Farrell, 1988). Carli et al. (1983) demonstrated that resting plasma levels of growth hormone were not affected by swim training of boys ages 12 to 16 years.

There is evidence that strenuous exercise in individuals with suboptimal nutritional habits can diminish plasma somatomedin levels. Smith, Clemmons, Underwood, Ben-Ezra, and McMurray (1987) reported somatomedin values in six healthy males ages 20 to 31 years who were studied during 1-week blocks of dietary restriction, exercise training (with a limit on caloric intake such that a negative nitrogen balance was achieved), and control. During the exercise training phase, mean plasma somatomedin level fell from 1.15 U/ml to 0.62 U/ml, similar to that observed during dietary restriction. This effect was felt by the authors to be secondary to an insufficient supply of nutrients to meet the augmented caloric expenditure of exercise training. The authors concluded from these findings that proper nutrition during athletic training might be particularly important in growing children.

Reassuring in this regard was the report of Denison and Ben-Ezra (1989) of somatomedin-C levels in 8- to 10-year-old trained swimmers. These athletes consumed an average of 2,301 kcal per day compared to 2,072 kcal by nontraining controls. Both groups ate an average of twice the daily recommended intake for protein for this age group. The mean plasma somatomedin-C level among the 37 swimmers was 1.39 U/ml, with an average of 0.91 in the control subjects. These values were significantly different, but both were within the normal range for age.

Growth Studies. Considering the potential risk of stress-induced skeletal damage and variations in growth-stimulating hormones, do linear growth and skeletal maturation deviate from the norm in prepubertal and adolescent athletes? The many cross-sectional and short-term longitudinal studies examining this question in a wide variety of sports have been extensively reviewed (Bailey, Malina, & Rasmussen, 1978; Broekhoff, 1986; Malina, 1989; Malina, Meleski, & Shoup, 1982). The conclusion is that regular athletic training has no apparent effect on growth and skeletal maturation in children. Variations are observed, as expected, according to sex and sport. For instance, advanced skeletal maturation is typical of male athletes in sports such as baseball, basketball, football, and swimming. Girls who participate in track, gymnastics, and ballet are usually delayed in skeletal maturity. There is no convincing evidence that athletic training during the growing years either accelerates or retards stature or skeletal maturity.

Recent studies of intensely training prepubertal athletes support this conclusion. The 10 distance runners ages 8 to 17 years studied by Nudel et al. (1989) had been training for an average of 8.4 years, with a current weekly mileage of 30 to 105 mi per week; seven runners had completed marathons. Radiological determination of bone age indicated no evidence of delayed bone maturation. Growth percentiles were normal, as were predicted heights compared to parental heights.

Seefeldt, Haubenstricker, Branta, and Evans (1988) evaluated rates of growth over a 2-year period of 32 trained runners ages 9 to 15 years and found no differences in standing height, sitting height, biacromial diameter, biiliac diameter, and sum of three skin folds, compared to nontraining youths. The authors concluded that ''a review of the scientific literature provides little evidence that long-distance running is detrimental to children's growth'' (p. 247). Conversely, neither does it give firm assurance that these intensive training regimens are entirely harmless, considering (a) the recognized vulnerability of growth plates to repetitive stress, (b) the high incidence of overuse injuries in young athletes, indicative of the effects of repetitive microtrauma on the musculoskeletal system, and (3) the total absence of any long-term evaluation of the ultimate skeletal consequences of intensive training in the prepubertal years.

Adverse Effects on Sexual Development

The observation that onset of menstruation (menarche) is often delayed in competitive young athletes has raised concern that training may adversely affect sexual development and reproductive function. The average age of menarche in healthy North American girls is 12.3 to 12.8 years, and most studies indicate that athletic females experience onset of menses at age 13 to 14 years or even later (Rogol, 1988). Such delays have been consistently found in most sports; swimming was once felt to be the exception, but recent information indicates that swimmers also may experience delayed menarche as well (Wells & Plowman, 1988). Frisch (1987) suggested that the age of menarche is related to the number of years of training prior to onset of menses. Her study indicated that on the average, a .4-year delay in menarche can be expected for each year of prepubertal training.

Whether delayed menarche in athletes is truly a direct consequence of training remains controversial. Frisch and Revelle (1971) proposed that intense exercise prior to puberty creates energy loss, thereby preventing girls from reaching a critical body weight or fat content necessary to trigger onset of menses. According to this concept, a critical weight (48 kg) or percent body fat (17%) is required before menarche can be achieved, and the effects of training prevent or delay the athlete from reaching these thresholds. The experimental methodology used to reach these conclusions has been criticized, and the concept of a critical fat or weight for onset of menses remains in doubt (Scott & Johnston, 1982). However, data support the role of changes in body composition and exercise stress in delaying menarche (Vanderbroucke, van Laar, & Valkenburg, 1983).

Alternatively, Malina (1983) argued that girls with delayed menarche are more likely to engage in sport. Girls with delayed puberty typically have narrow hips, slender physiques, long legs, and low body fat, characteristics that prove advantageous in sports such as ballet, running, and gymnastics. According to this concept, the observed association between delayed menarche and athletic training does not indicate a causal relationship; rather, the training-delayed menarche relationship is the result of a selective process. Competitors with delayed onset of menses possess a body habitus that allows them to be more successful in sports.

Questions of etiology aside, does delayed menarche present risks to young athletes? Late onset of menses may be accompanied by low levels of circulating estrogen, which can result in impaired development of bone density. However, this effect is not appreciable if menarche occurs before 18 years of age (Shangold, 1986). Long-term effects of delayed menarche on reproductive function have not been well evaluated, but anecdotal information and limited research data have failed to indicate any negative influence on ultimate fertility (Eriksson, Engstrom, & Lundin, 1978). At the present time, then, there are no clear-cut reasons for withholding prepubertal girls from intensive athletic training because of concerns over effects on future reproductive function.

Little information is available on sexual development in athletic boys. Cross-sectional studies of young male competitors have indicated no evidence of disturbed achievement of secondary sexual characteristics. Rowland, Morris, Kelleher, Haag, and Reiter (1987) described no changes in serum testosterone levels in 15 adolescent postpubertal male cross-country runners during the course of an 8-week competitive season. Low serum testosterone levels have been reported, however, in adult runners who trained at least 40 mi per week (Wheeler, Wall, Belcastro, & Cumming, 1984).

Hyperthermia

Research information suggests that prepubertal athletes may be at greater risk for heat stress injuries than adults. Bar-Or (1980) described several features that may predispose children to hyperthermia during athletic competition, particularly in warm, humid climates. Children produce more heat per unit of body mass at both maximal and submaximal levels of exercise than adults and demonstrate a lower cardiac output at a given oxygen uptake. This may interfere with skin perfusion and limit convection and radiation heat loss. Children sweat less than adults, a manifestation of diminished rates of sweat gland production; in hot environments, sweating may amount to 60 to 70% of adult production. Also, children are less able to acclimatize to a new warm environment (i.e., to achieve reduced heart rate and core temperature and increased sweating rates) than adults. These limitations in children appear to be significant, given that prepubertal subjects have been reported to be impaired in their abilities to exercise in a hot environment compared to adults.

The actual risk of hyperthermic disease (heat exhaustion, heat stroke) in children is unknown. Anecdotally, there have been no reports that heat stress injury is more common in prepubertal competitors than in adults. Also, studies of thermic responses to exercise in children have all involved nontrained subjects. Whether child athletes possess the same limitations of response to exercise in the heat as nonathletes is not known. Nonetheless, young athletes should be provided guidelines to prevent heat injuries (e.g., ensure adequate fluid replacement, avoid competing in hot, humid weather).

Susceptibility to Infection

There is growing recognition that physical training can affect immunologic function, but the nature of these responses and their relevance to clinical susceptibility to infection is unclear (Calabrese, 1990). Animal studies have produced conflicting results; increased antibody titers, T-lymphocyte hyporesponsiveness, and depletion of splenic lymphocytes have all been described in mice after a period of treadmill running training. In humans, a study of adult marathon runners showed no abnormalities of blood counts, T-cell numbers, phagocytic function, or levels of complement and immunoglobulins (Gren, Kaplan, Rabin, Stanitski, & Zdziarski, 1981). However, Soppi, Varjo, Eskola, and Laitinen (1982) reported a decreased ability to mobilize immunocompetent cells with exercise stress after a 6-week training program involving nonathletic men.

The commonly held assumption that athletes tend to be more resistant to infection has no research support. In fact, some data suggest quite the contrary. Exercising animals, for instance, can suffer increased severity of certain viral infections (poliomyelitis, myocarditis). And Douglas and Hanson (1978) reported that members of a rowing team experienced more frequent and prolonged viral upper respiratory infections than a group of nonathletic control subjects.

Osterback and Qvarnberg (1987) provided the only information on child athletes' susceptibility to infection. They studied a group of 12-year-old swimmers, hockey players, and gymnasts and compared their incidence of respiratory infections, antimicrobial treatment, days with fever, and absence from school to that of nonathletic controls. No differences between the athletes and control groups were observed in any of these parameters.

Poor Nutrition

Proper nutrition during childhood is essential for all phases of physical and mental growth. Inadequate dietary practices and the effect of training on nutrient requirements may therefore create health risks for the child athlete. This chapter has cited evidence suggesting that inadequate caloric intake during training might affect somatomedin levels. It is well recognized that athletes in certain sports (wrestling, gymnastics, ballet) limit nutrient intake in efforts to improve performance or gain competitive advantages. Such caloric restriction may instead result in muscle weakness, diminished bone density, calcium loss, iron deficiency, and menstrual irregularities.

Little information is available regarding iron status in prepubertal athletes, but progressive iron depletion caused by training, particularly distance running, is not uncommon in adolescent competitors (Rowland, Black, & Kelleher, 1987). Iron needs are particularly high during the growing years, and deficiencies may influence not only hematopoietic but also cognitive, gastrointestinal, and immunologic functions. An iron-rich diet may therefore be particularly important for child and adolescent athletes.

Inadequate dietary intake of other minerals is also common in young athletes. Benardot, Schwarz, and Heller (1989) found that of 29 7- to 10-year-old junior elite gymnasts, 50% had deficient calcium intakes and 38% had inadequate iron intakes. Schemmel, Ryder, Moeggenberg, and Conn (1988) compared nutrient intakes of 74 elite wrestlers and runners, ages 8 to 15 years, using a 3-day food diary. Both groups consumed twice the recommended daily amount of protein, and low mineral intakes were common. Half of the athletes in each group consumed less than 67% of the RDA for zinc, whereas approximately a third were similarly deficient in magnesium, iron, and iodine intake. These observations are probably not unique to athletes, however. Conn et al. (1988) reported that dietary consumption and serum levels of magnesium were not significantly different in 22 competitive prepubertal swimmers ages 9 to 12 years and control subjects.

Benefits of Intensive Training in Prepubertal Athletes

Considering the extensive commitments paid to the development of young athletes it is surprising that little research has specifically addressed the benefits of early training regimens. A paucity of information is available to document the physiological and performance improvements gained from such training, and there has been only a limited investigation of potential positive effects of early competition on health.

Physiological and Performance Gains

Daniels and Oldridge (1971) studied physiological changes in 14 boys ages 10 to 15 years in the course of a 22-month period of steady running training. Most of the subjects had been involved in previous running activities. Although absolute level of $\dot{V}O_2max$ improved 22% during the training period, maximal aerobic power per kilogram of body weight remained unchanged (about 59 ml/kg/min). Submaximal $\dot{V}O_2/kg$ (running economy) steadily decreased, but only in those boys who trained less than 750 mi per year. Race times improved over 13 months, an average of 32 s in the mile and 63 s over 2 mi.

These findings appear to indicate that training of young athletes may not improve maximal oxygen delivery more than that resulting from growth alone, yet gains in performance can be expected. However, nontraining controls were not included in this study. Testing of untrained boys in the American Alliance for Health, Physical Education, Recreation and Dance Health Related Physical Fitness Test (1980) indicated an average yearly decrease of 40 s in 1-mi run times between the ages of 8 and 12 years (greater than the improvement observed by Daniels and Oldridge in their trained subjects).

Van Huss et al. (1988) studied maximal aerobic power longitudinally in 42 elite runners ages 9 to 15 years over a 3-year period and found similar results. No significant improvements in $\dot{V}O_2max/kg$ were observed in either boys or girls (mean initial values 65.9 and 54.9 ml/kg/min, respectively). Clarke, Vaccaro, and Andresen (1985) described gains in muscle strength after 3 months of wrestling training of 7- to 9-year-old subjects but no found improvements in maximal aerobic power compared to controls.

Hakkinen et al. (1989) examined the effects of 1 year's training by prepubertal runners, sprinters, weight lifters (four in each group), and control subjects. $\dot{V}O_2max/kg$ on treadmill testing did not change significantly during the 12 months in any of the groups. Significant improvement in maximal isometric force (+21.4%) was observed only in the weight lifters.

Other studies have indicated improvements in weight-related $\dot{V}O_2max$ with training of child athletes. Paterson, McLellan, Stella, and Cunningham (1987) demonstrated a progressive yearly rise in mean $\dot{V}O_2max$ from 62.3 to 67.3 ml/

kg/min in 18 athletic boys during the 3 years prior to the age of peak height velocity. Brown, Harrower, and Deeter (1972) reported increased $\dot{V}O_2max/kg$ of 18.5% by 6 weeks of running training in nine preadolescent girls and 26.2% by 12 weeks. Although these girls were recruited from track clubs, average $\dot{V}O_2max$ at the beginning of the study was only 46.3 ml/kg/min.

There is little information available regarding the effect of training on skill and performance outcomes in athletic children. MacNab (1979) compared performance markers in 15 highly trained hockey players and controls for 5 years beginning at age 8 years. Skating and puck skills were significantly better in the trained skaters, but their rates of change with increasing age appeared to parallel those of control subjects. Likewise, performances on sit-ups, 50-yd dash, flexed arm hang, broad jump, and 300-yd run were superior in the trained players, but their rates of improvement with age were not greater than those of the controls.

Based on these scant experimental data, it is unclear whether training of highly fit endurance prepubertal athletes can improve maximal aerobic power beyond improvements caused by growth alone. Failure to demonstrate such gains might reflect the observation that adults' gains in $\dot{V}O_2max$ with training are inversely related to pretraining fitness levels. However, we cannot exclude the possibility that prepubertal subjects have a diminished capacity for improving aerobic power.

The extent to which endurance performance can be improved in child athletes through intensive training—a question of greater interest to the athlete—is unknown. Studies indicating improved strength following resistance training in prepubertal subjects suggest that performance in sports involving muscle strength might improve following such a training regimen (Kraemer, Fry, Frykman, Conray, & Hoffman, 1989).

Reduced Coronary Artery Disease Risk Factors

Given that regular exercise appears to reduce risk factors for adult coronary artery disease, we might expect that athletes would similarly benefit from physical training. In fact, cross-sectional studies have indicated that prepubertal athletes possess a favorable lipoprotein profile in respect to risk for future atherosclerosis (Atomi, Kuroda, Asami, & Kawahara, 1986; Smith, Metheny, Van Huss, Seefeldt, & Sparrow, 1983; Smith, Sparrow, Heusner, Van Huss, & Conn, 1985; Valimaki, Hursti, Pihlakosk, & Viikari, 1980; Zonderland et al., 1988). All five such reports—involving track athletes, runners, swimmers, and soccer players—show higher levels of HDL-C in young competitors compared to nonathletic children (Table 6.2). Consistent differences in other serum lipids have not been observed. No studies have examined the effects of training by child athletes on serum lipids, however, so it is not certain to what extent the favorable elevated HDL-C levels reflect participation in athletics per se. In nonathletic children exercise training has produced few changes in lipid values (Rowland, 1990).

Both cross-sectional and longitudinal studies indicate that most groups of prepubertal athletes, both males and females, have lower percent body fat than

Table 6.2   Serum Lipoproteins in Trained Prepubertal Athletes

Study	Sport	Subjects (N)	Sex	Age (years)	Total cholesterol	HDL-C	LDL-C	Triglycerides
Zonderland et al. (1988)	Swimming	21	F	12	0	+	0	0
	Gymnastics	25	F	12	0	0	0	0
Smith et al. (1983)	Running	28	M & F	10-15	0	+	0	-
Smith et al. (1985)	Swimming	18	M & F	9-12	0	+	-	0
Atomi et al. (1986)	Soccer	21	M	12	+	+	*	0
Valimaki et al. (1980)	Track	9	M	11-13	0	+	0	0
		7	F	11-13	0	+	0	-

Note. Plus sign = increased compared to nontraining controls; zero = no difference from controls; minus sign = decreased compared to controls. HDL-C = high-density lipoprotein cholesterol; LDL-C = low-density lipoprotein cholesterol; asterisk = no LDL-C reported.

nonathletic children (Bailey et al., 1978; Daniels & Oldrige, 1971; Thoren & Asano, 1984). Whether prepubertal athletes have resting blood pressures that vary from the norm is uncertain. When compared to nonathletic controls, child athletes have been reported as having lower (Van Huss et al., 1988), the same (Sundburg & Elovainio, 1982; Thoren & Asano, 1984), or higher (Rowland, Delaney, & Siconolfi, 1987) systolic pressures.

Summary

Major gaps in our understanding of the physiological responses to exercise training in the prepubertal years hamper our ability to offer child athletes guidelines for safe training and competition. However, the available scientific evidence regarding the risks and benefits of early training is, in general, reassuring.

Prepubertal athletes are physiologically different than nonathletic children, and these differences mimic those observed between athletic and sedentary adults, although to a lesser extent. That intensive training truly triggers these physiological adaptations in the child athlete has not been documented. Virtually all information is of cross-sectional nature and fails to differentiate genetically acquired traits from those resulting from a training effect. Likewise, it is not clear to what extent training during the childhood years improves performance outcomes. Verification of a true physiological and performance training effect in child athletes is further complicated by the observation that the changes characteristic of normal biological maturation are similar to those achieved through training.

The potential risks of training stresses on growing children have raised concern, but there is little evidence that developing body systems suffer adverse long-term effects from early intensive training. None of the cardiovascular or pulmonary characteristics of child athletes appear to be detrimental to health; on the contrary, the differences that separate prepubertal athletes from nonathletes appear to reflect superior functional efficiency, which is translated into improved athletic performance. However, overuse injuries to epiphyseal regions of the elbows and wrists of young baseball pitchers and gymnasts, respectively, provide evidence that the potential for damage to growth centers exists.

Recommendations

From a physiological standpoint, based on current information, sport scientists, physicians, and physical educators can give cautious approval to athletic training during the prepubertal years. However, the same data suggest several caveats that we should observe before sanctioning intensive sport participation for children.

1. Child athletes should obtain appropriate medical clearance to ensure that they are free of medical conditions that would pose a health risk during training and competition.

2. All prepubertal athletes should be assessed on an ongoing basis to detect signs of adverse physiological effects (particularly cardiac, growth, musculoskeletal, and body composition) of excessive training.

3. Proper nutrition is important for all athletes but particularly for children, who require adequate diets for normal growth. Athletic participation places additional nutritional demands on the child, and counseling the young competitor in healthy dietary practices is essential.

4. Child athletes should be coached and supervised in their training by individuals who are knowledgeable about proper equipment and training techniques, particularly as they relate to young competitors.

5. The amount of training that might suppress a child's skeletal growth (if this can occur at all) is unknown and presumably varies from child to child. In the absence of direct markers of excessive epiphyseal compression, coaches and trainers must strive to prevent and seek early treatment for soft tissue overuse injuries ("shin splints," tendinitis, etc.), which indicate excessive microtrauma.

References

Allen, H.D., Goldberg, S.J., Sahn, D.J., Schy, N., & Wojcik, R. (1977). A quantitative echocardiographic study of champion childhood swimmers. *Circulation*, **55**, 142-145.

American Alliance for Health, Physical Education, Recreation and Dance. (1980). *Health related physical fitness test manual*. Washington, DC: Author.

Amirov, I., Dowdeswell, R.J., Plit, M., Panz, V.R., Joffe, B.I., & Seftel, H.C. (1990). Growth hormone response to exercise in asthmatic and normal children. *European Journal of Pediatrics*, **149**, 443-446.

Andrew, G.M., Becklake, M.R., Guleria, J.S., & Bates, D.V. (1972). Heart and lung function in swimmers and nonathletes during growth. *Journal of Applied Physiology*, **32**, 245-251.

Apple, D.F. (1985). Adolescent runners. *Clinics in Sports Medicine*, **4**, 641-655.

Arkin, A.M., & Katz, J.F. (1956). The effects of pressure on epiphyseal growth. *Journal of Bone and Joint Surgery*, **38A**, 1056-1076.

Atomi, Y., Kuroda, Y., Asami, J., & Kawahara, T. (1986). HDL_2-cholesterol of children (10 to 12 years of age) related to $\dot{V}O_2$max, body fat, and sex. In J. Rutenfranz, R. Mocellin, & F. Klimt (Eds.), *Children and exercise XII* (pp. 167-172). Champaign, IL: Human Kinetics.

Bailey, D.A., Malina, R.M., & Rasmussen, R.L. (1978). The influence of exercise, physical activity, and athletic performance on the dynamics of human growth. In F. Falkner & J.M. Tanner (Eds.), *Human growth* (pp. 475-505). New York: Plenum Press.

Bailey, D.A., & Mirwald, R.L. (1988). The effects of training on the growth and development of the child. In R.M. Malina (Ed.), *Young athletes: Biological, psychological, and emotional perspectives* (pp. 33-47). Champaign, IL: Human Kinetics.

Bar-Or, O. (1980). Climate and the exercising child—a review. *International Journal of Sports Medicine*, **1**, 53-65.

Bassett, S., Ruttenburg, H., Johnson, S.C., & Sands, W. (1990). Cardiac dimensions of highly trained prepubescent female gymnasts (abstract). *Medicine and Science in Sports and Exercise*, **22**(Suppl.), S101.

Benardot, D., Schwarz, M., & Heller, D.W. (1989). Nutrient intake in young, highly competitive gymnasts. *Journal of the American Dietetics Association*, **89**, 401-403.

Blimkie, C.J.R., Cunningham, D.A., & Nichol, P.M. (1980). Gas transport capacity and echocardiographically determined cardiac size in children. *Journal of Applied Physiology*, **49**, 994-999.

Bloomfield, J., Blanksby, B.A., Beard, D.F., Ackland, T.R., & Elliott, B.C. (1984). Biological characteristics of young swimmers, tennis players, and noncompetitors. *British Journal of Sports Medicine*, **18**, 97-103.

Blount, W.P., & Clarke, G.R. (1949). Control of bone growth by epiphyseal stapling. *Journal of Bone and Joint Surgery*, **31A**, 464-478.

Borms, J. (1986). The child and exercise: An overview. *Journal of Sports Science*, **4**, 3-20.

Bouchard, C. (1986). Genetics of aerobic power and capacity. In R.M. Malina & C. Bouchard (Eds.), *Sport and human genetics* (pp. 55-98). Champaign, IL: Human Kinetics.

Broekhoff, J. (1986). The effect of physical activity on physical growth and development. In G.A. Stull & H.M. Eckert (Eds.), *The effects of physical activity on children* (pp. 75-87). Champaign, IL: Human Kinetics.

Brown, C.H., Harrower, J.R., & Deeter, M.F. (1972). The effects of cross country running on preadolescent girls. *Medicine and Science in Sports and Exercise*, **4**, 1-5.

Buti, T., Elliott, B., & Morton, A. (1984). Physiological and anthropometric profiles of elite prepubescent tennis players. *The Physician and Sportsmedicine*, **12**, 111-116.

Cahill, B.R. (1977). Stress fracture of the proximal tibial epiphysis: A case report. *American Journal of Sports Medicine*, **5**, 86-87.

Caine, D.J. (1990). Growth plate injury and bone growth: An update. *Pediatric Exercise Science*, **2**, 209-229.

Calabrese, L.H. (1990). Exercise, immunity, cancer, and infection. In C. Bouchard, R.J. Shephard, T. Stephens, J.R. Sutton, & B.D. McPherson (Eds.), *Exercise, fitness, and health: A consensus of current knowledge* (pp. 567-580). Champaign, IL: Human Kinetics.

Carli, G., Martelli, G., Viti, A., Baldi, L., Bonifazi, M., & diPrisco, C. (1983). Modulation of hormone levels in male swimmers during training. In A.P. Hollander, P.A. Huijing, & G. deGrout (Eds.), *Biomechanics and medicine in swimming* (pp. 33-40). Champaign, IL: Human Kinetics.

Carlson, J.S., & Cera, M.A. (1984). Cardiorespiratory, muscle strength, and anthropometric characteristics of elite Australian junior male and female tennis players. *Australian Journal of Science and Medicine*, **16**, 7-13.

Clarke, D.H., Vaccaro, P., & Andresen, N.M. (1985). Physiological alterations in 7- to 9-year old boys following a season of competitive wrestling. *Research Quarterly for Exercise and Sports*, **55**, 18-22.

Conn, C.A., Schemmel, R.A., Smith, B.W., Ryder, E., Heusner, W.W., & Ku, P-K. (1988). Plasma and erythrocyte magnesium concentrations and correlations with maximum oxygen consumption in nine-to-twelve year old competitive swimmers. *Magnesium*, **7**, 27-36.

Crawford, M.H., & O'Rourke, R.A. (1979). The athlete's heart. *Advances in Internal Medicine*, **24**, 311-329.

Cunningham, D.A., Telford, P., & Swart, G.T. (1976). The cardiopulmonary capacities of young hockey players: Age 10. *Medicine and Science in Sports*, **8**, 23-25.

Daniels, J., & Oldridge, N. (1971). Changes in oxygen consumption of young boys during growth and running training. *Medicine and Science in Sports*, **3**, 161-165.

deKnecht, S., Saris, W.H.M., Daniels, O., Elvers, J.W.H., & deBoo, T.M. (1984). Echocardiographic study of the left ventricle in sedentary and active boys aged 8-9 years. In J. Ilmarinen & I. Valimaki (Eds.), *Children and sport* (pp. 170-176). Berlin: Springer-Verlag.

Dempsey, J.A., Aaron, E., & Martin, B.J. (1988). Pulmonary function and prolonged exercise. In D.R. Lamb & R. Murray (Eds.), *Perspectives in exercise science and sports medicine: Vol. I. Prolonged exercise* (pp. 75-124). Indianapolis: Benchmark Press.

Denison, B.A., & Ben-Ezra, V. (1989). Plasma somatomedin-C in 8- to 10-year old swimmers. *Pediatric Exercise Science*, **1**, 64-72.

Douglas, D.J., & Hanson, P.G. (1978). Upper respiratory infection in the conditioned athlete (abstract). *Medicine and Science in Sports*, **10**, 55.

Douglas, P.S. (1989). Cardiac considerations in the triathlete. *Medicine and Science in Sports and Exercise*, **21**(Suppl.), S214-218.

Douglas, P.S., O'Toole, M.L., Hiller, W.D.B., Hackney, K., & Reichek, N. (1987). Cardiac fatigue after prolonged exercise. *Circulation*, **76**, 1206-1213.

Eichner, R.E. (1988). Other medical considerations in prolonged exercise. In D.R. Lamb & R. Murray (Eds.), *Perspectives in exercise science and sports medicine: Vol. I. Prolonged exercise* (pp. 415-442). Indianapolis: Benchmark Press.

Eriksson, B.O., Engstrom, L., & Lundin, A. (1978). Long term effect of previous swim training in girls: A 10-year follow-up on the "girl swimmers." *Acta Paediatrica Scandinavica*, **67**, 285-291.

Frisch, R.E. (1987). Body fat, menarche, fitness, and fertility. *Human Reproduction*, **2**, 521-533.

Frisch, R.E., & Revelle, R. (1971). Height and weight at menarche and a hypothesis of menarche. *Archives of Diseases of Childhood*, **46**, 695-701.

Godshall, R.W., Hansen, C.A., & Rising, D.C. (1981). Stress fractures through the distal femoral epiphysis in athletes. *American Journal of Sports Medicine*, **9**, 114-116.

Gratas, A., Dassonville, J., Beillot, J., & Rochcongar, P. (1988). Ventilation and occlusion pressure response to exercise in trained and untrained children. *European Journal of Applied Physiology*, **57**, 591-596.

Gren, R.J., Kaplan, S.S., Rabin, B.S., Stanitski, C.L., & Zdziarski, U. (1981). Immune function in the marathon runner. *Annals of Allergy*, **47**, 73-75.

Gutin, B., Mayers, N., Levy, J.A., & Herman, M.V. (1988). Physiologic and echocardiographic studies of age-group runners. In E.W. Brown & C.F. Branta (Eds.), *Competitive sports for children and youth* (pp. 117-128). Champaign, IL: Human Kinetics.

Hakkinen, K., Mero, A., & Kauhanen, H. (1989). Specificity of endurance, sprint, and strength training on physical performance capacity in young athletes. *Journal of Sports Medicine*, **29**, 7-35.

Hamilton, P., & Andrew, G.M. (1976). Influence of growth and athletic training on heart and lung function. *European Journal of Applied Physiology*, **36**, 27-38.

Henry, W.L., Ware, J., Gardin, J.M., Hepner, S.I., McKay, J., & Weiner, M. (1978). Echocardiographic measurements in normal subjects. *Circulation*, **57**, 278-285.

Kabara, J.J., & Morris, L. (1988). Biochemical scan reports: A tool for evaluating athletes and their training program. In E.W. Brown & C.F. Branta (Eds.), *Competitive sports for children and youth* (pp. 77-97). Champaign, IL: Human Kinetics.

Kato, S., & Ishiko, T. (1966). Obstructed growth of children's bones due to excessive labor in remote corners. In K. Kato (Ed.), *Proceedings of International Congress of Sports Sciences* (pp. 479-486). Tokyo: Japanese Union of Sports Sciences.

King, D.W., & Gollnick, P.D. (1970). Ultrastructure of rat heart and liver after exhaustive exercise. *American Journal of Physiology*, **218**, 1150-1155.

Kraemer, W.J., Fry, A.C., Frykman, P.N., Conray, B., & Hoffman, J. (1989). Resistance training and youth. *Pediatric Exercise Science*, **1**, 336-350.

Loucks, A.B. (1988). Osteoporosis prevention begins in childhood. In E.W. Brown & C.F. Branta (Eds.), *Competitive sports for children and youth* (pp. 213-223). Champaign, IL: Human Kinetics.

MacNab, R.B.J. (1979). A longitudinal study of ice hockey in boys aged 8-12. *Canadian Journal of Applied Sports Science*, **4**, 11-17.

Maffulli, N., & Helms, P. (1988). Controversies about intensive training in young athletes. *Archives of Diseases of Childhood*, **63**, 1405-1407.

Maher, J.T., Goodman, A.L., Francesconi, R., Bowers, W.D., Hartley, L.H., & Angelakos, E.T. (1972). Responses of rat myocardium to exhaustive exercise. *American Journal of Physiology*, **222**, 207-212.

Mahlamaki, S.T., Pekkarinen, H.A., Partanen, J.V., & Michelsson, J-E. (1989). Neurologic signs and neurophysiological findings in the lower extremities of young cross-country skiers and control children. In S. Osied & K-H. Carlton (Eds.), *Children and exercise XIII* (pp. 415-420). Champaign, IL: Human Kinetics.

Malina, R.M. (1983). Menarche in athletes: A synthesis and hypothesis. *Annals of Human Biology*, **10**, 1-24.

Malina, R.M. (1989). Growth and maturation: Normal variation and effect of training. In C.V. Gisolfi & D.R. Lamb (Eds.), *Perspectives in exercise science and sports medicine: Vol. 2. Youth, exercise, and sport* (pp. 223-272). Indianapolis: Benchmark Press.

Malina, R.M., Meleski, B.W., & Shoup, R.F. (1982). Anthropometric, body composition, and maturity characteristics of selected school-age athletes. *Pediatric Clinics of North America*, **19**, 1305-1323.

Maron, B.J. (1986). Structural features of the athlete heart as defined by echocardiography. *Journal of the American College of Cardiology*, **7**, 190-203.

Maron, M.B., Hamilton, L.H., & Maksud, M.G. (1979). Alterations in pulmonary function consequent to competitive marathon running. *Medicine and Science in Sports*, **11**, 244-249.

Mayers, N., & Gutin, B. (1979). Physiologic characteristics of elite prepubertal cross country runners. *Medicine and Science in Sports and Exercise*, **11**, 172-176.

Medved, R., Fabecic-Sabadi, V., & Medved, V. (1986). Echocardiographic findings in children participating in swimming training. *International Journal of Sports Medicine*, **7**, 94-99.

Micheli, L.J., & Smith, A.D. (1982). Sports injuries in children. *Current Problems in Pediatrics*, **12**, 1-54.

Niemela, K.O., Palatsi, I.J., Ikaheimo, M.J., Takkunen, J.T., & Vuori, J.J. (1984). Evidence of impaired left ventricular performance after an uninterrupted competitive 24-hour run. *Circulation*, **70**, 350-356.

Nudel, D.B., Hassett, I., Gurian, A., Diamant, S., Weinhouse, E., & Gootman, N. (1989). Young long distance runners: Physiologic and psychologic characteristics. *Clinical Pediatrics*, **28**, 500-505.

Osterback, L., & Qvarnberg, Y. (1987). A prospective study of respiratory infections in 12 year old children actively engaged in sports. *Acta Paediatrica Scandinavica*, **76**, 944-949.

Paterson, D.H., McLellan, T.M., Stella, R.S., & Cunningham, D.A. (1987). Longitudinal study of ventilation threshold and maximal O_2 uptake in athletic boys. *Journal of Applied Physiology*, **62**, 2051-2057.

Rasmussen, B.S., Elkjaer, P., & Juhl, B. (1988). Impaired pulmonary and cardiac function after maximal exercise. *Journal of Sports Sciences*, **6**, 219-228.

Raven, P.B., & Stevens, G.H.J. (1988). Cardiovascular function and prolonged exercise. In D.R. Lamb & R. Murray (Eds.), *Perspectives in exercise science and sports medicine: Vol. 1. Prolonged exercise* (pp. 43-74). Indianapolis: Benchmark Press.

Rogol, A.D. (1988). Pubertal development in endurance-trained female athletes. In E.W. Brown & C.F. Branta (Eds.), *Competitive sports for children and youth* (pp. 173-194). Champaign, IL: Human Kinetics.

Rost, R., Gerhardus, H., & Schmidt, K. (1985). Auswirkungen eines Hochleistungstrainings im Schwimmport mit Beginn im Kindersalter auf das Herz-Kreislaufsystem [Effects of high performance swim training on the cardiovascular system of children]. *Medizin und Welthausen*, **36**, 65-71.

Rost, R., & Hollman, W. (1983). Athlete's heart—a review of its historical assessment and new aspects. *International Journal of Sports Medicine*, **4**, 147-165.

Rowland, T.W. (1985). Aerobic response to endurance training in prepubescent children: A critical analysis. *Medicine and Science in Sports and Exercise*, **17**, 493-497.

Rowland, T.W. (1990). *Exercise and children's health* (pp. 110-115). Champaign, IL: Human Kinetics.

Rowland, T.W., Black, S.A., & Kelleher, J.F. (1987). Iron deficiency in adolescent endurance athletes. *Journal of Adolescent Health*, **8**, 322-326.

Rowland, T.W., Delaney, B.C., & Siconolfi, S.F. (1987). Athlete's heart in prepubertal children. *Pediatrics*, **79**, 800-804.

Rowland, T.W., Morris, A.H., Kelleher, J.F., Haag, B.L., & Reiter, E.O. (1987). Serum testosterone response to training in adolescent runners. *American Journal of Diseases of Children*, **141**, 881-883.

Schemmel, R.A., Ryder, E., Moeggenberg, J.A., & Conn, C.A. (1988). Comparison of nutrient intakes between elite wrestlers and runners. In E.W. Brown & C.F. Branta (Eds.), *Competitive sports for children and youth* (pp. 27-38). Champaign, IL: Human Kinetics.

Schumucker, B., & Hollmann, W. (1974). The aerobic capacity of trained athletes from 6 to 7 years of age on. *Acta Paediatrica Belgica*, **28**(Suppl.), 92-101.

Scott, E.C., & Johnston, F.E. (1982). Critical fat, menarche, and the maintenance of menstrual cycles. A critical review. *Journal of Adolescent Health Care*, **2**, 249-260.

Seals, D.R., Rogers, M.A., Hagberg, J.M., Yamamoto, C., Cryer, P.E., & Ehsani, A.A. (1988). Left ventricular dysfunction after prolonged strenuous exercise in healthy subjects. *American Journal of Cardiology*, **61**, 875-879.

Seefeldt, V., Haubenstricker, J., Branta, C.F., & Evans, S. (1988). Physical characteristics of elite young distance runners. In E.W. Brown & C.F. Branta (Eds.), *Competitive sports for children and youth* (pp. 247-258). Champaign, IL: Human Kinetics.

Shangold, M.M. (1986). Gynecological concerns in young and adolescent physically active girls. *Pediatrician*, **13**, 10-13.

Shepherd, T.A., Eisenman, P.A., Ruttenburg, H.D., Adams, T.D., & Johnson, S.C. (1988). Cardiac dimensions of highly trained prepubescent boys (abstract). *Medicine and Science in Sports and Exercise*, **20**, S53.

Siegel, A.J., Silverman, L.M., & Holman, L. (1981). Elevated creatine kinase MB isoenzyme levels in marathon runners. *Journal of the American Medical Association*, **246**, 2049-2051.

Smith, A.T., Clemmons, D.R., Underwood, L.E., Ben-Ezra, V., & McMurray, R. (1987). The effect of exercise on plasma somatomedin-C/insulinlike growth factor I concentrations. *Metabolism*, **36**, 533-537.

Smith, B.W., Metheny, W.P., Van Huss, W.D., Seefeldt, V.D., & Sparrow, A.W. (1983). Serum lipids and lipoprotein profiles in elite age-group endurance runners (abstract). *Circulation*, **68**, 191.

Smith, B.W., Sparrow, A.W., Heusner, W.W., Van Huss, W.D., & Conn, C. (1985). Serum lipid profiles of pre-teenage swimmers (abstract). *Medicine and Science in Sports and Exercise*, **17**, 220.

Soppi, E., Varjo, P., Eskola, J., & Laitinen, L.A. (1982). Effect of strenuous physical stress on circulating lymphocyte number and function before and after training. *Journal of Clinical and Laboratory Immunology*, **8**, 43-46.

Strobino, L.J., French, G.O., & Colonna, P.C. (1952). The effect of increasing tensions on the growth of epiphyseal bone. *Surgery, Gynecology, and Obstetrics*, **95**, 694-700.

Sugimoto, T., Allison, J.L., & Guyton, A.C. (1973). Effect of maximal workload on cardiac function. *Japanese Heart Journal*, **14**, 146-153.

Sundberg, S., & Elovainio, R. (1982). Cardiorespiratory function in competitive runners aged 12-16 years compared with normal boys. *Acta Paediatrica Scandinavica*, **71**, 987-992.

Sutton, J.R., & Farrell, P. (1988). Endocrine responses to prolonged exercise. In D.R. Lamb & R. Murray (Eds.), *Perspectives in exercise science and sports medicine: Volume 1. Prolonged exercise* (pp. 153-212). Indianapolis: Benchmark Press.

Telford, R.D., McDonald, I.G., Ellis, L.B., Chennells, M.H.D., Sandstrom, E.R., & Fuller, P.J. (1988). Echocardiographic dimensions in trained and untrained 12-year old boys and girls. *Journal of Sports Sciences*, **6**, 49-57.

Tertti, M., Paajanen, H., Kujala, U.M., Alanea, A., Salmi, T.T., & Kormano, M. (1990). Disc degeneration in young gymnasts: A magnetic resonance imaging study. *American Journal of Sports Medicine*, **18**, 206-208.

Tharp, G.D., Thorland, W.G., Johnson, G.O., & Peter, J.B. (1986). Cardiac dimensions in elite young track athletes. *Research Quarterly for Exercise and Sport*, **57**, 139-143.

Thoren, C.A.R., & Asano, K. (1984). Functional capacity and cardiac function in 10 year old boys and girls with high and low running performance. In J. Ilmarinen & I. Valimaki (Eds.), *Children and sport* (pp. 170-176). Berlin: Springer-Verlag.

Vaccaro, P., & Poffenbarger, A. (1982). Resting and exercise respiratory function in young female child runners. *Journal of Sports Medicine*, **2**, 102-107.

Valimaki, I., Hursti, M.L., Pihlakosk, L., & Viikari, J. (1980). Exercise performance and serum lipids in relation to physical activity in school children. *International Journal of Sports Medicine*, **1**, 132-136.

Vanderbroucke, N.P., van Laar, A., & Valkenburg, H.A. (1983). Synergy between thinness and intensive sport activity in delaying menarche. *British Medical Journal*, **284**, 1907-1908.

Van Huss, W., Evans, S.A., Kurowski, T., Anderson, D.J., Allen, R., & Stephens, K. (1988). Physiologic characteristics of male and female age-group runners. In E.W. Brown & C.F. Branta (Eds.), *Competitive sports for children and youth* (pp. 143-158). Champaign, IL: Human Kinetics.

Webber, L.M., Byrnes, W.C., Rowland, T.W., & Foster, V.L. (1989). Serum creatine kinase activity and delayed onset muscle soreness in prepubescent children: A preliminary study. *Pediatric Exercise Science*, **1**, 351-359.

Wells, C.L., & Plowman, S.A. (1988). Relationship between training, menarche, and amenorrhea. In E.W. Brown & C.F. Branta (Eds.), *Competitive sports for children and youth* (pp. 195-212). Champaign, IL: Human Kinetics.

Wheeler, G.D., Wall, S.R., Belcastro, A.N., & Cumming, D.C. (1984). Reduced serum testosterone and prolactin levels in male distance runners. *Journal of the American Medical Association*, **252**, 514-516.

Yost, L.J., Zauner, C.W., & Jaeger, M.J. (1981). Pulmonary diffusing capacity and physical working capacity in swimmers and non-swimmers during growth. *Respiration*, **42**, 8-14.

Zauner, C.W., Maksud, M.G., & Melichna, J. (1989). Physiological considerations in training young athletes. *Sports Medicine*, **8**, 15-31.

Zonderland, M.L., Erich, W.B.M., Peltenburg, A.L., Bernink, M.J.E., Havekes, L., van Erp-Baart, A.M.J., & Saris, W.H.M. (1988). Lipoprotein profiles and nutrition of prepubertal female athletes. In R.M. Malina (Ed.), *Young athletes: Biological, psychological, and emotional perspectives* (pp. 177-191). Champaign, IL: Human Kinetics.

PART IV

Clinical/Pathological Perspectives

William E. Garrett, Jr.

The popularity of sports is a phenomenon quite obvious in Western society. One need go no further than the daily newspaper or the evening news to be reminded of our society's general interest in athletic participation. The increasing involvement in sports is most evident in our youth, for whom competitive sports are a feature of childhood. Furthermore, there is an increasing awareness that this participation in sports may involve very high levels of duration and intensity even in very young or prepubescent children.

There is a great need for parents, medical personnel, and others involved with sports to determine the effects of intensive participation in youth sports on the health of the children involved. Unfortunately, very few epidemiological studies have been conducted to establish the risks and benefits of this type of training. Further, as became apparent during workshop discussions, many of the studies that have evaluated injury in youth participants do not specify the maturity levels of the children studied. In the process of consensual validation used in this workshop, participants recognized that our discussions were often based on inconclusive studies and were significantly influenced by the personal experiences of participants as individuals and as a group. Nevertheless, we agree on a number of issues relevant to the effects of intensive training and participation in youth sports. This summary will present the areas of broad agreement about musculoskeletal injury in these active children.

Injuries in Youth Sports

Children Are Not Small Adults

The degree of risk of musculoskeletal injury and the types of injury that occur are often very different in children than in adults. In addition, the motivations for intense participation in children often come from parents and other adults. An adult may acknowledge and accept risk of personal injury through sport participation; however, our medical community and society should be more concerned about musculoskeletal injuries incurred by children, who are unable to make decisions about risks. We must understand and seek to define further the differences in youth and adult sport participation, in order to avoid acute and chronic injury in children.

Injury Rates in Youth Sports

The public often assumes that injury rates are higher in youth sports than in adult sports, but a number of studies demonstrate that this is not necessarily true. As a matter of fact, it appears that injury rates for most sports increase significantly from prepubescent to junior high to high school age groups. This has been addressed for a number of sports, including football (Larson, 1973; Mueller & Blyth, 1982), soccer (Schmidt-Olsen, Bünemann, Lade, & Brassøe, 1985; Sullivan, Gross, Grana, & Garcia-Moral, 1980), and sports in general (Zaricznyj, Shattuck, Mast, Robertson, & D'Elia, 1980). These data show that sport participation in general does not present a higher risk, and probably presents lower risk, to the prepubescent athlete as compared to adults.

However, these studies do not address the intensity of the training. No good epidemiological studies exist that demonstrate the relative risk incurred by young athletes who train more than 20 hr per week at certain sports such as gymnastics or tennis. It is quite likely that the relatively low injury rate for preadolescents reflects the lower intensity of their training. But just as there are no data to prove there is not an abnormally high injury rate in preadolescents, there is little reason to suspect that the risk of injury is less! When the training intensity is sufficient to injure adolescents and older children, we must be at least as concerned for the preadolescent.

In addition, these studies generally look for acute injury data and therefore may not address the large problem of overuse injury in youth sports. An overuse injury is due to the repeated application of many small stresses that by themselves create no apparent injury. However, when these stresses are applied at a rate that is faster than the body's ability to recover from each stress, the cumulative effect can lead to injuries such as stress fractures and tendinitis (Clain, Hershman, & Goldberg, 1989; Micheli, 1983). Therefore, cumulative stresses that begin in prepubescence may not be manifest as an injury until adolescence.

Characteristic Injury Patterns

A number of studies have shown that the injuries sustained by preadolescents are different than those of adults and further that the injuries appear to be relatively sport specific. Those involved with youth sports should be particularly aware of these characteristic injury patterns.

Examples of these are discussed by Dr. Mandelbaum in chapter 8. Young gymnasts are prone to a number of injuries involving the wrist and the lumbar spine (Jackson, Wiltse, Dingeman, & Hayes, 1981; Mandelbaum, Bartolozzi,

Davis, Teurlings, & Bragonier, 1989; Roy, Caine, & Singer, 1985). Preadolescent and adolescent baseball players, especially pitchers, frequently have problems related to the shoulder and to the elbow (Barnett, 1985; Gugenheim, Stanley, Woods, & Tullos, 1976; Larson, Singer, Bergstrom, & Thomas, 1976). Most of these injuries that follow characteristic patterns are overuse injuries. There is strong reason to believe that early diagnosis and proper treatment will lead to resolution without permanent disability.

Youth sport in general seems to demonstrate injuries to different structures than adult sport. The growing bone of the preadolescent and adolescent athlete is very different than adult bone. When the bone is still growing and the physes are open, injuries often involve the physeal and apophyseal areas (Micheli, 1983; Wilkins, 1980). Quite often these injuries are mild and self-limited, such as Osgood-Schlatter disease of the tibial apophysis or Sever's disease of the calcaneal apophysis. However, these injuries must be distinguished from more serious injuries such as stress fractures, which are also being seen more frequently in the intensively training youth athlete (Maffulli, 1990).

Injuries to the growing epiphyses are characteristic of childhood injuries in general. However, it is not established that adolescent and preadolescent sport participation greatly increases the risk of epiphyseal injury, either acute or chronic (Garrick & Requa, 1979; Zaricznyj et al., 1980).

Intensive Training Alters Fitness and Flexibility

This topic received significant attention in Part III on the physiological affects of intense training in youth sports. In general, most of these changes are beneficial and not only help performance capacity but also diminish potential for injury. However, as chapter 7, by Dr. Kibler, stresses, changes may also occur in strength and flexibility that increase the risk of musculoskeletal pain or injury, for example, the inflexibilities and weaknesses in the shoulders of tennis players. Young baseball players also demonstrate changes in strength and flexibility in the shoulders and elbows. And flexibility changes in ballet and dance are often discussed (Hamilton, 1990). It is likely that these adaptations help the performance of the individual sport, but these adaptations may also predispose the athlete to overuse injury. For example, the inflexibility of shoulder internal rotation in tennis players and throwers certainly exists in adolescents and preadolescents. These changes may predispose these athletes to injury of rotator cuff or to intra-articular injury, as discussed by Dr. Kibler. Coaches and trainers must be aware of adaptations in young athletes that may predispose them to subsequent injury. Potentially harmful adaptations can be identified and rectified early.

Pain Associated With Youth Sports

The presence of pain in youth sports is cause for concern; pain should not be considered a normal adaptation resulting from intensive training. Adults associated with youth sports should pay careful attention to complaints of pain and have each problem evaluated if the etiology is not clear. A high index of suspicion is appropriate for parents, coaches, and others dealing with youth sports. Pain should not be masked by medications such as nonsteroidal anti-inflammatory drugs unless the diagnosis is clear and the condition is felt to be nonprogressive. Failure to identify and treat painful conditions not only constitutes a risk to the health of the athlete but also contributes to diminished training and performance capacity. Coaches and trainers should consult with appropriate sports medicine personnel whenever there is any question about the cause and the risk of a condition causing pain in the young athlete.

Injury Prevention Among Young Athletes

When parents, coaches, and sports medicine personnel understand the nature of the injuries incurred by preadolescent athletes, the next logical step is an intensive effort to prevent musculoskeletal injury in participating youth.

The Preparticipation Evaluation

Presently, participation in many youth sports requires a preparticipation medical evaluation. Most often these evaluations are very general and include only a cursory examination of the health of the child. Although this may be appropriate for most children participating in sports, a more thorough and sport-specific evaluation may be appropriate for those involved in intensive training and participation.

The medical history should identify general health problems, previous acute and chronic injuries, and psychological and nutritional problems such as anorexia and bulimia. Evaluations should be sport specific; that is, evaluations should look for different things in different athletes. For example, eating disorders are much more likely to occur in the gymnast or dancer than in the football or basketball player.

A thorough physical examination is important, and general maturational status should be carefully observed. Particularly in the adolescent years there is a wide variation of musculoskeletal maturity levels in children of the same chronological age. The examination should identify specific musculoskeletal problems and general health problems as well as sport-specific patterns of weakness and inflexibility in tennis players and throwing athletes. Because conducting exhaustive examinations of all youth sport participants is impractical, it is recommended that a general examination be supplemented by a sport-specific examination that concentrates on the musculoskeletal issues specific to certain sports. Chapter 8 discusses this in detail. It has also been emphasized that anatomical alignment can be a significant factor in predisposing a child to injury (Micheli, 1983). For example, pronated or flat feet predispose the athlete to foot, leg, and knee pain. Femoral anteversion affects turnout in dancers and may cause injury if the child attempts to force turnout by stressing the lower extremity at levels below the hip. Malalignment is often present in young athletes with musculoskeletal injury.

Controlled Training Progression

It is believed that one of the most common causes of overuse injury is improper and, usually, too rapid progression in the intensity of the training. The adults controlling the training must ensure that increases in intensity are gradual (Micheli, 1983). It is generally believed that the body adapts to increased training stresses, but adaptations take some time. The increased rate of applied stresses should not exceed the capacity of the body to adapt. Coaching and sports medicine personnel should document adaptation before increasing the stresses of training.

Protective Equipment

In some sports protective equipment may be used for reasons of safety, and this equipment is often optional for adults. It is recommended that the use of protective equipment be mandatory in youth sports. Examples include shin guards in soccer, batting helmets in baseball, and properly fitted football helmets (Reider et al., 1990). Attention to shoes is also important, because proper shoes for running and field sports may significantly reduce overuse and acute injuries.

Recommendations

Our responsibility to children engaged in intensive training and participation in sports involves two sometimes conflicting goals. We must be cognizant of participants' needs and desires to improve performance, and we are therefore concerned with the beneficial responses of training as it regards health and performance in youth. On the other hand, we are responsible for preventing injury and minimizing the morbidity of acute and chronic injuries due to intensive training and participation in youth sports, so it behooves us to better understand the risks and benefits of intensive training. In many ways this recommendation considers physical training as the analogy of a pharmacological agent: We must optimize the dose based on its beneficial and harmful effects on the organism.

Encourage Epidemiological Studies of Injury in Youth Sports

Because information is often lacking on the frequency and severity of injury, epidemiological studies must be conducted to establish a baseline for the incidence of injury. These data are necessary to point out the problem areas of each sport and each age group. Once the problems are evident, then further epidemiological studies will be needed to demonstrate the efficacy of intervention strategies to prevent or reduce the morbidity of musculoskeletal injury. These data should be useful for youth sports in general and especially for intense training and sport participation.

Establish a Dose-Response Relationship of Exercise Based on Its Benefits and Risks

Pharmacological studies establishing the efficacy and risk of medications are obligated to demonstrate the efficacy and the harmful effects of the agent as they relate to dose. Similarly, data are needed to establish the dose-response curve of physical training. Increased training obviously will yield improvements in performance. But at what level of training will the side effects of musculoskeletal injury, psychological burnout, and "competitive staleness" outweigh the beneficial responses of training? These questions are generally unanswered for youth sports. Further, there are few studies underway to establish these data for the young athlete.

There are a few examples of attempts at limiting the dose of children's exercise in order to prevent musculoskeletal injury; notable is the widespread limitation on the numbers of innings of competitive pitching in baseball (Bryan, 1990). Rules such as these impress on players, coaches, and parents the need to control the dose of potentially harmful exercise. However, these limitations only apply to formal competition and not to practice and play periods, which probably account for a larger percentage of the exercise dose. Furthermore, some feel that the limitations are not based on any careful studies demonstrating a relationship between the intensity of participation and permanent injury (Slager, 1977).

Certainly many factors are involved in establishing a dose-response relation for physical training. These include, among others,

- the age and maturational level of the child,
- the length and the intensity of the training and rest periods,
- the age at onset of training and specialization,
- the progression of training, and
- the presence of risk factors such as body habitus, strength deficits, and inflexibility.

The challenge is now before those involved with youth sports, and in particular with youth undergoing intense training and participation, to establish the safety of the participation. The desire to excel and the benefits derived from athletic success are often perceived to be so high that some coaches and athletes will not adopt arbitrary limitation of training without clear indications that limitations are warranted. In addition, one must consider whether ever-increasing levels of training intensity yield higher levels of performance. There is likely a level of diminishing returns.

Summary

Participation in competitive youth sports is now an accepted part of our society, and there is increasing awareness that involvement in sports has become intense for a number of adolescent and preadolescent children. This presents a clear challenge to sports medicine personnel. The safety of participation must be established in order to protect the health of these children. Injuries must be prevented when possible, and the morbidity of injury must be minimized. However, it is not acceptable to consider injury alone. We must better understand the physiological response to exercise and the potential for improving performance.

Ultimately, we must better define for our young athletes the overall balance between exercise dose, improved performance, and the risk of injury.

References

Barnett, L.S. (1985). Little League shoulder syndrome: Proximal hymeral epiphyseolysis in adolescent baseball pitchers. *Journal of Bone and Joint Surgery*, **67A**, 495-496.

Bryan, W. (1990). Baseball. In B. Reider (Ed.), *Sports medicine: The school age athlete* (pp. 447-483). Philadelphia: Saunders.

Clain, M.R., Hershman, E.B., & Goldberg, B. (1989). Overuse injuries in children and adolescents. *The Physician and Sportsmedicine*, **17**(9), 111-123.

Garrick, J.G., & Requa, R.K. (1979). Injury patterns in children and adolescent skiers. *American Journal of Sports Medicine*, **7**(4), 245-248.

Gugenheim, J.J., Stanley, R.F., Woods, G.W., & Tullos, H.S. (1976). Little League survey: The Houston study. *American Journal of Sports Medicine*, **4**(5), 189-200.

Hamilton, W.G. (1990). Ballet. In B. Reider (Ed.), *Sports medicine: The school age athlete* (pp. 485-519). Philadelphia: Saunders.

Jackson, D.W., Wiltse, L.L., Dingeman, R.D., & Hayes, M. (1981). Stress reactions involving the pars interarticularis in young athletes. *American Journal of Sports Medicine*, **9**(5), 304-312.

Larson, R.L. (1973). Epiphyseal injuries in the adolescent athlete. *Orthopedic Clinics of North America*, **1**, 839-851.

Larson, R.L., Singer, K.M., Bergstrom, R., & Thomas, S. (1976). Little League survey: The Eugene study. *American Journal of Sports Medicine*, **4**(5), 201-209.

Maffulli, N. (1990). Intensive training in young athletes: The orthopaedic surgeon's viewpoint. *Sports Medicine*, **9**(4), 229-243.

Mandelbaum, B.R., Bartolozzi, A.R., Davis, C.A., Teurlings, L., & Bragonier, B. (1989). Wrist pain syndrome in the gymnast: Pathogenetic, diagnostic, and therapeutic considerations. *American Journal of Sports Medicine*, **17**(3), 305-317.

Micheli, L.J. (1983). Overuse injuries in children's sports: The growth factor. *Orthopedic Clinics of North America*, **14**, 337-360.

Mueller, F., & Blyth, C. (1982). Epidemiology of sports injuries in children. *Clinics in Sports Medicine*, **1**(3), 343-352.

Reider, B. (1990). Football. In B. Reider (Ed.), *Sports medicine: The school age athlete* (pp. 559-589). Philadelphia: Saunders.

Roy, S., Caine, D., & Singer, K.M. (1985). Stress changes of the distal radial epiphysis in young gymnasts. *American Journal of Sports Medicine*, **13**(5), 301-308.

Schmidt-Olsen, S., Bünemann, L.K.H., Lade, V., & Brassøe, J.O.K. (1985). Soccer injuries of youth. *British Journal of Sports Medicine*, **19**(3), 161-164.

Slager, R.F. (1977). From Little League to big league, the weak spot is the arm. *American Journal of Sports Medicine*, **5**(2), 37-48.

Sullivan, J.A., Gross, R.H., Grana, W.A., & Garcia-Moral, C.A. (1980). Evaluation of injuries in youth soccer. *American Journal of Sports Medicine*, **8**(5), 325-327.

Wilkins, K.E. (1980). The uniqueness of the young athlete: Musculoskeletal injuries. *American Journal of Sports Medicine*, **8**(5), 377-382.

Zaricznyj, B., Shattuck, L.J.M., Mast, T.A., Robertson, R.V., & D'Elia, G. (1980). Sports-related injuries in school-aged children. *American Journal of Sports Medicine*, **8**(5), 318-324.

Chapter 7

Musculoskeletal Adaptations and Injuries Associated With Intense Participation in Youth Sports

W. Ben Kibler
T. Jeff Chandler

The importance of physical activity to health and fitness is recognized today more than ever. Many youth participate intensely in sports and activities, and we assume the result is positive. But for physical activity to have life-long positive benefits, the athlete should either make a career of sport or receive some positive alteration in quality or length of life. Few young athletes go on to professional athletic careers, so lifestyle improvements should be the goal of participation in physical activities.

Cardiorespiratory fitness has been shown to be vitally important in preventing diseases of the heart and lungs. Fitness of the musculoskeletal system is also important in terms of minimal strength, flexibility, and muscular endurance. These ''health-related'' benefits of exercise add to the quality of life, especially as one ages. Physical activity should result in physiological changes leading to greater fitness and longevity, retardation of some of the effects of aging, and prevention of chronic disease. It may be possible, however, to reach a point where continued intense physical activity leads to chronic or stress-induced injuries, impaired organ function, and decreased longevity. Perhaps athletic activity is like a mountain, with a lot of physical effort required to get to the top, and a steep downside if too much activity is attempted. More information is needed on the effects of intense participation in physical activity, particularly for preadolescents, so we can determine both the benefits and possible dangers of such activities.

More and more young people are participating or aspiring to participate in national-level sports. We routinely see 12- to 14-year-old females participating in national competitions in gymnastics, swimming, cheerleading, and tennis and youngsters of both sexes competing for several hours a day in national-level contests. The financial and other rewards available to successful athletes mean this tendency will not likely be diminishing.

Despite the benefits of exercise and the increasing participation in high-level sport, the President's Council on Physical Fitness has determined that the fitness level of young people as a whole in the U.S. is on the decline, and young people are being urged to participate in sports and other activities for either personal or societal reasons. Many youths attend summer sports camps where they play a variety of sports, including tennis, soccer, football, basketball, and baseball; in these camps 3 to 4 sessions of practice per day are not uncommon. But do we understand the adaptations their bodies go through when their participation becomes intense?

It has been estimated that well over 20 million children ages 6 to 16 are participating in recreational youth sport programs (Martens, 1978; Seefeldt & Haugenstricker, 1978). Young children are becoming increasingly involved in competitive programs that involve year-round practice, competition, and conditioning, in either single or multiple sports. More youngsters are specializing in a single sport at an earlier age with consequent increased intensity of training. It has been reported that children as young as 6 years old have completed marathons and have trained up to 80 mi per week. Eight-year-old swimmers are reportedly swimming up to 20,000 m per day ("Shoulder pain," 1980).

This chapter reviews the literature on the effects of intense athletic participation on the musculoskeletal systems of prepubertal youth and evaluates the clinical manifestations of these effects. Additionally, data is presented from our work comparing soccer and tennis players to normally active youth. These sports were selected to highlight stresses on the upper body in tennis and the lower body in soccer.

This chapter addresses several questions from a clinical standpoint. First, does the prepubertal athlete's musculoskeletal system respond to the exercise dose in the same fashion as the older athlete's? Second, are the injury mechanics the same for children and adults, and do they produce the same type of injury? Third, do the same flexibility and strength adaptations take place in children and adults? Fourth, is the standard musculoskeletal fitness exam appropriate for prepubertal athletes? Last, is a prehabilitation conditioning program, that is, an exercise program to prevent injury, important in this age group?

Injury Incidence in Young Athletes

Injury studies of athletes are prevalent in the scientific literature, but injury studies of young athletes are less common. Cahill (1978) reported on the incidence and severity of high school football knee injuries, concluding that preseason conditioning reduced both the total number and the severity of traumatic knee injuries. Brady (1982) studied weight-training injuries in the high school athlete and reported that out of 80 injuries, 43 could be attributed directly to weight training and the remaining 37 could possibly be attributed to other sport activities.

Of the 43 injuries, 29 were classified as lumbosacral pain, 6 as anterior iliac spine avulsion, 4 as torn knee meniscus, and 4 as cervical sprains.

Other studies have looked more closely at overload injuries. According to Micheli (1982), this type of injury usually results not simply from overuse but also from improper training techniques and anatomic malalignment. Kibler (1989) suggested that the strength and flexibility of the musculotendinous unit are also factors in such injuries. Rarick and Seefeldt (1976) stated that the overloading of immature and growing joints is the primary cause of epiphyseal injury.

Wilkins (1980) commented on the differing responses of young athletes and adults to musculoskeletal injuries. The capacity of bone to remodel is greater in children than in adults, leading to more rapid healing of fractures and stress fractures. Also, actions that may result in torn ligaments in adults often result in epiphyseal fractures in children, because children's ligaments are relatively stronger than their epiphyseal plates. Rapid growth may change the stress patterns on children's ligaments, muscles, and tendons in a short period of time. According to Wilkins, sex is not a factor in determining injury predisposition in the prepubescent.

Adams (1965) reported on elbow X rays of 9- to 14-year-old baseball pitchers, baseball position players, and nonthrowing controls. Changes in the medial epicondylar epiphysis and opposing articular surfaces of the capitulum and head of the radius in the throwing arm appeared to be in direct proportion to the amount and type of throwing. All of the pitchers' X rays showed some degree of accelerated growth, separation, and fragmentation of the medial epicondylar epiphysis. Similar changes were seen in only 28% of the position players and 14% of the controls.

Kibler, McQueen, and Uhl (1988) reported on the injury incidence of elite junior tennis players and recreational tennis players. In the elite juniors, overload injuries accounted for 63% of the injuries, sprains 25%, and fractures 12%. In recreational players, overload injuries accounted for 62% of the injuries, sprains 22%, and fractures 14%.

These reports as well as our observations show that prepubertal athletes do suffer injuries and that these are likely to be overload injuries. Specifically, we have looked at two sports in which intense youth participation is common: In both tennis and soccer, players begin elite competition as early as age 10.

Intense Youth Participation in Tennis

In 1990, the United States Tennis Association (USTA) had 30,148 members ages 12 and under and 28,873 members ages 13 to 14. All levels of activity are represented in the USTA, but the vast majority of members, estimated at 85%, belong because membership is a prerequisite for playing in USTA-sanctioned tournaments. In 1990, through the USTA, tennis players ages 14 and under had the opportunity to participate nationally in one of four "zonal" competitions and two national competitions, one on hard courts and one on clay; tennis players ages 12 and under could participate in one of four zonal competitions and one national tournament. Approximately 600 players competed in each age group in these tournaments in 1990. In a given year, these athletes can compete in approximately 400 local tournaments, and they often practice many hours per week. Tennis players at tennis academies have been reported to spend as many as 6 hr per day in court play and practice (Kibler et al., 1988).

Intense Youth Participation in Soccer

Soccer continues to increase in popularity in the United States. In March 1989, the U.S. Under-20 Team placed fourth in the World Youth Championships. The U.S. Under-16 Team qualified for the Under-16 World Tournament in Scotland. In 1990, a team representing the U.S. qualified for the World Cup for the first time since 1950. Thus U.S. is now competitive in the world arena.

In 1989, approximately 1.5 million youth soccer players were registered with the U.S. Soccer Federation, up from 103,000 in 1974. According to statistics from the National Collegiate Athletic Association (NCAA) and the National Association of Intercollegiate Athletes (NAIA), more U.S. colleges and universities field intercollegiate soccer teams than football teams. According to a survey by the Soccer Industry Council, more than 6 million youngsters under the age of 12 played soccer in 1990. Soccer is the second most popular team sport in the nation for players under 12 years old; soccer leagues and tournaments are abundant at the local, state, national, and international levels. Thus we would expect an increase in soccer injuries, because of both the increase in the number of participants and the fact that those athletes are participating at higher levels of competition.

It is obvious that prepubescents intensely participate in sport. What we do not know is the effect of this intense participation on the musculoskeletal system. To determine this effect, we must examine studies of injuries and other musculoskeletal parameters such as strength and flexibility.

The Overload Injury Model and Prepubertal Athletes

Kibler (1990a,b,c) described the overload injury cycle in older athletes. This chapter will study its applicability to prepubescent athletes. Many overload injuries are caused by an athlete's performing at too high an absolute load, called *absolute tensile overload*, or performing excessive repetitions of a normal load, called *relative tensile overload* (Figure 7.1). An example of an absolute overload injury, then, is an injury caused when an athlete attempts too much weight on a 1-RM bench press. An injury caused when an athlete performs too many sets and repetitions of the bench press after the muscle is fatigued is a relative overload injury.

Following a tensile overload injury muscle tissue is damaged, either microscopically or macroscopically. With repeated use of the muscle, repeated microscopic tears could become larger. If the muscle tear encompasses less than 3 g of tissue, the muscle is allowed ample time to heal, and muscle strength and flexibility are adequate, the athlete can return to competition with little or no decrease in

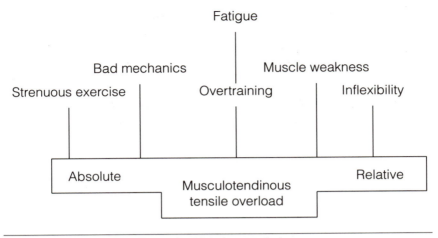

Figure 7.1   Causes of tensile overload injuries to soft tissue.

performance. If the athlete returns too early, or continues to participate in spite of a muscle injury, the muscle may repeatedly tear and eventually scar (Figure 7.2).

Certain clinical symptoms are evident following some muscle injuries. The athlete will experience pain and swelling in the area of the injury. Instability of a joint resulting from muscle weakness or muscle strength imbalance will in some instances prevent the athlete from participating, and certainly the athlete is at increased risk of further injury if participation continues.

However, in a lot of cases of mild muscular injury, few symptoms are overtly manifest following the initial insult. If the athlete does not rest or rehabilitate properly the healing that takes place is insufficient and is largely scar tissue. This causes inflexibility due to contracture.

The Cascade Effect

If participation continues after any injury, these inflexibilities and muscle weaknesses may worsen as more scar tissue forms, interfering with the muscle's ability to contract efficiently and move through a normal range of motion. Pain may lessen the intensity and frequency with which the athlete uses her or his muscles, and this adds to muscle weakness through neural inhibition. Due to the body's clinical and subclinical adaptations to tensile overload, efficient biomechanical movement patterns become difficult; this usually leads the athlete to change movement patterns, thus decreasing the skill with which an activity is performed. The athlete may undertake these substitute actions subconsciously to avoid pain or consciously because he or she lacks the strength, endurance, or flexibility to perform the movement. Examples include the baseball pitcher who unintentionally alters his throwing motion to accommodate for pain, weakness, or inflexibility; the runner with plantar fasciitis who decreases his stance time due to pain; and

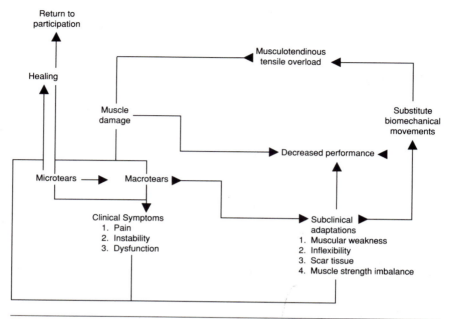

Figure 7.2   The overload injury cycle: Possible results of overload injuries to the musculotendinous unit.

the bench presser who alters the bar position to accommodate for pain. All of these factors—clinical adaptations, subclinical adaptations, and substitute biomechanical actions—may markedly decrease performance. Additionally, the tight weak muscle is more susceptible to continued tensile overload. This "cascade effect" moves the athlete to the point at which participation in the sport is no longer possible, the athlete no longer experiences success at sport, or overt injury occurs. This overt injury may occur locally due to continued injury to the damaged tissue. Or overt injury may occur at a different site due to altered mechanics such as plantar fasciitis due to tight plantar flexor muscles, or superior glenoid labral tears due to tight posterior shoulder capsular and muscular tissues.

The etiology of these maladaptations to activity is largely unknown. The changes in flexibility are almost certainly due to tensile stretch and resulting scar tissue formation. This has been demonstrated in a study of lateral epicondylitis (Nirschl, 1979), a study of plantar fasciitis (Clancy, 1982), and in a study involving rabbit muscle (Garrett, 1988). Steindler's (1956) point, that contractures that develop secondary to inflammatory changes of muscle are the most resistant to correction, has special relevance for athletically induced tensile injuries, which usually involve inflammation (Kibler, 1990b).

The nature of the muscle weakness and imbalance that are part of the cascade effect is less clear. Muscle damage does occur with intense muscle contraction (Armstrong, 1990) or with tensile overload (Garrett, 1990), and this damage may be a factor in loss of strength, as it is in loss of flexibility. However, no clinical study has documented the exact correlation of muscle strength loss with muscle damage.

Neurological adaptation may be another factor in strength alteration. The pain resulting from muscle tears or resulting inflammation is a potent inhibitor of muscle contraction (Herring, 1990). In addition, eccentric work is done with the firing of fewer motor units than required for concentric work, because the tension developed in eccentrically working fibers is greater than in concentrically working fibers (Armstrong, 1990). It may be that neural adaptation to chronic tensile load decreases the number of motor units firing, thereby decreasing total muscular strength. If so, this local adaptation would have adverse consequences for the entire kinetic chain.

Preventing the Overload Injury Cycle

Ideally, athletes can avoid the overload injury cycle by achieving a sport-specific level of strength and flexibility of the muscular system prior to participation. One way to determine the preseason strengths and weaknesses of the athlete is by performing an adequate preparticipation fitness evaluation (Kibler, 1990b; Kibler, Chandler, Uhl, & Maddux, 1989).

The strength and flexibility component of this evaluation should focus on the areas of the musculoskeletal system that are under high tensile loads during activity. For example, tennis players demonstrate a loss of internal rotation flexibility of the shoulder (Chandler, 1992) as well as a decrease in shoulder external rotation strength (Chandler, 1992). Similar adaptations of the shoulder musculature have been demonstrated in baseball pitchers and in swimmers (Kibler, 1986). Runners with plantar fasciitis show weakness of the dorsiflexors of the foot (Kibler, Chandler, & Goldberg, 1991). Runners also demonstrate weakness in the hamstring muscles and tightness in the hamstrings and low back (Kibler, 1986). The extent to which these adaptations occur in prepubescents is discussed later.

Muscular hypertrophy may play a role in the development of these maladaptations. It may be, however, that the preadolescent muscle, because of cross-sectional size, fiber size, force-generating capacity, load-resisting capacity, or biochemical characteristics, does not respond like more mature muscle. This factor may preclude our drawing conclusions from research on older athletes and applying the results to prepubescent athletes.

Musculoskeletal Profiles of Young Athletes

Fitness levels of athletes can be measured and studied with a variety of techniques. Kibler (Kibler, 1990c; Kibler et al., 1989) outlined a musculoskeletal profile for evaluating the fitness of athletes' musculoskeletal systems. In a study of junior high, high school, and college athletes, the researchers noted losses in flexibility using goniometric measurements of flexibility in the muscle groups primarily used in the athletes' sports. Significant differences were noted between males and females on all flexibility measurements. Upper body athletes showed decreased upper body flexibility compared to lower body athletes and lower body athletes showed decreased lower body flexibility compared to upper body athletes. Males were stronger than females on all strength measurements.

Adaptations to Joint Range of Motion

The frequency of muscle tightness and injuries in senior division soccer players, mean age 24.6 years, was reported by Ekstrand and Gillquist (1982). Soccer players were generally less flexible than a group of age-matched nonplaying controls. All measurements were performed on the lower body and included hip flexion with the knee straight, hip extension, hip abduction, knee flexion with the subject lying prone, and ankle dorsiflexion with the knee straight. Sprains of the knees and ankles were the predominant injuries.

Chandler (1990a) reported that flexibility comparisons of junior elite tennis players to other athletes indicated specific musculoskeletal adaptations in areas of the body under highest stress. Tennis players demonstrated less flexibility than other athletes on shoulder internal and external rotation on the dominant and nondominant sides as well as less low back flexibility. These tennis players, mean age 15.4, spent approximately 6 days per week, totaling 22 hours, on the tennis court.

Although less data are available on the flexibility of prepubertal athletes, recent information demonstrates that the same flexibility patterns may occur with intense participation in this age group. Researchers compared strength and flexibility measurements of preadolescent tennis and soccer players to active but not intensely trained controls. Three groups of athletes ages 10 to 14 were measured using the sit and reach, sit-ups, push-ups, grip strength, and goniometric range of motion of the hamstrings, quadriceps, gastrocnemius, and shoulder internal and external rotators. Groups consisted of intensely trained tennis players from a resident tennis camp ($n = 143$), intensely trained soccer players from elite city soccer clubs ($n = 41$), and active but not intensely trained controls ($n = 123$). Results are presented in Table 7.1. Soccer players showed less quadriceps flexibility than the other groups, and tennis players showed less hamstring and shoulder internal rotation flexibility. Controls performed significantly more sit-ups, and tennis players performed significantly more push-ups. Values for sit-and-reach and grip strength were not significantly different. The authors concluded that flexibility and strength adaptations to intense participation in soccer and tennis are specific to the sport.

Adaptations to Muscular Strength

Muscle strength adaptations have been reported elsewhere in the scientific literature (Anderink & Kuck, 1986; Chandler, 1990; Cook, Gray, Savinar-Nogue, & Medeiros, 1987; Hinton, 1988; Ivey, Calhoun, Rusche, & Biershenk, 1985; Kibler, 1990c; Parker, Ruhling, Holt, Bauman, & Drayna, 1983). Chandler (1992) demonstrated that college-level tennis players increase the strength of the shoulder

Table 7.1   Flexibility and Strength Comparisons of Prepubertal Intensively Trained Tennis Players, Soccer Players, and Normally Active Controls

	Tennis: mean (cm)/ standard deviation		Soccer: mean (cm)/ standard deviation		Control: mean (cm)/ standard deviation		
Low back	4.9	8.0	4.8	5.3	6.1	8.7	NS
Dominant quadriceps	131.1	10.2	123.4	13.5	126.2	16.1	*1
Nondominant quadriceps	130.4	9.6	124.6	12.3	130.3	7.7	*2
Dominant hamstring	84.5	9.8	89.1	9.6	85.7	15.4	*3
Nondominant hamstring	84.1	10.7	87.9	16.0	85.5	15.0	NS
Dominant gastrocnemius	12.5	10.3	12.1	4.9	10.1	6.2	NS
Nondominant gastrocnemius	11.1	5.2	12.6	4.8	10.4	6.5	*4
Dominant shoulder internal rotator	58.2	13.8	63.9	16.2	66.3	16.2	*5
Nondominant shoulder internal rotator	66.3	11.5	70.0	13.6	70.8	15.6	*6
Dominant shoulder external rotator	118.2	17.2	122.2	11.3	107.7	28.3	*7
Nondominant shoulder external rotator	119.6	13.4	121.4	15.9	108.9	14.6	*8
Sit-ups	42.4	9.4	41.9	9.8	50.6	13.7	*9
Push-ups	33.8	14.1	23.1	14.6	30.7	19.0	*10
Dominant grip	59.3	20.4	58.2	21.2	54.4	16.0	NS
Nondominant grip	48.4	16.3	49.0	18.2	48.3	17.5	NS

Note. NS = nonsignificant differences.
*1 Tennis = soccer, $p < .01$, tennis = control, $p < .05$.
*2 Tennis = soccer, $p < .05$, soccer = control, $p < .01$.
*3 Tennis = soccer, $p < .01$.
*4 Soccer = control, $p < .05$.
*5 Tennis = soccer, $p < .05$, tennis = control, $p < .01$.
*6 Tennis = control, $p < .01$.
*7 Tennis = control, $p < .01$, soccer = control, $p < .01$.
*8 Tennis = control, $p < .01$, soccer = control, $p < .01$.
*9 Tennis = control, $p < .01$, soccer = control, $p < .01$.
*10 Tennis = soccer, $p < .01$, soccer = control, $p < .05$.

musculature in internal rotation without subsequently strengthening the external rotator muscle group, creating a functional muscle imbalance that may predispose athletes to injury. Using their nondominant arms as controls, these tennis players demonstrated significantly greater strength in internal rotation in peak torque at 60° per second and 300° per second and in average power at 60° per second and 300° per second. In external rotation, the tennis players were significantly stronger on only one of the four measurements; peak torque at 300° per second. By increasing the strength of the internal rotator muscle groups without subsequently strengthening the external rotators, the athlete creates a muscle imbalance that may predispose him or her to overload injury.

These studies indicate a sport-specific adaptation of the musculoskeletal system, relative to strength and flexibility, in athletes of all ages. From the data presently available, it appears that prepubescent athletes show the same musculoskeletal adaptations as older athletes, even though these adaptations may become more marked with continued participation as the athlete ages.

Summary

Adaptations to the musculoskeletal systems of athletes correspond with the sites of primary tensile overload. In postpubertal athletes, these adaptations have been documented in measurements of both strength and flexibility. In prepubertal athletes, these adaptations have been demonstrated as decreased flexibility of the musculotendinous unit. More research is needed on the adaptations of young athletes in regard to muscle strength, although preliminary evidence indicates muscle weaknesses are present.

The importance of these findings is related to two areas. The first is that the prepubescent's musculoskeletal base responds in the same manner to tensile loads as the postpubertal athlete's. Therefore, preparticipation evaluations and precompetition conditioning programs are valid and are necessary for intensively trained prepubescent athletes. Second, data from a tennis academy show that these inflexibility patterns in young athletes resist normalization over short periods of time (Kibler, 1986). As long as 1 year was needed to normalize the internal rotation contractures in the older adolescents studied. Therefore, coaches and trainers should strive for early recognition and should employ aggressive programs to correct these maladaptions.

Previously, overload injuries may have comprised the most overlooked category of athletic injuries in terms of research and diagnosis. Although the recognition of such injuries is increasing, the actual role of strength and flexibility deficits in the cause and prevention of these injuries is not completely clear. It appears that these deficits create abnormal mechanics that predispose the tissues to injury with continued use. The injuries occur either locally or at a distance from the mechanical deficit. These injuries comprise a significant part of injuries sustained in sports, and they greatly affect performance. Understanding the dynamics of muscle function in athletic activity, including force generation, force regulation, load absorption, and neurological control, as well as understanding the consequences that alterations in these functions will have on injury and performance, is critical to reducing the risk of injury to athletes, including children.

In terms of understanding the effect of an intensive exercise dose, young athletes deserve special attention both because of their different physiology and because of their documented increased participation in intensive sports. Overload injuries historically seen in older athletes after years of participation are increasing in younger athletes, which is likely due to increasing intensity of competition and practice and a lack of sport-specific conditioning.

Several predisposing factors cause these injuries: anatomy of children, changes to the musculoskeletal base due to athletic activities, and intrinsic demands of the sport. Anatomically, growing bone has a looser periosteum and tendinous attachments than mature bone, which means that less force can cause traction overloads. The epiphyses and apophyses are also weak links in the bone-tendon-muscle unit, because they are susceptible to tensile overloads. Also, as a consequence of differential growth patterns in the length of bones relative to muscles, many of the larger muscle groups of both upper and lower extremities and the back show decreased flexibility. This condition may be present in up to 88% of prepubescent males (back and hamstrings) and 78% of prepubescent females (back) (Kibler, 1986). This tightness also affects muscle strength by interfering with the normal length-tension relationship. A tight and weak muscle is the most susceptible to overload injury.

In the average intensively trained young athlete, inflexibilities, which have been demonstrated in key anatomic areas, create a less than optimal base for athletic performance. However, it is the extrinsic factors resulting from the demands of the sport, when added to this deficient base, that result in overt injuries. These factors include increased size required for the sport; improper biomechanics of weight training, throwing, running, or jumping; traumatic injuries or inadequate rehabilitation; and the large amount of time spent competing, practicing, or conditioning.

Improper biomechanics may involve poor form or altered biomechanical patterns due to fatigue, weakness, inflexibility, pain, or injury. The throwing athlete or tennis player with inflexible and weak external rotators of the shoulder may change the mechanics of the overhead motion, which may help temporarily but also will likely cause more problems in the future and may decrease performance. The same is also likely in long-distance runners with ankle plantarflexor weakness and inflexibility who will shorten their stride or have function pronation that predisposes plantar fasciitis. Similarly, hamstring weakness and inflexibility may cause increased patellofemoral joint load and anterior knee pain in running athletes.

In both conditioning for a sport and practicing the skills involved, athletes must follow proper principles of conditioning to allow time for muscles to recover. Proper sequence and progression of both skill work and conditioning are imperative so the athlete does not attempt skills that are too advanced.

Traumatic injuries and inadequate rehabilitation place extra strains on the athlete, predisposing him or her to reinjury or causing new injuries in other parts of the kinetic chain. It is said that prevention of the second ankle sprain begins with proper rehabilitation of the first sprain.

Structured athletic programs are the means through which most young athletes participate. It is possible for an athlete to play an organized sport every day of the year and to play several sports at the same time of year. This places extra load on the athlete in two ways. First, competition is often continuous, allowing little rest, and second, because different sports have different musculoskeletal requirements, so muscles may not be fit for all activities.

Proper musculoskeletal preparation is based in the sport-specific preparticipation exam, which can elucidate information about the athlete's muscular ability to participate in a particular sport and can suggest proper conditioning practices to obtain maximum muscular fitness, proper from perspectives of both health and athletic fitness. Proper mechanics result from good coaching and emphasis on practicing skills rather than from spending all of the practice time playing the sport. Proper mechanics improve the efficiency of muscle action and decrease the chance of fatigue and overload to the muscle.

In summary, musculoskeletal problems in adolescent and preadolescent athletes are very common and appear to be similar to musculoskeletal problems in older athletes. These problems can be strongly related to the intensity of participation as well as the musculoskeletal base the athlete brings to the sport. Thus, prepubertal and postpubertal athletes respond in the same manner to overload. Maladaptations of the musculoskeletal system occur in preadolescent athletes in the areas of strength and flexibility. These maladaptations likely predispose the prepubertal athlete to overload injuries, which are the predominant injuries in athletes of this age. Risks of injury and responses to intense athletic participation appear to be the same in pre- and postpubertal athletes. Prehabilitation prevention strategies suggested for postpubertal athletes could be the same with proper modification for size and strength. Conditioning exercises designed to correct these maladaptations, along with reasonable guidelines for intensity and frequency of participation, will likely reduce the frequency of overload injuries in the prepubertal athlete.

Future directions to explore in this area include expansion of the preparticipation exam to larger populations in other sports, the implementation of prehabilitation conditioning programs to improve the musculoskeletal base the athlete brings to the sport, and longitudinal tracking systems for long-term evaluation of the effects of intensive exercise on clinical symptoms and sport performance.

References

Adams, J.E. (1965). Injury to the throwing arm: A study of traumatic changes in the elbow joints of boy baseball players. *California Medicine*, **102**(2), 127-132.

Anderink, G.J., & Kuck, D.J. (1986). Isokinetic shoulder strength of high school and college-aged pitchers. *Journal of Orthopaedic and Sports Physical Therapy*, 163-172.

Armstrong, R.B. (1990). Initial events in exercise-induced muscular injury. *Medicine and Science in Sports and Exercise*, **22**(4), 429-435.

Chandler, T.J., Kibler, W.B., Uhl, T.L., Wooten, B., Kiser, A., & Stone, E. (1990). Flexibility comparisons of junior elite tennis players to other athletes. *The American Journal of Sports Medicine*, **18**(2), 134-136.

Chandler, T.J., Kibler, W.B., Kiser, A.M., & Pace, B.P. (1992). Shoulder strength, power, and endurance in college tennis players. *American Journal of Sports Medicine*, **20**(4), 455-458.

Clancey, W. (1982). Tendinitis and plantar fasciitis in runners. In R. D'Ambrosia & D. Drez (Eds.), *Prevention and treatment of running injuries* (pp. 77-87). Thorofare, NJ: Slack.

Cook, E.E., Gray, V.L., Savinar-Nogue, E., & Medeiros, J. (1987). Shoulder antagonistic strength ratios: A comparison between college-level baseball pitchers and nonpitchers. *Journal of Orthopaedic and Sports Physical Therapy*, **8**(9), 451-461.

Ekstrand, J., & Gillquist, J. (1982). The frequency of muscle tightness and injuries in soccer players. *The American Journal of Sports Medicine*, **10**(2), 75-78.

Garrett, W.E. (1990). Muscle strain injuries: Clinical and basic aspects. *Medicine and Science in Sports and Exercise*, **22**(4), 436-443.

Herring, S.A. (1990). Rehabilitation of muscle injuries. *Medicine and Science in Sports and Exercise*, **22**(4), 453-456.

Hinton, R.Y. (1988). Isokinetic evaluation of shoulder rotational strength in high school baseball pitchers. *American Journal of Sports Medicine*, **16**(3), 274-279.

Ivey, F.M., Calhoun, J.H., Rusche, K., & Biershenk, J. (1985). Isokinetic testing of the shoulder strength: Normal values. *Archives of Physical Medicine and Rehabilitation*, **66**, 384-386.

Kibler, W.B., Chandler, T.J., & Goldberg, C. (1991). Functional biomechanical deficits in running athletes with plantar fasciitis. *American Journal of Sports Medicine*, **19**(1), 66-71.

Kibler, W.B., Chandler, T.J., Pace, B.P., Odom, C.J., Strasner, E.S. (1992). A comparison of musculoskeletal fitness profiles of intensely trained tennis players, soccer players, and controls. Manuscript submitted for publication.

Kibler, W.B., Chandler, T.J., Uhl, T., & Maddux, R.E. (1989). A musculoskeletal approach to the preparticipation physical examination, preventing injury and improving performance. *The American Journal of Sports Medicine*, **17**(4), 525-531.

Kibler, W.B., McQueen, C., & Uhl, T. (1988). Fitness evaluations and fitness findings in competitive junior tennis players. *Clinics in Sports Medicine*, **7**(2), 403-416.

Kibler, W.B. (1986). Unpublished raw data.

Kibler, W.B. (1990a). Clinical aspects of muscle injury. *Medicine and Science in Sports and Exercise*, **22**(4), 450-452.

Kibler, W.B. (1990b). Concepts in exercise rehabilitation of athletes. In W. Ledbetter (Ed.), *Sports induced inflammation: Clinical and basic science concepts* (pp. 759-769). Chicago: American Orthopaedic Society for Sports Medicine.

Kibler, W.B. (1990c). *The sport preparticipation fitness examination*. Champaign, IL: Human Kinetics.

Martens, R. (1978). *Joy and sadness in children's sports*. Champaign, IL: Human Kinetics.

Micheli, L.J. (1982). Upper-extremity injuries: Overuse injuries in the recreational adult. In R.C. Cantu (Ed.), *The exercising adult* (pp. 121-128). Lexington, MA: Collamore Press.

Nirschl, R.P. (1979). Tennis elbow. *Journal of Bone and Joint Surgery*, **61A**, 832-839.

Parker, M.G., Ruhling, R.O., Holt, D., Bauman, E., & Drayna, M. (1983). Descriptive analysis of quadriceps and hamstrings muscle torque in high school football players. *Journal of Orthopaedic and Sports Physical Therapy*, **5**, 2-6.

Rarick, G.L., & Seefeldt, V. (1976). Characteristics of the young athlete. In J.R. Thomas (Ed.), *Youth sports guide for coaches and parents.* Washington, DC: American Association for Health, Physical Education, and Recreation.

Seefeldt, V.B., & Haugenstricker, J. (1978). Competitive athletics for children: The Michigan study. *Journal of Health, Physical Education, and Recreation*, **49**, 38-41.

Shoulder pain in swimmers: Introduction. (1980). *The Physician and Sportsmedicine*, **8**, 35.

Steindler, A.J. (1956). Contracture of soft tissue. In *Kinesiology of the human body.* Springfield, IL: Charles C Thomas.

Wilkins, K.E. (1980). The uniqueness of the young athlete: Musculoskeletal injuries. *The American Journal of Sports Medicine*, **8**(5), 377-382.

Chapter 8

Intensive Training in the Young Athlete: Pathoanatomic Change

Bert R. Mandelbaum

Historically, musculoskeletal adaptation to inactivity, activity, and overactivity has been a challenge with respect to health and disease. At one time scientists believed that bone was truly an inert material that was unable to dynamically respond to stimuli. It was not until 1892 that Wolff presented and eventually popularized the concept that mechanical force applied to bone resulted in adaptation. Only in recent years has the sophistication of biochemical and other laboratory techniques allowed us to define, characterize, and quantify the responses of bones to these stimuli. We now understand that bone is a complex, composite structure that has dynamic functions and that responds with a high gain or loss in density during performance, health, and disease. Analogously, the sciences of connective-tissue physiology and biochemistry have been in the embryonic stage and in fact may be at the same stage as cardiovascular physiology earlier in this century. Thus, with the development of new assessment techniques combined with objectively quantifiable methods of directing exercise specificity, the clinical scientist can better define bone structure and function and can understand the impact of multiple modulation factors on the local, regional, and systemic levels. This understanding is vital, given that a stress injury or a developmental chronic disorder can result in pain, diminution of performance, and inability to participate. These are the specific clinical problems and solutions that are significant to physician, athlete, and parent. In view of this, the goals of the health care team include maximizing performance, minimizing morbidity, and preventing injury. Consequently, it is imperative that the connective tissue scientist, in collaboration with clinician, develop a sophisticated understanding of complex dose-response relationships. Therefore, the purpose of this chapter is as follows:

1. To define the specific dose-response relationships in the child and adolescent during intensive training and exercise.

2. To define the dose factors with respect to the duration, intensity, and frequency that have most impact on the adaptive response.

3. To define the adaptive response factors on the local, regional, and systemic levels. This includes physeal susceptibility; physical, biochemical, and cellular factors of bone; and physiological, endocrine, and nutritional details that contribute to the response adaptation.

4. To make specific recommendations as a result of the sport and its requirements, age of initiation, qualitative and quantifiable progression of training, and specificity of athlete for a particular sport.

Historical Perspective of Injury Prevention

Injury and prevention have been challenges since the Old Testament. In the *Book of Genesis*, Jacob was described as "wrestling with a man resulting in a hallow in his thigh." In the writings of Kung Fu the Chinese civilization first developed the relationship between quality of life and exercise. Unfortunately, most early sports injury in the Greek civilization related to battlefield trauma. Hippocrates' treatises regarding the humors of injury in principles of surgery and health and disease were a product of this battlefield laboratory. Furthermore, by approximately 700 B.C. the concept of body and mind integration through sports such as gymnastics and running was popularized. As a result, in honor of the god Zeus, the first Olympiad was created in 762 B.C. The Athenians identified gymnastics as a sport worthy of Olympic competition. The Spartans titled the sport *gymnastics*, meaning "to perform exercises while naked." Aristotle, with interests in "marathon" running between Sparta and Athens, stated that Olympic victors were those who did not squander their powers by early training. In the Roman civilization Claudius Galen was the first sports physician to further develop the relationship between body and mind in athletics. In addition, he popularized and advanced the concept that tendons would "waste away" if they were idle. After the fall of the Roman Empire, concepts of physical activity, health, and exercise became of secondary importance. Through the Renaissance and the Islamic civilizations, Mercuriale and Avicenna further developed issues of response to injury, early motion, and the import of muscle activity. In 1892, Wolff stated that tissues could respond and adapt to mechanical forces placed upon them. "In relation, every change and form of function of bone is followed by definite changes in internal architecture and equally definite secondary alterations in its mathematical laws" (Wolff, 1892, p. 272). The end of the 19th century brought us Darling's classic text, *On the Effects of Training*.

The 20th century has been remarkable for conceptual developments by individuals such as Paul Dudley White, who underscored the adaptive effects of the cardiovascular system. He not only described the "athletic heart" syndrome and the mechanical, structural, and physiological transitions of the cardiovascular system that result from physical training, but he held that dose-response relationships—when within normal limits—are a normal response to activity and overactivity.

Little was done until the post–World War II era in 1961 when John F. Kennedy first defined the importance of physical fitness by creating the foundation of the President's Council on Physical Fitness. The next 2 decades resulted in the growth and popularity of sports, and in the 1972 and 1976 Olympics, stars such as Olga Korbut and Nadia Comaneci introduced the world to gymnastics through the media and telecommunications. They illuminated the beautiful sport, which requires grace, determination, discipline, and, in their cases, perfection. As a consequence, gymnastics as a sport has grown to include more than 2 million gymnasts on the club, school, and collegiate levels. In addition, the remainder of the population continues to cultivate commitments to a multitude of sports and activities. Our society at all levels and ages has become increasingly involved in physical activity. At one time a marathon was the end-all of long distance running, but now many have set ultramarathons and triathlons as the extreme point of athletic endeavors.

This increased activity has increased dose-related problems such as stress fractures, physeal injuries, and developmental disorders. At best we have only descriptive and epidemiological data regarding the etiology and pathogenesis of these disorders. Runners will now run anything from 10K races to marathons without using detailed systematic approaches to training progression and competition. Gymnasts begin their participation at the age of 5 or 6, training up to 24 hr per week, 365 days a year, during growth and development. The current trend toward gathering elite young gymnasts in regional training centers has added the stress of isolation from their families to the physiological and psychological demands placed on the developing adolescents. The U.S. Soccer Federation now has 7 million members, most of whom are between the ages of 5 and 18; stress injuries are these athletes' major problem. Among dancers, musculoskeletal injuries to the hip and spine have become common, as has delayed menarche, or amenorrhea, a serious problem that requires professional health care.

In summary, our population now engages in a wide spectrum of activity (and overactivity). As a consequence athletes bring to our health care system a variety of clinical problems caused by traumatic and overuse injuries, which have both physiological and psychological consequences. Therefore the sports physician must attempt to answer the following questions:

1. How do we define the dose of a specific sport, qualitatively and quantitatively?
2. How does one objectively define the response of adaptation with respect to performance and injury?
3. What specific indicators tell us at what age a child can begin to participate in a specific sport?
4. What constitutes optimal specificity for a specific sport relative to dose-response relationships?
5. What temporal details and training progressions are appropriate for a specific sport and a specific athlete?
6. How does participation ultimately affect specific organs and how does this relate to local, regional and systemic factors?

The Clinical Problem: Human Response

There is little information regarding the exact response of growing bone to various loads. Few studies have shown the adaptation of immature bone to stressful exercise and the resultant spectrum of anatomic and pathoanatomic changes. Possible local changes include physical changes to the size of the extremity, biochemical changes including the organic matrix and the inorganic phase, and cellular changes to the osteoclast and osteoblast. Regional changes include the increasing size of an extremity, both bony as well as soft tissue, and systemic changes include changes to the neuroendocrine axis. The physical hypertrophic response to long-term overloading has been noted in the humerus and radius of professional tennis players. Alexseev (1977) suggested a similar response in the hands and feet of ski racers; in this study, comparisons between skiers and nonskier controls indicated that the skiers had larger hands and feet than controls. If we consider the fact that congenital absence of the tibia results in fibular hypertrophy, it follows that hypertrophy of the growing bone in response to physical loading or overload is the normal adaptive response. Despite the structural asymmetry, most athletes who experience such hypertrophy continue to perform at high levels with few or no subjective or objective problems.

A significant number of clinical reports indicate that high-level physical activity causes significant injury to the epiphyseal plate and consequent pathoanatomic changes. Objective pathoanatomic changes may include epiphyseal plate fragmentation, cystic changes, and irregularities of the metaphyseal margin, therefore resulting in a beaking in the distal aspect of the metaphysis.

A multitude of clinical problems result from relative overuse of and overloading to the adolescent athlete's extremities. These problems are ubiquitous in structured developmental programs such as Little League and in children's gymnastics and tennis, where the age of initiation is low and the intensity of participation is high. The upper extremities of young baseball pitchers received attention in 1953, when Dotter described the "Little League shoulder." Adams (1976) further characterized this as a syndrome consisting of pain felt during the end of a hard throw. X rays of affected athletes whom Adams studied indicated widening of the proximal humeral epiphysis and demineralization and fragmentation. In these cases, the process was self-limited; treatments included rest and palliative management. Symptoms resolved in 6 weeks, resulting in complete clinical recovery at the end of 8 weeks. Cahill, Tullos, and Fain (1974), Barnett (1985), and Drvaric and Albert (1990) described the same syndrome, cautioning against overuse syndrome and making recommendations for diagnosis, treatment, and prevention.

The elbow has been another site of overuse in the Little League baseball pitcher. This injury has been titled the "Little League elbow." Pathoanatomic radiographic changes occur most commonly on the medial side in 23% of all players. Torg (1972) identified three separate processes involved in Little League elbow: medial condylar apophysitis, osteochondritis of the radial head, and osteochondritis of the humeral capitellum. Adams (1976) described radiographic changes in the medial epicondylar epiphysis in pitchers; these radiographic findings included physeal enlargement, augmentation, and premature closure and separation or widening of the epiphysis. Thus, specific anatomic and pathoanatomic changes result from intensive baseball pitching.

Wrist pain in the gymnast is a difficult diagnostic and therapeutic challenge, the causes of which are unknown. Wrist pain is a significant problem given that most gymnastics skills involve upper extremity weight bearing; pain can result in loss of participation time and, ultimately, reduction in performance. This problem, therefore, serves as a clinical model of overuse in the pediatric and adolescent athlete. Researchers in the initial study, after clinically observing increasing wrist pain, evaluated 38 collegiate gymnasts clinically and radiographically (Mandelbaum, Bartolozzi, Davis, Teurlings, & Bragonier, 1989). The incidence of wrist pain was 75% in the males and 33% in the females. A subsequent study of 43 gymnasts with a mean age of 11.7 years demonstrated incidence of 72% with pain lasting longer than 4 months. In addition, these studies indicated a trend toward increasing occurrence and intensity of wrist pain in the younger and female gymnast. Further, characterization of this problem demonstrates that the pain is insidious at onset and is generally not caused by an acute injury or mechanism. Pain follows a typical progression; initially the pain occurs only during gymnastics activity, then it is present only during and after the activity, and then pain becomes constant. Coincidentally, the incidence of wrist pain has increased with the introduction of the ''Urtchenko'' vault. During this vault the gymnast hyperextends her hand with a high-velocity impact shear force prior to hitting the springboard. In the second phase of the vault, the hand is placed in a hyperextended position against the top of the horse. Both of these positions cause pain by increasing stress forces within the wrist.

The dose-response relationship in gymnastics was further characterized with development of Total Hours of Gymnastics (THG), an index to quantify the dose of gymnastics. Theoretically, the dose includes the weight-bearing forces of the upper extremity multiplied by the duration, intensity, and frequency of activities. The incidence of pain is correlated to increasing age and increasing total hours of gymnastics. Response factors include clinical factors of pain and radiographic factors. Roy, Caine, and Singer (1985) reported on stress changes, as revealed by X ray, in the distal radial physis in 21 young high-performance gymnasts. Aldridge, Carter, and Read (1981) identified similar radiographic changes in the distal radial physis. As a consequence of these pathoanatomic changes to the ''end organ'' of the distal radial physis, there is an apparent direct effective decrease in the growth of the distal radius. At the same time the distal ulnar physis remains open resulting in positive ulnar variance. Initial studies in collegiate gymnasts, mean age 21 years, demonstrated statistical differences between gymnasts and nongymnast controls to $p < 0.001$ (BRM) (Mandelbaum, Bartolozzi, Davis, Teurlings, & Bragonier, 1989). In another study, younger gymnasts (average age $p < 11.7$ years) demonstrated a variance of +0.35 mm, whereas the age-matched nongymnast controls demonstrated a variance of −0.30 mm, statistically different at $p < .05$. Another group of gymnasts, mean age of 16 years, was studied at the World Championships in Rotterdam. The mean ulnar variance in this group was +0.68 mm. This data is on the same curve as the data from the studies of 11- and 21-year-old gymnasts. We can derive several conclusions from these studies:

1. Gymnastic wrist pain is increasingly common and is becoming more debilitating.
2. Wrist pain is correlated with the total hours spent in gymnastics and with increase in the age of the gymnast and thus has a specific dose-response relationship.
3. As shown radiographically, the gymnast has an increased tendency toward positive ulnar variance.

Overuse in adolescent runners has caused injury to the tibial physis. Cahill (1976) reported a proximal tibial epiphyseal stress fracture in a 15-year-old male cross-country runner. Goodshall, Hansen, and Raising (1981) reported a distal femoral epiphyseal stress injury in a 15-year-old football player on a running fitness program. Clinically, these patients present with pain and radiographically demonstrate widened epiphyseal plates. Kato and Ishiko (1964) reported 116 cases of arrested epiphyseal growth in the lower extremities of Japanese children performing strenuous labor. This factor led to reduced lower extremity height, but in these cases there may have been other modulators such as poor nutrition (Kato & Ishiko, 1964). In addition, injuries of the lower extremity included apophyseal problems, because some of these injuries occur in patients whose epiphyses were still open. Such injuries occurred in girls twice as often as in boys. The most common signs of apophyseal problems were knee problems and a painful tibial tubercle (indicating the classic diagnosis of Osgood-Schlatter disease) and a painful heel (indicating Sever's disease). Injuries were reportedly treated with rest and were self-limited by virtue of their healing potential. Thus, it appears that running and overuse during running can injure the distal femoral or tibial physis, decreasing overall growth or causing stress fracture. These processes are self-limited and can easily heal with time and rest. It appears, therefore, that dose factors qualitatively and quantitatively can determine whether significant injury to the immature skeleton occurs.

Other problems that have been presented regarding overuse to the growing adolescent extremity include that of ''break dancer's wrist.'' In a case report, Gerber, Griffin, and Simons (1986) reported on an injury to the distal ulnar physis as a result of upper extremity weight-bearing during break dancing.

Therefore, the literature has identified several injuries to the extremities resulting from activity and overactivity. The pathogenetic sequence includes hypertrophy on both the regional level and on the local level causing changes within the physis. Pathoanatomic changes within the physis cause growth cartilage to transform into bone, which results in a growth inhibition or, in the most extreme circumstance, a partial growth or full arrest. Although the quantitative details and the specifics of the dose-response relationships have not been studied clinically, clearly we may conclude that there is a threshold point above which are significant negative consequences such as pain, pathoanatomic changes defined radiographically, and diminished training and performance.

Animal Studies

In recent years significant literature has investigated the dose-response activity of the immature skeleton of a variety of animals. In the past there has been a dearth of sensitive, accurate, and reproducible techniques to identify various components and how they respond to physical, mechanical, and biochemical stimuli. Existing parameters fall into four groups: physical, inorganic, organic, and strength. Physical parameters include measurements of bone size, length, cortical diameter, and width. The inorganic fraction is best measured with total body calcium, bone mineral density, and bone mineral concentration. The organic fraction can be assayed through metabolites of collagen metabolism including hydroxyproline and the respective cross-links. Measurements of bone strength have been limited to tensile strength in animal studies and fracture rate and fracture details in human studies. Because assay techniques are now more sensitive, we can evaluate Wolff's law, which states (in translation) that "every change in form of function or bone results in a change in internal architecture" (Wolff, 1892, p. 271). To this end, evaluation of the dose of specific activity and response is analogous to a pharmacological evaluation of a drug's dose and consequence response. The dose involves a spectrum of factors, such as duration, intensity, frequency, and the activity itself (which can range from weightlessness in space, to bed rest, to immobilization). In addition, the assessment must consider the specific athlete and how the respective activity is administered. Therefore, the system must be modeled after the work of a pharmacologist, who interprets a drug and its impact on the organism as a dose-response curve. The route of administration, mechanism, the age of the organism, and other details define the athlete's response to the dose for the spectrum from immobilization to strenuous exercise. Therefore, it is imperative that the spectrum be developed from zero loading, which includes weightlessness in space, to immobilization, low-intensity exercise, and high-intensity exercise, and the appropriate responses.

Space Flight and Weightlessness

Animal studies conducted with rats during the various Cosmos and Space Lab III flights demonstrate that weightlessness decreases bone mass, periosteal new bone formation, and physical parameters of strength and stiffness.

Immobilization

Allison demonstrated that immobilization decreases the overall length of bones and increases the canal diameter (Allison & Brooks, 1921). Steinberg demonstrated in immature rats that immobilization decreases whole-body weight as well as length thickness and mass of the long bones (Steinberg & Trueta, 1981); articular surfaces and epiphyseal lines were irregular, bone formation was retarded, and the circulation to the femoral head was diminished. Reactivation of these animals resulted in increases in weight and in length, thickness, and mass of the bone. Immobilization in mature animals led to a decrease in bone mass, whereas activity resulted in an increase. Allison and Brooks (1921) reported that immobilizing the extremities (in casts) of immature dogs resulted in decreased length and increased canal diameter. Laros demonstrated that immobilization of pig tibias resulted in decreased bone mass (Laros, Tipton, & Cooper, 1971); the histological changes included an increased scalloping and an increased number of osteoclasts. Gillespie (1954) demonstrated increased muscle and bone mass in immobilized rats. Vogel (Vogel & Whittle, 1976) demonstrated that immobilization resulted in atrophy of muscle and bone. Deitrick demonstrated that immobilization resulted in increased hydroxyproline and calcium excretion (Dietrick, Whedon, & Schorre, 1948). In addition, there is an increase in osteoclast number as well as release of organic and inorganic phases, which results in a net bone resorption relative to a decreased bone formation. Thus, immobilization results in a decrease in mineral and organic phases of bone. This appears to result in a net bone resorption and decreased bone mass.

Historically, exercise has been thought to exert a positive effect on bone. Sayille created a bipedal rat model that resulted in increased size of the femur and increased breaking strength (Sayille & Smith, 1966; Sayille & White, 1969). Chamay exercised a dog radius, which resulted in ulnar hypertrophy (Chamay & Tschantz, 1972). Goodship exercised pig ulna, resulting in a radial hypertrophy (Goodship, Lanyon, & McFieh, 1979).

Low-Intensity Exercise

Woo, et al. (1981), in a pig treadmill study, documented increased cortical thickness as a result of exercise as a discrete entity; there were also increases in the mineral and organic phases. Vailas, in a running rat model, demonstrated an increase in glycosaminoglycans (Vailas, Martinez, Shaw, Zernicke, & Grindeland, 1987). Heikkinen, using a growing mice training model, demonstrated increased collagen metabolism (Heikkinen & Vuori, 1972). Liu, in a running dog model, demonstrated that on the days the animals were run, calcium excretion in the urine decreased (Liu & McCay, 1953). Thus, that animal study shows that bone responds to exercise, with exercise typically increasing the physical size and also positively affecting the mineral and organic phases, thus increasing the material properties and strength of bone.

High-Intensity Exercise

Booth and Gould hypothesized that low-intensity exercise increases bone length and growth whereas high-intensity exercise may inhibit bone growth (Booth et al., 1981). Relating to the Hueter-Volkmann principle of epiphyseal pressures, there is an inverse relationship between status compressive forces parallel to the axis of epiphyseal growth and the rate of growth of that cartilage. Furthermore, via Wolff's law of transformation (1892), physical load stimulates hypertrophy of growing bone with direct response to additional strain. Gelbke (1950), using a dog model, concluded that the strong compressive forces resulted in increased enchondral ossification. In addition, the extremes of tension and pressure cause a disappearance of the epiphyseal growth plate and diminution in growth. The Hueter-Volkmann principle further states that compression stimulates longitudinal growth of the epiphysis. However, excess compressive loads can diminish growth. Simon (1978), using a bipedal fifth metatarsal amputation model, illustrated an increased compressive load with intermittent dynamic loading. As a consequence, he demonstrated an inverse U-curve such that low levels of compression were essential to stimulate accelerated physeal growth; however, when the threshold was attained, compressive force caused suppression of the physeal cartilage and consequent enchondral ossification. In addition, self-proliferation rate in the growth plate decreased with increasing progressive stress, which parallels the decrement in long bone growth (Shinoyaka, Tsuri, Nagmumma, Moss, & Salentjul, 1984). Vasan (1983) showed that in rats, training at a very low dose and low intensity had actually no effect on bone size. Sayille corroborated this finding 40 years later with a rat model (Sayille & Smith, 1966). Kiskinnen and Heikkinen (1973b; Kiiskinen, 1977) demonstrated in growing mice that increasing intensity resulted in longer, heavier bones. In addition, increasing duration caused significantly shorter and lighter bones. These studies were eventually corroborated by Tipton. Matsuda et al. (1986), studying immature growing chickens, demonstrated that very strenuous, high-level intensive exercise decreased size and strength of bones and biochemically decreased nonreducible cross-link collagen by products. Vailas et al. (1987), studying 3-week-old chicks on a treadmill, demonstrated decreased long bone growth in the tarsometatarsal and increased physeal height of 42%. Observing increased cellularity and decreased chondrocyte mitosis, he concluded that there was a retardation of maturation with very intense exercise. Pedrini-Mille, Peprini, Maynard, & Vailas (1986), using very intense exercise with 4-week-old chicks, demonstrated decreased protoglycans, decreased matrix, and a widened physis. The material properties of bone, including bending stiffness and overall strength, also decreased. Therefore, it appears that the physis has a degree of susceptibility to the dose of mechanical load, in which the qualitative and quantitative factors may be significant.

Response Modulators

Physeal susceptibility may depend not only on dose factors but also on response modulators. These modulators may include endocrine as well as nutritional factors.

Endocrine Factors

Vanbuul-Offers, Smeets, and Vandenbrande (1984) illustrated that growth hormone and Thyroxine influence the thickness of various cell zone layers of the physis. Growth hormone increases the thickness of both the proliferating and the hypertrophic cell layers, whereas T4 stimulates primarily the resting zone. Burch (1984) found that calcitonin increases cartilage growth primarily via cell hypertrophy rather than hyperplasia. In addition, calcitonin was determined to increase matrix formation. It appears that cortisol increases the rate of collagen synthesis in the short term; however, prolonged glucocorticoid treatment decreases collagen synthesis. This may be quite a significant factor, given that research has shown that mammals' levels of glucocorticoids increase with high-intensity exercise (Burch, 1984; Vanbuul-Offers et al., 1984). In fact, this may explain why there is a decreased collagen synthesis and suppression of long bone growth in the transition from moderate to very intense exercise, and it further supports the theory of increased physeal susceptibility with increasing intensity of activities and the increased sensitivity to a complex endocrinological milieu of stimulators.

Nutritional Factors

Nutritional factors have been found to directly impact physeal reactivity. Nutritional integrity depends on adequate levels of protein, calories, trace elements, and vitamins. A deficiency in any or all of these components may significantly impact the modulatory response of bone adaptation during exercise. Severe protein deficiency in prisoners of war and in patients with anorexia nervosa has been associated with a significantly decreased growth rate, decreased cortical thickness, and increased endosteal bone resorption. These osseous changes only occur when protein deficiency less than the 15th percentile is reached. Caloric intake does have indirect effects to the bone adaptive response. Specifically, adipose tissue is responsible for the conversion of androstenedione to estrone. Therefore, adipose tissue is involved with a peripheral conversion of the adrenal steroid precursors to estrogen. In addition, body weight directly correlates to estrone production and directly relates to menstrual abnormalities. Calcium, in view of its direct role in the mineral phase of bone, has a significant and direct impact on growth, development, adaptive response, and maintenance of integrity. Studies indicate that the intake of calcium is directly proportional to the maintenance of positive calcium balance. In addition, positive calcium balance is proportional to bony adaptation and to the ability of bone to respond to stress. Poor calcium dietary intake is directly proportional to bony maladaptation. Studies indicate that lactase-deficient patients and patients who have low calcium intakes have a significantly increased fracture rate and low bone mineral densities. Therefore, positive calcium balance is essential at all ages to ensure normal growth and development and to maintain adequate bone density and, therefore, mechanical strength of bone relative to its important functions of support, protection, and mineral storage.

Several trace elements may have a significant impact in bone adaptation and maladaptation. Zinc impacts the musculoskeletal system on multiple levels including growth, development, and adaptive response of bone to stress. It has been shown that zinc-deficient rats had tibial epiphyses that were narrower and thinner than those of normal rats. In addition, the trabeculae of the test rats were thinner and had less hypertrophy of cells and osteoblasts. It has been demonstrated that zinc-deficient chickens had significant collagenase deficiency and a decrement in collagen turnover, resulting in a tibial deformity called *perosis*. This decrement in collagen synthesis is associated with decreased alkaline phosphatase activity and decreased tibial collagenase. A study using a rat tibia fracture model demonstrated the effect of zinc deficiency and supplementation on fracture healing; zinc contributed to a more proliferative callus but did not significantly affect the time of fracture healing. A study using a rat femur model demonstrated that zinc was necessary for osteogenesis and that strength of the cancellous bone was directly proportional to zinc intake. In addition, zinc was found to accumulate at the sites of osteogenesis, and this accumulation could be accelerated by increasing zinc intake.

These studies identified the importance of zinc in bone growth, the adaptive response, and healing. Alkaline phosphatase is a zinc-dependent metalloenzyme, and is therefore dependent on accumulation of this trace element. Human studies have concentrated less on the effects of growth and osteogenesis and more on dietary intake in population studies. It is essential to provide adequate levels of zinc to the target tissue of bone, in order to maintain adequate homeostasis and positive zinc balance. In recent years, changes in the American diet, especially in younger athletes, have resulted in decreased zinc intake. The collegiate athlete, who commonly consumes a diet devoid of beef and other meat, may be 50% short of the recommended daily allowance of zinc; thus dietary intake is being decreased concomitant with an increase in physical and physiological requirements. This ongoing deficit may result in bone maladaptation and theoretically may increase physeal susceptibility to injury. Zinc homeostasis can be corrected by supplementation, which has significant positive implication.

Therefore, early nutritional integrity appears to be an essential component of bone's response to stress. Deficiencies in protein, calories, and specific trace elements may impact that adaptive response. Nutritional elements that relate to this modulation include calcium, phosphate, magnesium, zinc, and manganese. Those nutritional elements that have no relationship include sodium, fluoride, fiber, and Vitamin D. There are several other possible modulators of bone adaptation, including the maximum oxygen capacity and the degree of aerobic fitness. Anthropometric details and genetics are significant but are beyond the scope of this project. The important implication is that bone has a degree of "contractility," which means that there is a cyclic integration of modulators that allows a progressive increased responsiveness to increasing doses of exercise and training. This concept is illustrated by our schematic diagram (Figure 8.1), which shows a dose-response curve. The X-axis illustrates responsive adaptation; the Y-axis represents activity dose relative to weightlessness, bed rest, and the duration, intensity, and frequency of exercise. On the spectrum of the curve between weightlessness and bed rest, which both lack ground reactive forces, performance negatively adapts and results in decreased bone mineral density, decreased tensile strength, and decreased new periosteal bone formation. The exercise portion of the curve demonstrates that it is essential that bone adapt in a cyclically progressive fashion. All points below the cyclical curve allow a positive adaptation, which prevents the organism from injury.

Increasing the activity dose in a way inconsistent with the organism's pattern and quantity of response to adaptation, such as those practiced in a progressive training program, results in a maladaptive response and injury. In addition, in the moderate and high doses of exercise, dose response is key, as in any specific training program, in understanding and integrating details of the adaptive response. This includes not only quality and quantity but also temporal relationships. Negative modulation such as hormonal deficiency, nutritional deficiency, or increase in the duration, intensity, and frequency outside of the temporal response will also cause this negative response to adaptation. When the maximal dose ("D max") is exceeded, there will also be a negative response and maladaptation, as demonstrated by Simon (1978). Based on animal studies, it appears that the dose-response curve and the cyclical progression curve may comprise an appropriate working hypothesis from which new concepts can be generated and developed.

The Working Hypothesis: The Dose-Response Curve

The child is not a small adult. Cardiovascular, pulmonary, neuroendocrine, nutritional, and musculoskeletal factors are significantly different in children and

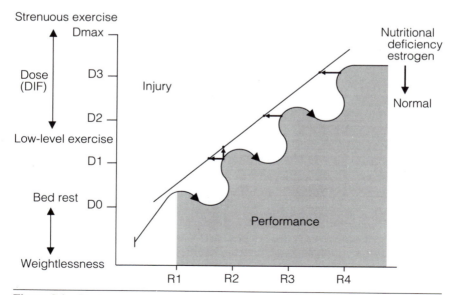

Figure 8.1 Dose-response curve.

adolescents as compared to adults. During the transition through puberty, these changes become less and less significant, but the end organ of the physis may have varied susceptibility. The pathogenesis of injury in intensively training youth may have several different etiologic progressions. Physeal susceptibility is increased between the ages of 6 and 9 but may significantly change at any time throughout growth and development. In addition, the susceptibility and response to various dose factors may change relative to response modulators. These modulators include presence of secondary sexual characteristics and Tanner scaling (the classification schema of the puberty spectrum), size, and age of menarche. Endocrine variables including estrogen, testosterone, growth hormone, cortisol, and perhaps prolactin. The complex interaction of all these modulators significantly impacts physeal susceptibility.

Among the most significant concerns in the young female athlete are eating disorders and nutritional abnormalities. The age of menarche in a young, growing gymnast or dancer is in fact delayed by almost 2 years. The exact etiology may relate to intensive exercise and training required by the sport as well as to specific nutritional deficiencies. Eating disorders such as anorexia nervosa and bulimia are common in this population. The intensity and the obsession these athletes use to perfect their athletic techniques may be manifest as an extreme parallel consequence of the eating disorder. Loss of nutritional integrity, relative malnutrition, and loss of calories, protein, vitamins, and trace elements may result in incompetence of the musculoskeletal system and maladaptation.

By recognizing the clinical problem of overuse injury in the intensively participating adolescent population, and by using basic animal science studies, we can better assess dose-response relationships in performance and injury.

Recommendations

Following are several recommendations:

1. Specific attention must be paid to dose factors. We must be able to quantify the duration, intensity, frequency, and specific forces during an activity. We must communicate to athletes, coaches, and parents that the details of how many miles, how many pitches, what kind of pitches, and how many hours spent in the gym during what particular activity are essential to successful participation and performance. This identification and quantification of dose factors will allow a greater control of training behaviors and progressions.
2. Athletes must avoid progressive training behaviors. At all times the athlete should maintain a cyclical progression to allow stereotypical transitions in the musculoskeletal system as a temporal relationship.
3. We must recognize that the child is not a small adult! A corollary of this is that more is not better; we must also condemn the concept of ''no pain, no gain.''

4. We must identify athletes who are at "physeal risk." It appears as though there is a direct relationship between physeal age, bone age, and chronological age. The activity doses of athletes who have delayed pubescence should not be equal to the doses of athletes who are at a greater physeal, bone, and chronological ages. Individuals who are at a delayed pubescence can be recognized by Tanner scaling and through identification of specific physeal progressions. We must pay close attention to details of the individual's physical and anatomic development.

5. We must identify delayed menarche, which is characteristic of many athletes but which may be associated with a decreased body weight or nutritional deficiency. The delay in menarche should signal full medical evaluation of all factors and modulators. Consequently, specific directives regarding training progressions should be based on the complexities of these details. Lack of identification or ignorance of these components has resulted in bone maladaptation, pain, and injury.

6. Attention should be paid to the end organ relative to the specific demands of that sport. For example, gymnasts who are at risk for developing wrist problems should be assessed with frequent X rays to identify potential of partial physeal arrest or structural abnormalities. Coaches of young gymnasts should have a high index of suspicion for wrist injuries and should take appropriate preventive diagnostic steps. The health care team should understand the potential problems associated with a specific sport. Instruction of coaches, parents, and athletes in the details of prevention is essential to increase awareness of problems and therefore prevent them. As an example, spine problems were quite prevalent in the gymnastic population during the early 1970s. As a consequence of collaboration between physicians, coaches, parents, and athletes, dismount habits and techniques were modified. This lowered the incidence of back pain and pathoanatomic change in this intensively participating population.

Summary

Human and animal studies have demonstrated some details regarding the immature skeleton's response to exercise. The spectrum of skeletal response varies. It is a complex phenomenon that is nonstereotypic, that varies temporally, and that depends on a multitude of local, regional, and systemic modulators. Dose factors include duration, intensity, frequency, forces, age of initiation, and training progression. Response modulators include level of fitness, bone age, chronological age, constitutional and anthropometric details, and nutritional and neuroendocrine integrity. The dynamic changes in the dose-response curve and resultant physeal susceptibility are essential concepts. Complete identification and assessment of these details may ensure safe participation, training, and competition, attainment of the sports physicians' goals, and a recognition of Aristotle's early warning.

References

Adams, J.E. (1976). Little League survey: The Eugene study (editorial). *American Journal of Sports Medicine*, **4**(5), 207-209.

Albert, M.J., Drvaric, D.M. (1990). Little League shoulder: case report. *Orthopedics*, **13**, 779-781.

Alekseev, B.A. (1977). The influence of skiing races on the hand and foot skeleton of young sportsmen. *Arkhiv Anatomii Gistologii Embriologii* (Leningrad), **72**, 35-39.

Allison, N., & Brooks, B. (1921). Bone atrophy. *Surgery, Gynecology and Obstetrics*, **33**, 250-260.

Barnett, L.S. (1985). Little League shoulder syndrome: Proximal humeral epiphysiolysis in adolescent baseball pitchers. *Journal of Bone and Joint Surgery*, **67A**, 495-496.

Booth, F.W., Gould, E.W., Woo, S.L., Kueis, S.C., Amiel, D., Gomez, M.A., et al. (1981). The effect of prolonged physical training on the properties of long bone: A study of Wolff's law. *Journal of Bone and Joint Surgery*, **63A**(5), 780-786.

Burch, W.M. (1984). Calcitonin stimulates growth and maturation of embryonic chick pelvic cartilage in vitro. *Endocrinology*, **114**, 1196-1202.

Cahill, B.R. (1976). Stress fracture of the proximal tibial epiphysis: A case report. *American Journal of Sports Medicine*, **19**(5), 186-187.

Cahill, B.R., Tullos, H.S., & Fain, R.H. (1974). Little League shoulder. *American Journal of Sports Medicine*, **2**, 150-153.

Carter, D.R., Harris, W.H., & Vasu, R. (1981). The mechanical and biological response of bone to in vivo strain histories. Mechanical properties of bone. *American Society of Mechanical Engineering*, **45**, 81-92.

Chamay, A., & Tschantz, P. (1972). Mechanical influences in bone remodeling: Experimental research on Wolff's law. *Journal of Biological Mechanics*, **51**, 173-180.

Deitrick, J.E., Whedon, G.D., & Schorre, E. (1948). Effects of immobilization upon various metabolic and physiologic functions in normal men. *American Journal of Medicine*, **4**, 3-36.

Dotter, W.E. (1953). Little League shoulder/fracture of the proximal humeral epiphyseal cartilage due to baseball pitching. *The Guthrie Clinical Bulletin*, **23**, 68-72.

Gelbke, H. (1950). Tierexperimentelle. Unterbuchugen zur Frage des enthandralen Knochenwachstums unter zug. *Arch Deutsche Ztschr Chir*, **266**, 271-284.

Gerber, S.D., Griffin, P.P., & Simons, B.P. (1986). Break dancer's wrist: A case report. *Journal of Pediatric Orthopedics*, **6**, 98-99.

Gillespie, J.A. (1954). The nature of the bone changes associated with nerve injuries and disuse. *Journal of Bone and Joint Surgery*, **36B**, 464.

Godshall, R.W., Hansen, C.A., & Ryising, D.C. (1981). Stress fractures through the distal femoral epiphysis in athletes. *American Journal of Sports Medicine*, **9**, 114-116.

Goodship, A.E., Lanyon, L.E., & McFieh, H. (1979). Functional adaptation of bone to increased stress. *Journal of Bone and Joint Surgery*, **61A**, 539-546.

Heikkinen, E., & Vuori, I. (1972). Effect of physical activity of collagen in aged mice. *Acta Physiologica Scandanavica*, **81**, 543-549.

Kato, S., & Ishiko, T. (1964). Obstructed growth of children's bones due to excessive labor in remote corners. In K. Kato (Ed.), *Proceedings of the International Congress of Sports Scientists* (p. 476). Tokyo: Japanese Union of Sports Sciences.

Kiiskinen, A. (1977). Physical training and connective tissues in young mice—physical properties of Achilles tendons and long bones. *Growth*, **41**, 123-137.

Kiiskinen, A., & Heikkinen, E. (1973a). Effects of physical training on development and strength of tendons and bones in growing mice. *Scandanavian Journal of Clinical Laboratory Investigation*, **29**(Suppl. 123), 20.

Kiiskinen, A., & Heikkinen, E. (1973b). Effect of prolonged physical training on the development of connective tissues in growing mice (abstract). *Proceedings of the International Symposium on Exercise Biochemics* (2nd ed., p. 25).

Kiiskinen, A., & Heikkinen, E. (1978). Physical training and connective tissues in young mice: Biochemistry of long bones. *Journal of Applied Physiology*, **44**, 50-54.

Laros, G.S., Tipton, C.M., & Cooper, R.R. (1971). Influence of physical activity on ligament insertions in the knees of dogs. *Journal of Bone and Joint Surgery*, **53A**, 275-286.

Liu, C.H., & McCay, C.M. (1953). Studies of calcium metabolism in dogs. *Journal of Gerontology*, **8**, 264-271.

Mandelbaum, B.R., Bartolozzi, A.R., Davis, C.A., Teurlings, L., & Bragonier, B. (1989). Wrist pain syndrome in the gymnast. Pathogenic, diagnostic, and therapeutic considerations. *American Journal of Sports Medicine*, **17**, 305-317.

Margulies, J.Y., Simkin, A., Leichter, I., Bivas, A., Steinberg, R., Giladi, M., Stein, M., Kashtan, H., & Milgrom, C. (1986). Effect of intense physical activity on the bone-mineral content in the lower limbs of young adults. *Journal of Bone and Joint Surgery*, **68A**, 1090-1093.

Matsuda, J.J., Zernicke, R.F., Vailas, A.C., Peprini, V.A., Pedrini-Mille, A., & Maynard, J.A. (1986). Structural and mechanical adaptation of immature bone and strenuous exercise. *Journal of Applied Physiology*, **60**, 2028-2034.

Pedrini-Mille, A., Peprini, V.A., Maynard, J.A., & Vailas, A.C. (1986). Effects of strenuous exercise on physes and bones of growing animals. *Orthopedic Transactions*, **11**, 164.

Price-Jones, C. (1927). The effect of exercise on the growth of white rats. *Journal of Experimental Psychology*, **16**, 61-67.

Priest, J.D., Jones, H.H., Tichenor, C.J.C., & Nagel, D.A. (1977). Arm and elbow changes in expert tennis players. *Minnesota Medicine*, **60**, 399-404.

Roy, S., Caine, D., & Singer, K.M. (1985). Stress changes of the distal radial epiphysis in young gymnasts. *American Journal of Sports Medicine*, **13**, 301-308.

Sayille, P.D., & Smith, R.E. (1966). Bone density: Breaking force and leg muscle mass as functions of weight in bipedal rats. *American Journal of Physical Anthropology*, **25**, 35-40.

Sayille, P.D., & Whyte, M.P. (1969). Muscle and bone hypertrophy: Positive effect of running exercise in the rat. *Clinical Orthopaedics*, **65**, 81-88.

Shaw, S.R., Vailas, A.C., Grindeland, R.E., & Zernicke, R.F. (1988). Effects of a one week space flight on the morphological and mechanical properties of growing bone. *American Journal of Physiology*, **254**, R78-83.

Shinozuka, M., Tsurui, A., Nagumuma, T., Moss, M., & Moss-Salentjul, L. (1984). A stochastic-mechanical model of longitudinal long bone growth. *Journal of Theoretical Biology*, **108**, 413-436.

Simon, M.R. (1978). The effect of dynamic loading on the growth of epiphyseal cartilage in the rat. *Acta Anatomical*, **102**, 176-183.

Steinberg, M.E., & Trueta, J. (1981). The effects of activity on rat bone growth. *Clinical Orthopedics*, **56**, 52-60.

Terjung, R. (1979). Endocrine response to exercise. In R.S. Hutton & D.I. Miller (Eds.) *Exercise and Sports Science Reviews (Vol. 7)* (pp. 153-180). Philadelphia: Franklin Institute Press.

Torg, J. (1972). Little League pitcher. *American Family Physician*, **6**(2), 71-76.

Vailas, A.C., Deluna, D.M., Lewis, L.L., Curwin, S.L., Roy, R.R., & Alford, E.K. (1988). Adaptation of bone and tendon to prolonged hind limb suspension in rats. *Journal of Applied Physiology*, **65**, 373-376.

Vailas, A.C., Martinez, D., Shaw, S., Zernicke, R.F., & Grindeland, R.E. (1987). Biochemical morphological and mechanical characteristics of cortical bone in young growing rats exposed to seven days of space flight: Results from the SL-3 flight mission. *NASA Life Sciences*, **1**, 173-175.

Van Buul-Offers, S., Smeets, T., Van den Brande, J.L. (1984). Effects of growth hormone and thyroxine on the relation between tibial length and the histological appearance of the proximal tibial epiphysis in Snell dwarf mice. *Growth, 48*, 166-175.

Vasan, N. (1983). Effects of physical stress on the synthesis and degradation of cartilage matrix. *Connective Tissue Research, 12*, 49-58.

Vogel, J.M., & Whittle, M.W. (1976). Bone mineral changes: The second manned skylab mission. *Aviation Environmental Medicine*, **47**, 396-400.

Vose, G.P. (1974). Review of roentgenographic bone demineralization studies of the Gemini space flights. *American Journal of Roentgenology Radium Therapy and Nuclear Medicine*, **121**, 1-4.

Wolff, J. (1892). *Das gesetz der transformation der knochen*. Berlin: Hirschwald.

Woo, S.L., Kuei, S.C., Amiel, D., Gomez, M.A., Hayes, W.C., White, F.C., & Akeson, W.H. (1981). The effect of prolonged physical training on the properties of long bone: A study of Wolff's law. *Journal of Bone and Joint Surgery*, **63A**, 780-787.

Index